CYCLIC ANALYSIS IN FUTURES TRADING

Contemporary Methods and Procedures

JACOB BERNSTEIN

WILEY

JOHN WILEY & SONS

NEW YORK   CHICHESTER   BRISBANE   TORONTO   SINGAPORE

Disclaimer

It should not be assumed that the theories, systems, methods or indicators presented herein will be profitable or that they will not result in losses. Futures trading involves the risk of loss as well as the potential for profit. The information contained herein has been obtained from sources believed to be reliable, but cannot be guaranteed as to accuracy or completeness, and is subject to change without notice.

Library of Congress Cataloging in Publication Data:

Bernstein, Jacob, 1946-
   Cyclic analysis in futures trading: contemporary methods and
procedures/Jacob Bernstein.
      p.   cm.

   Bibliography: p.
   Includes index.
   ISBN 0-471-01185-1
   1. Commodity exchanges.   I. Title
HG6024.A3848   1988   87-26350
332.64'4—dc19   CIP

Printed in the United States of America

10   9   8   7   6   5   4   3   2   1

Dedicated to
Becky, Eli, Sara, Linda, Virginia, George and Meyer.

Contents

Credits

The following figures are reprinted with permission of:

Commodity Quote Graphics, 6916 Hwy 82, Glenwood Springs, CO 81602

1.2	8.12	10.10
1.3	8.13	10.11
1.4	8.14	10.12
1.5	8.15	10.13
4.7	8.16	10.14
4.8	8.17	10.15
4.9	8.18	10.16
4.10	8.19	10.17
4.11	8.20	10.18
4.12	8.21	11.1
4.13	8.22	11.2
4.14	8.23	11.3
4.15	8.24	11.4
4.16	8.25	11.5
4.17	8.26	11.6
4.18	9.2	11.7
4.19	9.3	11.8
4.20	9.4	11.9
4.21	9.5	11.10
5.23	9.6	11.11
5.26	9.7	11.12
5.29	9.8	11.13
6.1	9.9	11.14
7.2	9.10	11.15
7.3	9.11	11.16
7.4	9.12	11.17
7.5a	9.13	11.18
7.5b	9.14	11.19
7.5c	9.15	11.20
7.5d	9.16	12.1
7.6	9.17	12.2
7.7	9.18	12.3
7.8	9.19	12.4
7.9	9.20	12.5
7.10	9.21	12.6
7.11	9.22	12.7
7.12	10.1	12.8
8.3	10.2	12.9

8.4	10.3	12.10
8.5	10.4	12.11
8.6	10.5	12.12
8.7	10.6	12.13
8.8	10.7	12.14
8.9	10.8	12.15
8.10	10.9	12.16
8.11		

Commodity Research Bureau, 30 South Wacker Drive, Suite 1820, Chicago, IL 60606

2.9	2.40	3.20
2.13	3.3	3.28
2.17	3.5	3.32
2.18	3.6	3.33
2.19	3.7	3.34
2.29	3.8	3.39
2.30	3.9	3.49
2.31	3.10	4.1
2.33	3.11	4.2
2.34	3.15	5.27
2.36	3.17	5.28
2.38		

Foundation for the Study of Cycles, 3333 Michelson Drive, Irvine, CA 92715

2.1	2.5	2.24
2.2	2.11	2.52
2.4		

Lambert-Gann Publishing Co., Richman Gulch, Pomeroy, WA 99347

5.1
5.2
5.3

Commodity Perspective, 30 South Wacker Drive, Suite 1820, Chicago, IL 60606

3.13	3.36	5.6
3.18	3.37	5.13
3.22	3.41	5.19
3.24	3.45	5.20
3.25	3.47	5.21
3.29	3.52	5.25
3.30	5.5	6.6

Commodity Price Chart, 219 Parkade, Cedar Falls, IA 50613

2.12	3.38	5.12
2.42	3.40	5.14
3.1	3.42	5.15
3.2	3.43	5.16
3.4	3.44	5.17
3.12	3.46	5.18
3.14	3.48	5.22
3.16	3.50	5.24
3.19	3.51	6.2
3.21	5.4	6.3
3.23	5.7	6.4
3.26	5.8	6.5
3.27	5.9	6.7
3.31	5.10	6.8
3.35	5.11	

Introduction

Although the study of cycles has gained more followers during the 1970's and 1980's than was the case during the 1950's and 1960's, the fact remains that precious few publications or sources of cyclic information exist to which the investor and/or futures trader can turn. The works of John Burns, Gertrude Shirk, and most certainly Edward R. Dewey at the Foundation for the Study of Cycles have been among the few continuing sources of cyclic study. Many traders and analysts express opinions and forecasts based on their understanding of cycles, yet such conclusions are not based on a central theory or system of cyclic analysis. With the exception of a few newsletter services that seek to educate the public, price cycles are generally misunderstood by most people. Yet the subject of recurrent events in the futures markets is one that has been sporadically studied for at least 75 years. Currently, the range of methodologies runs from the ultrasimple to the highly complex. Many different approaches to cyclic analysis have come into fashion, only to then lose favor and fade into obscurity.

The futures market is no less immune to fads than is any other area of human experience. Trading systems and methods seem to come and go. The 1950's and early 1960's witnessed unprecedented popularity in technical analysis. Many of the older techniques of fundamental analysis fell into disuse during these years. Yet it is the nature of investors and traders to never totally abandon any technique. The revival of technical analysis witnessed during this period was, in some respects, a reincarnation of techniques developed many years earlier by such persons as Samuel Wyckoff, W. D. Gann, Jesse Livermore, and others.

The exponential growth of computer technology can be cited as the probable stimulus for the renaissance of technical analysis that eased its way into the market in the 1960's. The revival was still going strong in the 1980's. The computer revolution of the early 1980's not only helped foster entirely new concepts in technical analysis, but also improved the forecasting ability of fundamental analysts. They could now "massage" ever greater amounts of data with their forecasting models.

Computer technology has rekindled research in areas previously difficult to study. The work of W. D. Gann, for example, has been an enigma to many traders. His use of seemingly magical technical methods and seasonal price tendencies can now be studied with greater ease by computer. Due to the complexity of

1

cyclical analysis, pioneers in the field of cycles, such as Samuel Brenner, E. R. Dewey, and Burton Pugh were frequently ridiculed by their contemporaries. Their theories were too difficult to test. Only in recent years has there been a revival in the study of cyclical principles and theories. Cycles are now popular in the futures market and in the stock market as well. The ready availability of affordable computer technology has facilitated a renewed interest in cyclic methods. In spite of this revival, only a handful of analysts or advisory services are seriously committed to the study and pragmatic implementation of cycles. My first work on cycles was prompted by growing public and professional interest in cyclic analysis that occurred partially as a consequence of my research efforts and publications in the areas of cycles, repetitive patterns, and seasonal price analyses.[1,2,3]

In spite of convincing research on the validity of cyclic events, many traders are still hesitant to acknowledge the value of repetitive price patterns. This phenomenon continues to amaze me, since the statistical evidence supporting repetitive price patterns slowly but surely builds with virtually every new research project. Furthermore, the significance of cyclic events in the biological and physical sciences is also becoming more evident daily. Nevertheless, recent years have fostered a small but growing cadre of those who appreciate cycles and other time-based patterns. This book has been written in order to partially satisfy the growing need for techniques and systems applicable to cyclic trading.

SYSTEMS ARE CYCLICAL

Cyclic and seasonal analysis achieved great popularity from the mid 1970's to the early 1980's. Recently, even more traders have been attracted to cyclic trading by advanced methods of computer analysis. As previously noted, the comings and goings of trading system popularity are, to a certain extent, themselves cyclical. A number of today's new techniques are in fact not new, but are, in fact sophisticated versions of methods that have been known and used for many years. Cyclical analysis itself enjoyed a period of popularity from the late 1950's through the mid 1960's, being reborn in the 1970's. The point-and-figure-chart technique, currently being used by some pit traders in the futures markets, was developed many years ago. A host of today's popular trading systems are yesterday's trading systems reincarnated. I have long maintained that to find tomorrow's trading systems, you need only look at yesterday's trading systems. As a further example, consider the "full moon/new moon" signals. In 1981, when I published *The Handbook of Commodity Cycles: A Window on Time,*[4] I referred to Burton Pugh and the "moon-effect" technique he used in the early 1900's. For many years, Pugh's system remained out of the public limelight, while more technical and mathematical techniques (such as moving averages) took the lead. In the 1970's, Larry Wil-

[1]MBH Weekly Commodity Letter, PO Box 353, Winnetka, IL 60093.
[2]MBH *Seasonal Cash Charts.* J. Bernstein. PO Box 353, Winnetka, IL 60093. 1987.
[3]MBH *Seasonal Futures Charts.* J. Bernstein. PO Box 353, Winnetka, IL 60093. 1986.
[4]Bernstein. J. *The Handbook of Commodity Cycles: A Window on Time.* New York: John Wiley & Sons, 1981.

liams published *How I Made a Million Dollars Trading Commodities Last Year.*[5] Pugh's work was mentioned, and a new generation of "moon watchers" was born.

For several years the full moon/new moon buy-and-sell signals (i.e., buy on full moon; sell on new moon) were watched, perhaps by thousands of traders. Even today, over 15 years after the Williams revival of Pugh's work, some traders still use lunar signals.

The 1970's also prompted a new generation of astrological trading systems. This was consistent with a general increase of public interest in astrology, astronomy, and other cosmic phenomena. In fact, each generation has had its astrological advocates and detractors. Some have argued that astrology is the ultimate source of all cyclic phenomena and that cycles in the markets are, therefore, best determined and predicted through the use of astrological methods (I do not share this viewpoint).

MARKET CHANGES AFFECT SYSTEMS

The growing interest in cycles may be due to the cyclic nature of public interest in trading systems as described earlier. In addition to these reasons, the late 1979 to mid 1985 period was marked by a severe disinflationary trend. During the inflationary economic trend that flourished from 1950 through 1979-1980, many futures traders were able to profit handsomely in the strong uptrends that enveloped virtually every futures market. This era bore witness to the proliferation and growth of myriad trading systems and methods. The profitability of these techniques was virtually certain, as long as they selected positions primarily on the long side, and assuming that their "drawdown" during losing periods was fairly small. Concurrently, many futures traders were cutting their eye teeth in the markets, and few (myself included) had ever experienced futures trading during sustained periods of economic disinflation. Therefore, our apprenticeships were shaped during an inflationary period. Our experiences were primarily limited to bull markets of fairly long duration and bear markets of comparatively brief duration. In short, many of today's traders entered the 1980's suffering from market myopia. The thought of selling short for longer term positions was not only an alien concept but a reckless one at that! No wonder that the change in futures price trends that began in the early 1980's took so many traders by surprise. Trading systems and methods previously held in high regard experienced difficult times. Similarly, many speculators, floor traders, and commodity-fund managers who previously could do no wrong in the secular uptrends, were forced back to the basics of futures research to develop more profitable systems. Some turned to cycles and seasonals for their salvation.

Since 1980, my trading experiences have not been too unlike the trials and tribulations of other traders nurtured on the milk of commodity price inflation. Responding to the bear-market climate that has dominated futures prices since 1980, traders have turned to new methods of research. Highly sophisticated computer technology has emerged as a significant tool for improving timing and

---

[5]Williams, Larry. *How I Made a Million Dollars Trading Commodities Last Year.* Brightwaters, NY: Windsor Books, 1978.

trade selection. The demand for greater efficacy has fostered an oversupply (indeed, a virtual avalanche) of trading systems. While moving-average followers have busily put their computers to work optimizing their methods, other systems followers such as point-and-figure chartists, Gann theorists, and, of course, cyclic analysts have been hard at work with their programs, seeking to adjust and fit current market behavior to their theoretical models. The cycles have again turned bullish on cyclic analysis.

OBJECTIVES

The current state of cyclic analysis, then, is clearly a result of forces and factors emanating from a variety of sources. To review, they are:

1. The cyclic nature of trading systems
2. The growing public awareness of cycles due to increased validation of cyclic concepts
3. Increased ability and use of computer testing models to cyclic concepts, and
4. Changes in secular market trends, prompting the search for more promising techniques and systems.

My research on cycles has also taken some new directions. Previously established concepts and indicators have been subjected to further study. New concepts and indicators have been developed and analyzed. Many promising avenues of research have been evaluated.

Though not too many years have passed since I wrote *The Handbook of Commodity Cycles: A Window on Time*[6], the changes just cited warrant publication of this second work. Therefore, this book has been written with the following objectives:

1. To provide futures traders with an in-depth analytical look at price cycles and repetitive patterns in the futures market.
2. To provide additional timing tools for determining when prices have established cyclic lows and highs.
3. To examine and report the current status and character of repetitive patterns in futures and cash-market data.
4. To examine current efficacy and relevance of previously delineated timing indicators.
5. To explore new areas of cyclical research made possible by current trends in computer technology.
6. To examine the current reliability of historically established cyclical periods in the futures markets (i.e., 5.7-year cycles, 28-day cycles, and 9- to 11-month cycles), and
7. To examine and report new findings in established data and cyclic activity in recently introduced futures markets.

[6]Bernstein, J. *The Handbook of Commodity Cycles: A Window on Time*, New York: John Wiley & Sons, 1981.

This task requires considerable effort and space. Take the material slowly, particularly if this book is your first exposure to cyclical analysis. I have done everything within my power to keep mathematics to a minimum, to keep examples clear, the concepts logical, and the explanations specific. Although a thorough understanding of *The Handbook of Commodity Cycles: A Window on Time* is not entirely necessary, readers with limited exposure to futures-trading concepts and/or repetitive price patterns should read it before starting this more advanced work.

Throughout the text, ample illustrations of concepts have been provided with profuse explanations to clarify the information. Nothing can replace your own study and practice with these concepts. Finally, the methods and concepts presented in this book have been made as objective and as operational as I can make them. Ultimately, a number of cases may require subjective judgments, but these cases have been kept to a minimum. The science of cyclical study will always contain some degree of art, but art is diminished and science is stressed in this book.

THEORY AND PRACTICE

Market theory and trading reality are two extremes of the futures continuum. The present work intends to bridge the gap, concluding its journey at a common ground upon which pragmatism and academia meet as partners with a similar objective. All too often, books on futures trading are either errant examples of charlatanism, or they are steeped in malicious theoretical obfuscations. I have avoided both extremes. Each chapter begins with a theoretical consideration and progresses to evidence that supports theory. I think that you will find the blend to your liking and, on a more pragmatic level, to your financial benefit.

In closing, a brief word to would-be critics: With the contemporary penchant toward operationalism, computerization, and the mechanization of trading systems, a book like this can leave the author open to harsh treatment by those who seek to impose rigid scientific standards on a theory that cannot yet be judged on this basis. While some of the work in this book is based on completely objective and operational findings, other aspects are merely theoretical. Areas where science and theory part company have been indicated. In presenting my latest ideas to you, my sincere hope is that these ideas will stimulate rigorous research and new directions in trading theory.

1
Cycles: Characteristics, Anatomy, and Phases

One of the most difficult ideas for new students of price cycles to accept is the underlying notion that price-trend history is repetitive. Although many instances supporting the existence of price cycles in all types of events are known, most people (Westerners, in particular) are prone to deny the fact that cyclic factors may play a role in virtually every aspect of life.

In spite of attempts to refute, disprove, or diminish the existence and role of cycles, a growing body of evidence supports the presence of repetitive patterns as a key force in our universe. In economics, a slow but growing trend toward the definition and application of cyclic factors has developed in the last five decades. In the physical sciences, research tends to lean very heavily on cyclic phenomena and theory.

Whether cycles really exist, what causes and controls them, what or who created them, and why cycles are not more easily discernible, are all questions that cannot be fully answered at present. The quest for ultimate answers to these questions remains an insurmountable challenge. The search for the "cycles generator" or the "grand plan" (if such an entity exists) will likely require more effort than the human race can muster at this time. To seek understanding, and to wish for order from what appears to be chaos and confusion, is only human. Yet, even if the force or forces governing cyclic patterns is ultimately discovered, its machinery would probably be so powerful, so vast, and immense, that any effort at control would certainly meet with failure. People all too commonly reject what they cannot understand or ridicule that which threatens the stability of their psychological, economic, social, political, or intellectual structure. Man's rejection of new ideas comes from this process, which is also the seed from which such unhealthy and destructive forces as racism, stereotyping, and bigotry are born. Today, the science of cyclic analysis finds itself at the leading edge of "radical intellectualism," and, as a consequence, is frequently rejected by traditional economists and social scientists.

The debate between students of cycles and students of other theoretical persuasions is not a new one, but little progress has been made toward a resolution.

Based on the growing body of cyclic evidence in all fields of science, those who adhere to the study of cycles and its pragmatic application in the social, economic, and biological sciences are slowly gaining an upper hand. But much still remains to be achieved. Since the ideas of cyclic analysis often refute current social, scientific, and philosophical tenets, these ideas remain a threat to many scientists and academicians.

WHAT CAUSES CYCLES?

The answer to this question could be ample material for several books. Were we to know the forces, source, energy, or process by which the "cycles clock" is powered and/or regulated, the answer might be as simple as one word, or it could require volumes of explanation. I suspect that *the* answer, if in fact one exists, could even prove to be surprisingly simple. Unfortunately, the current state of knowledge (or ignorance) prohibits a definitive answer. There have been many theories regarding the forces that trigger cyclic price behavior. These have ranged from the astrological on one extreme, to the environmental on the other extreme. While some triggers of cyclic phenomena are clearly known, many are still a mystery. Yet, their determination should not be a major concern of those who seek to employ cycles in a pragmatic fashion. The cycle is your automobile and you are the driver. It is not necessary to understand what makes the automobile function in order to drive it!

AMPLITUDE

Amplitude (as used in my approach to cyclic analysis) refers to height or magnitude. Amplitude can be expressed either in terms of percentage or actual price movement. If, for example, the average movement of the market has been 500 points following a 9- to 11-month cycle low, then the magnitude or amplitude is 500 points. Amplitude up and down can be used to describe the rising and falling portions of the cycle. Both figures can be expressed as a percentage gain from the cycle low or percentage loss from the cycle high. Using percentages normalizes amplitude. Excessively high or low price movement will not significantly affect the percentage. I prefer to express amplitude up and down in terms of percentage as opposed to average price movement, unless only the last few observation cycles are being considered for the sake of comparison to the current market cycle.

PERIOD

The term "period" refers to the length of a cycle. A cycle period is specified in units of time such as minutes, days, hours, or years. The time span, or period refers to the average length of the cycle, either from low to low, high to high, low to high, or high to low. The traditional measurement of cycle length, or period is from low to low. Therefore, when I refer to an 11 month cycle, I mean that the average length of the cycle, from low to low, has been approximately 11 months. As a point of information, I measure cycles in the financial markets (i.e., stocks, futures, etc.) in market days as opposed to calendar days. In other words, I count only days during which the markets are open. But other market analysts consider all days in their period count. I will explain my reasons for counting only market days later on. For now, suffice it to say that there are two ways in which daily cycle periods can be stated. The lengths stated in this book are in market days unless otherwise indicated. Weekly, monthly, and yearly cycles are stated in calendar terms.

PHASE

Cycles frequently tend to top, when they should ideally bottom. *Phase* refers to the timeliness of the cycle. Do not confuse the use of this word with its traditional use in physics or electronics.

If a cycle is considerably late or considerably early in topping or bottoming, the cycle is referred to as "not in phase" or "out of phase." Another use for this term is in describing the relationship of two cycles to each other. For example, live hog and cattle cycles normally tend to run together up and down. At other times, however, they are significantly different and "out of phase" with each other. *Phase* is not ordinarily used in the decision-making process, but rather in a descriptive sense to draw attention to a given situation.

RELIABILITY

The reliability of a cycle is the degree to which the cycle can be depended on for repetition. Cycles with high reliability tend to show fairly stable lengths from low to low and/or high to high, and tend to top and bottom within an acceptable[1] degree of ideal low or high time frame. Reliability is a very important concept, since it allows the speculator to have a greater or lesser degree of confidence in a given cycle or cycles. This book contains my most current evaluations of cycle reliability. Remember, markets are not static; therefore, reliability will most definitely change over time. Cycles that may have been reliable several years ago may cease to be reliable in the future. Reliability of these cycles may again improve with the passage of time.

Since reliability is important, cyclic traders would do well to regularly evaluate the reliability of cycles that they are following. As you use cycles you will develop a sense of their reliabilities, based on your results. However, do not become complacent in research, expecting that your performance will always alert you to changes in reliability. The best way to keep track of reliability is through ongoing research and evaluation.

Reliability is also important in making decisions on how often to trade a given market, how much of a position to commit to a given market, and the particular cycle currently being considered for a trade. You must always remember that there are no guarantees, and that the very nature of cycles, due to their interaction with other cycles and seasonal tendencies, is to be variable. No single cycle should be taken entirely out of context in the overall picture. The shorter the time frame of the cycle, the less significant the influence of other cycles will be upon it. Hence, a trader tracking the approximate 14-day cycle in cattle futures should be

[1]To be defined later on.

aware of the approximate 28- to 32-day cycle, as well as the 9- to 11-month cycle. However, the approximate 20-month cycle (and longer cycles) should not play a serious role in evaluating the short term cycles, although it is important.

Reliability can be evaluated numerically in many different ways, but a rigorous mathematical determination at any given point is not a strict requirement, due to other checks and balances imposed upon the cyclic approach to trading.

CONFLUENCE

Confluence is loosely defined as "a coming together of different paths." Of all the concepts in cyclic analysis I consider confluence to be the most significant. Since the publication of HCC[2] I've had considerable opportunity to study the role of confluence in cyclic analysis. What is presented here (though still preliminary in many respects) should help markedly improve your market understanding, and forecasting skills.

The purpose of understanding confluence is to alert you to situations in the marketplace that have high predictive validity. In studying confluence then, situations must be found where many different cycles are likely to top or bottom in the same time frame. Such situations (some of which will be illustrated by historical example) tend to produce trades with the least amount of risk and the highest amount of potential. Since different types of confluence exist, each type will be presented separately in sections, with appropriate historical examples.

CONFLUENCE OF TWO CYCLES

The most simple type of confluence is the coming together of two cycles, both at an ideal cycle low or cycle high time frame. For example, the confluence of a cycle and its half cycle (i.e., the cycle which is half its length, as in "28 day" and "14 day" cycles) tends to be a significant event, since fairly good lows or highs tend to occur when such cycles converge. Figure 1.1 illustrates the confluence of two cycles as it would appear in an ideal situation. Figures 1.2 and 1.3 illustrate confluence in a real time situation. Examine the notes on each of these examples. As a rule of thumb, confluence between two cycles that are not harmonics or fractions of each other is preferable to confluence of a cycle and its half cycle. As an example, if the 28-day cycle were split in half, the result would be two 14-day cycles within the 28-day cycle. On every second count, 14- and 28-day cycles will converge. However, if a 14-day cycle and a 21-day cycle were present in the same market coming together for a low or a high at the same time, the confluence would be more meaningful.

CONFLUENCE OF THREE OR MORE CYCLES

In some instances three or more cycles will converge within the same relative time frame for a low or a high. Such confluence is even more significant than the convergence of two cycles in a similar time frame. In fact, the more cycle work

[2]Bernstein. J. *The Handbook of Commodity Cycles: A Window on Time.* New York: John Wiley & Sons, 1981.

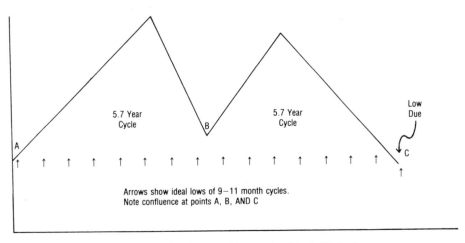

Figure 1.1 Confluence of two cycles (ideal situation).

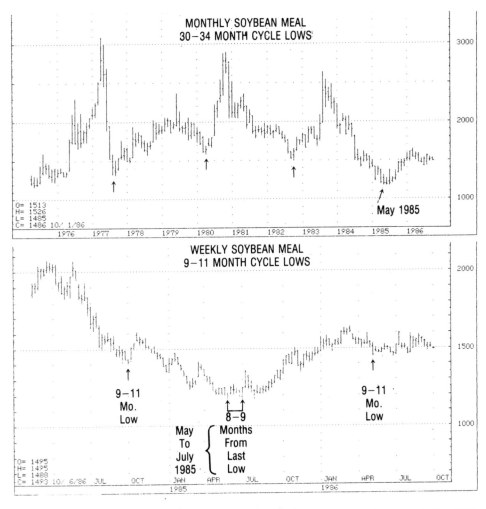

Figure 1.2 Confluence of 30−34-month and 9−11-month cycle lows in soybean meal. May 1985 marked the low of an approximate 30−34-month cycle while the May−July time frame marked a 9−11-month cycle low, thereby showing confluence of two cycles.

11

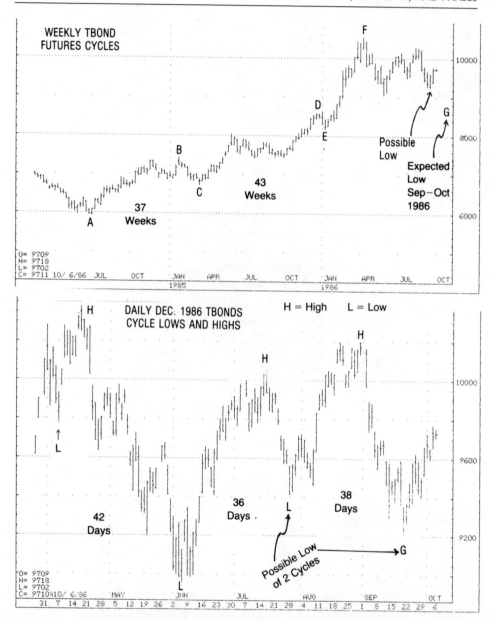

Figure 1.3 Weekly and daily confluence of lows. Weekly chart (TOP) shows projected approximate 38-week cycle low at "G". Daily chart shows approximate 38-day cycle low at "G" on daily chart. Weekly and daily cycles were in confluence at "G".

present during the same time frame, top or bottom, the more meaningful the cycle work is prone to be. Classic examples of highly significant confluence would be situations where 5.7-year, 9- to 11-month, 56-day, 28-day, and 14-day cycles all converge. The situations, might have even more significance during the time frame of an ideal seasonal top or bottom. Figures 1-4 and 1-5 provide some historical illustrations of this type of confluence at significant market turns. Though such situations do not develop frequently, they are highly signicant when they do.

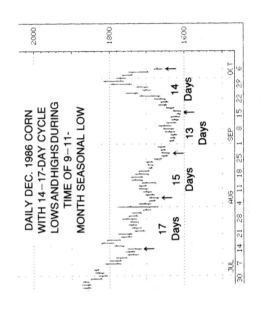

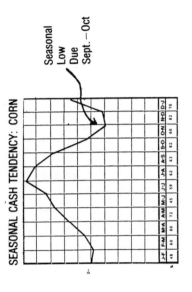

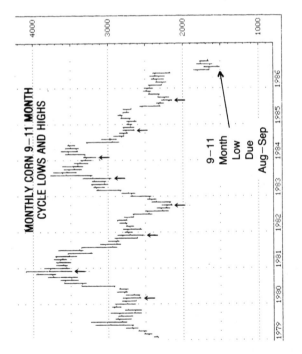

Figure 1.4 Confluence of 9–11-month, 14–17-day and cash seasonal lows all due in the August through October time frame, 1986.

13

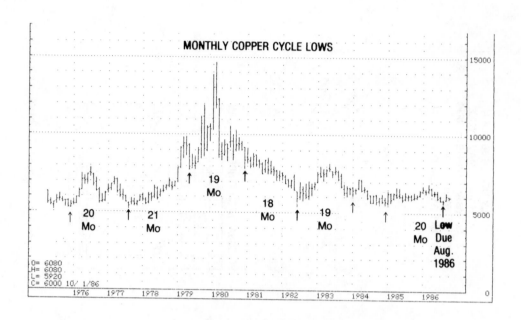

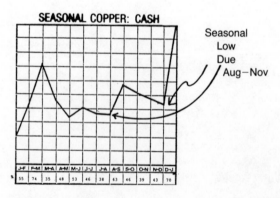

Figure 1.5   Confluence of monthly, daily and seasonal cycle lows in copper.

The cyclic trader interested in longer term opportunities can find triple confluence by continually monitoring the markets. Naturally, the very short-term trader need not be concerned with such types of occurrences. Remember, the confluence of long term and intermediate term cycles can, for brief periods of time, have a significant impact on the characteristics of short-term cycles. Typically, such influences would tend to significantly affect the phase of the short-term cycle, resulting in very early tops or bottoms, depending on the direction of the converging cycles. Again, the purpose of monitoring confluence is to alert you to trades that may have high probability of success or accuracy.

CONFLUENCE OF DIFFERENT CYCLES IN DIFFERENT MARKETS

Another interesting situation that occasionally arises is the confluence of different cycles in markets that are not directly related to each other. On some occasions, a number of different cycle lengths will converge for tops or bottoms of significance in many markets at the same time. In 1977, for example, the 5.7-year cycle in corn, the 6.2-year cycle in gold, the 5.9-year cycle in copper, and the approximate 10-year cycle in cattle all converged within the same relative time frame for a low. Interestingly, the lows established at that time turned out to be highly significant—not only in these markets but in a majority of the futures markets as well. Such confluence is very important on an economic level and usually correlates with significant turns in the economy.

CONFLUENCE OF SIMILAR CYCLES ACROSS DIFFERENT MARKETS

On occasion cycles of similar lengths will converge in a low or a high time frame in different markets. The so-called three- to four-year business cycle is evident in many markets; however, not all markets reflect lows or highs at the same time. The Commodity Research Bureau Futures Price Index is a prime indicator of confluence in futures prices in various cycles. Dating back many years, the CRB (which is comprised of most major commodity prices) has shown a most amazing degree of repetition. The CRB has a cycle of 9 to 11 months and larger cycle of approximately 2 ½ to 3 ½ years. When these two cycles top or bottom in conjunction, expect to see concurrent moves in most futures markets.

SUMMARY

As you study cycles, you will observe many of the relationships referred to in this chapter. Remember in all you do that the topic of cycles can be the stimulus for all manner and sorts of idealistic and romantic theories. But romance in the marketplace does not necessarily produce profits and can, indeed, produce losses. Therefore, seek to be free of romance while moving closer to *finance*. Don't get lured by the fantasy that cycles are perfect, or that they somehow represent some mystical force. Cycles, as discussed in this book are meant to be used as a tool. This is our primary goal.

2
Examining Some Long-Term Cycles

Long-term cycles are perhaps the most fascinating area of interest in cyclic analysis. Virtually no market, indicator, statistic, or price fails to exhibit a long-term cycle. Inasmuch as many cycles are interrelated or influenced by several master cycles, long-term cyclic lengths tend to be similar among various markets. The tendency of cycles to cluster in given time lengths was originally observed by E. R. Dewey. In addition, The Foundation for the Study of Cycles has published voluminous statistical research on long-term cycles and cyclic synchronicity.

Foremost among the long-term cycles is the approximate 50- to 60-year cycle, its harmonics, and its fractional cycles (i.e., 100–120 years, 25–30 years, etc.). By beginning with this master cycle, we can descend to cycles as short as 9–11 months. Cycles such as 27 years, 9 years, 5½ years are fractions of the 50–60 year economic cycle. A classic example of the approximate 50- to 60-year cycles is noted in Figure 2.1. This chart is taken from the work of E. R. Dewey. The chart shows an ideal 54-year cycle in bond yields (dashed line) and actual bond yields (solid line), based on various interest-rate instruments. At the time of its publication, Dewey made the then-radical forecast of rising interest rates through the late 1970's and early 1980's. His forecast likely raised many eyebrows. Yet, as history marched on, his analysis certainly proved to be an accurate one. Today, Dewey's forecast represents a major victory for long-term cyclic analysis. While, the 54-year cycle in bond yields is characteristic of a typical long-term cycle, Figure 2.2 shows a cycle on the other end of the long-term time scale in bond yields, the approximate 32.94-month cycle.

In addition to the ultra-long-term or secular cycles such as the approximate 50-to 60-year cycles, many shorter term lengths qualify as long-term cycles. These are also featured in this chapter along with comments regarding their history and reliability. I consider cycles of approximately 3 years to 60 years length as long term. For the purposes of this work, most long-term cycles featured cycles will fall in the approximate 3-year to 9½-year range (some a bit shorter, some a bit longer).

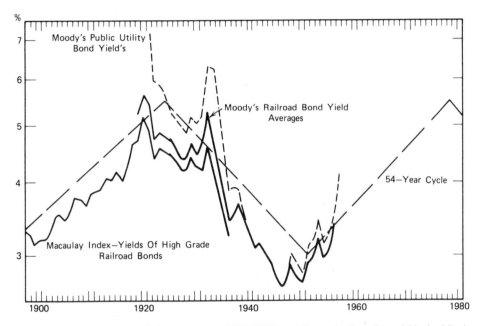

Figure 2.1 The 54-year cycle in interest rates, 1900-1957, and the projection of trend (dashed line) through 1980 (Dewey, 1970, p. 328). Reprinted with permission of The Foundation for the Study of Cycles.

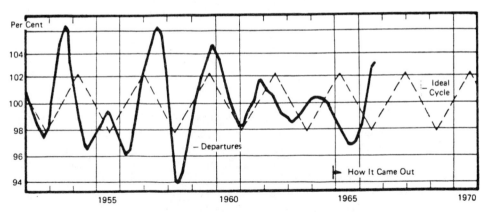

Figure 2.2 The 32.94-month cycle in industrial bond yields (*Cycles*, May 1968, p. 106). Reprinted with permission of The Foundation for the Study of Cycles.

ABOUT THE CHARTS

Now let's look at some charts which show various long-term cycles. It should be noted that various items of information are included in the cyclic analysis for each of the major markets:

1) Charts shown are, for the most part, monthly cash average charts. Some of the

lows and highs shown may not correlate exactly with highs and lows in futures, since at times there are differences in cash and futures tops and bottoms. Furthermore, the use of monthly average prices can distort actual low and high prices to a given extent. Such distortions, however, are not significant.

2) In addition to the up-to-date charts and cycles, charts from *The Handbook of Commodity Cycles* are included for reference purposes. They will assist you in evaluating projections and/or cycle-length changes that have taken place since HCC.

LIVE HOGS

The cycles in hogs have a long history. The work of Samuel Benner gave considerable attention to hog cycles. The Foundation for the Study of Cycles has also done extensive work on hog cycles. Figures 2.3, 2.4, and 2.5 show some of the historical studies of cycles in hogs. For our purposes, there are several cycles of interest and importance in hogs. They are the approximate 3.6-year, 7.2-year, 10-year, and 15-year cycles. Though the 15-year cycle has been especially accurate, it is not particularly useful for trading. The 10-year or mid-decade cycle has had a major effect on hog prices. Note the comments with Figure 2.3. The figure illustrates the ideal 3.61-year hog cycle (dashed line) and the actual cycles in the cash market as analyzed in *The Handbook of Commodity Cycles*. Figure 2.6 shows the 15-year cycles. A majority of the cycles in the hog market, cash, and futures are reliable and well worth the attention of long-term traders. Producers in particular should not consider themselves knowledgeable about the hog market unless they are familiar with the long-term cycles. In particular, the cycle shown in Figure 2.5 should interest producers.

LIVE CATTLE

This market has also shown a number of highly reliable cyclic tendencies. At one time my findings suggested the presence of an approximate 7-year cycle (see Figure 2.7); however, the approximate 45-month (i.e., 3.8-year), 10-year, and 15-year cycles have recently shown considerably more importance. The original projections (PH, PL, and dashed lines on Figure 2.7) were made on the basis of the 7-year and the 45-month cycles. In addition, a highly reliable 18- to 22-month cycle is prominent. However, this cycle falls into the intermediate-term time-length category. Figure 2.8 shows the approximate 10-year cattle cycles back to the year 1915. In terms of reliability, cattle futures can indeed be traded on the basis of cycles. As in the case of hogs, no producer should be ignorant of the cycles in this market.

PORK BELLIES

The pork bellies market has been a long-standing favorite of many traders. The cycles here have run essentially similar in length to those in the hog market (please refer to the hog cycles for specifics). Figure 2.9 shows the approximate 3.6-year cycle in cash pork bellies as it stood in 1980. The reliability of this cycle

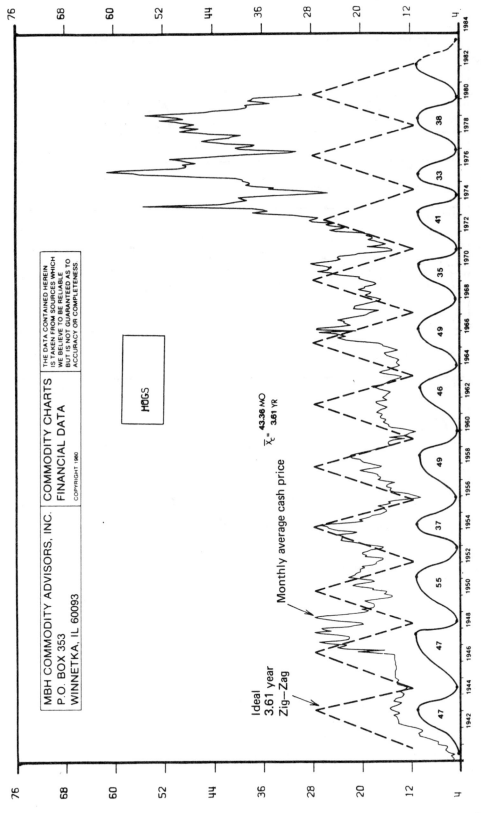

Figure 2.3 Cycles in cash live hogs 1940-1980. The zig-zag line shows an ideal 3.61-year (43.36-mo.) cycle. The actual cycles are shown at bottom of chart. Note that a large majority of the cycles fall within the 41—49-month range.

19

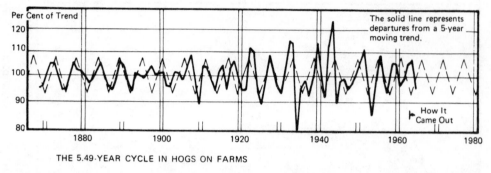

THE 5.49-YEAR CYCLE IN HOGS ON FARMS

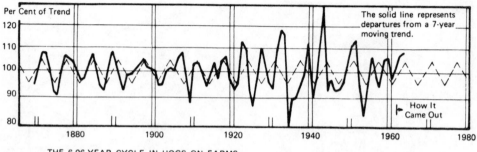

THE 6.06-YEAR CYCLE IN HOGS ON FARMS

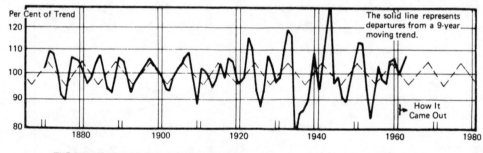

THE 8.78-YEAR CYCLE IN HOGS ON FARMS

Figure 2.4   Several cycles in hogs on farms (*Cycles*, May 1968, p. 108). Reprinted with permission of The Foundation for the Study of Cycles.

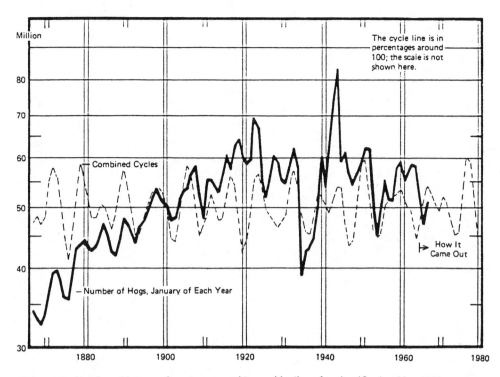

Figure 2.5   Number of hogs on farms compared to combination of cycles (*Cycles*, May 1968, p. 107). Reprinted with permission of The Foundation for the Study of Cycles.

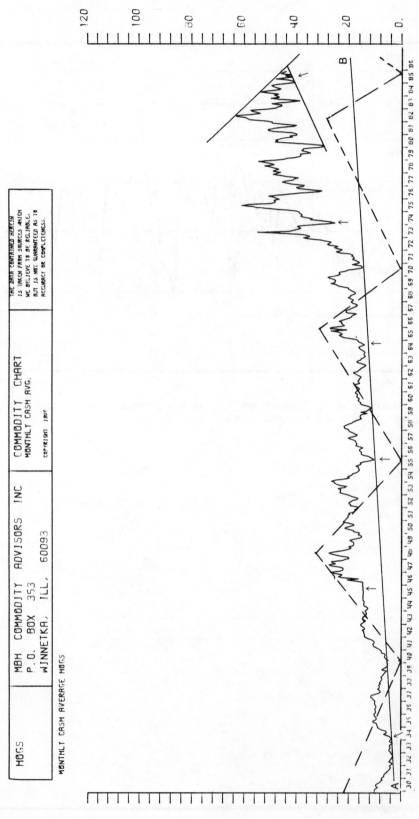

Figure 2.6 The approximate 15-year cycle in cash hogs (zig-zag). The approximate mid-decade cycle lows (10-yr. cycle) is shown with arrows. Long-term support trendline A—B.

22

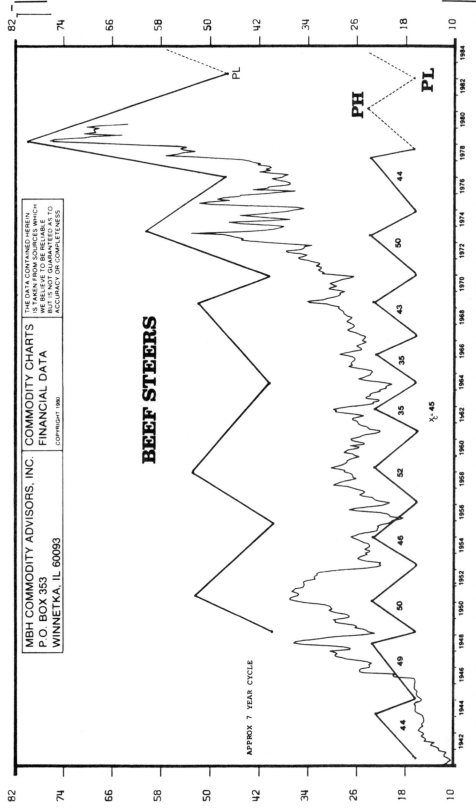

Figure 2.7 The approximate 7-year and 45-month cycles in beef steer prices. 1941-1982. PH = Projected high. PL = Projected low.

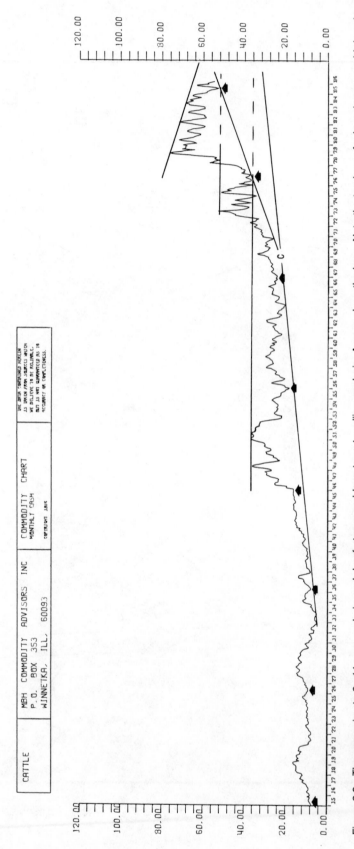

Figure 2.8 The approximate 9–11-year cycle in cash beef steers and long-term trendline analysis. Arrows show the lows. Note the tendency for lows to occur mid-decade and highs to occur about 3 years after the mid-decade lows.

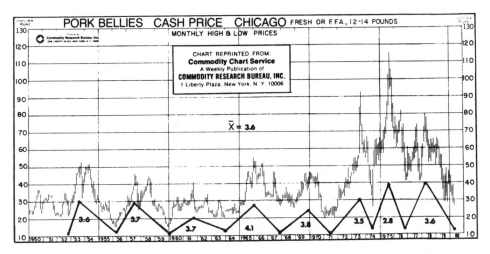

Figure 2.9   The 3.6-year cycle in cash pork bellies. Note the regularity of this cycle.

was excellent, and, furthermore, the price moves from cycle tops and bottoms were large. Figure 2.10 updates this cycle and illustrates another cyclic pattern that has proven valid. For those who trade bellies, these cycles are very valuable. Unfortunately, not too many traders can approach bellies from a longer term perspective without losing their objectivity when the wild price moves begin. But for those who can, the road to huge profits may be more readily visible.

WHEAT

The premier cycles in wheat have averaged about 54 years, 27 years, and 9 years, low to low, in their time span. Figure 2.11 shows the approximate 54-year cycle in European wheat prices from 1500 to 1850. Though this cycle is a reliable one, it is not of primary interest to the trader other than, perhaps, at projected major highs and lows. Figures 2.12 and 2.13 show some additional cycles in cash wheat, cycles that are more useful to traders and producers. (See the descriptive text accompanying each chart.) In addition, Figure 2.14 shows the approximate 9-year cycle (with traditional support/resistance lines) from 1915 to 1986. You can see for yourself that the approximate 9-year cycle in wheat prices is a viable and tradeable cycle. I rank long-term wheat cycles high in reliability.

CORN

The cycles in corn have run approximately 2.7 years, 5 to 6 years, 10.4 years, and 27 years in length. The work of Samuel Benner originally highlighted the important 5- to 6-year cycle. This cycle has been reliable for many years. Figure 2.15 shows the cycles as they were analyzed in *The Handbook of Commodity Cycles*. Figure 2.16 updates the 5–6-year corn cycle. Although many traders have lost interest in corn, moving instead to currencies, metals, stock index, and interest-rate futures in recent years, the cycles in corn are, nonetheless, still reliable. They are

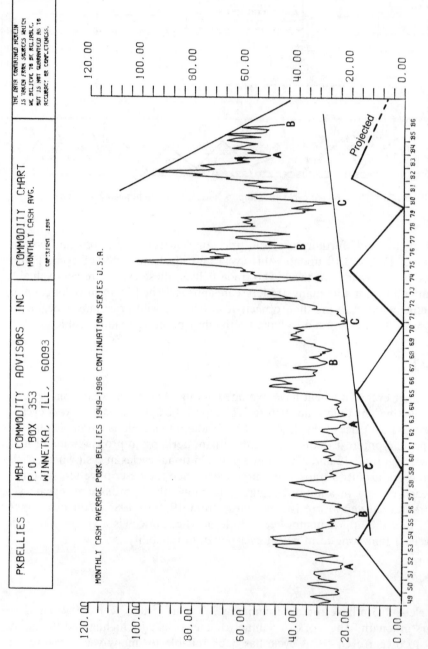

PKBELLIES | MBH COMMODITY ADVISORS INC P.O. BOX 353 WINNETKA, ILL. 60093 | COMMODITY CHART MONTHLY CASH AVG. COPYRIGHT 1986

MONTHLY CASH AVERAGE PORK BELLIES 1949-1986 CONTINUATION SERIES U.S.A.

Figure 2.10 The approximate 9—11-year cycle in cash pork bellies 1949-1986 with trendline analysis (support/resistance). A, B, C mark lows of approximate 3—6-year cycles. There have been approximately 3 repetitions of the 3—6-year cycle in each of the 9—11-year cycles.

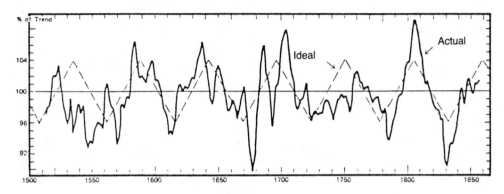

Figure 2.11 The approximate 54-year cycle in European wheat prices 1500-1850 (Dewey, 1962). Note that there have been some significant deviations from the ideal cycle (dashed line). Reprinted with permission of The Foundation for the Study of Cycles.

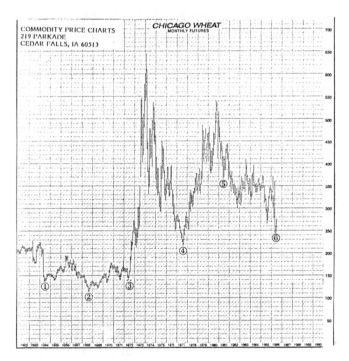

Figure 2.12 Cycles in wheat: numbers 1−6 mark approximate 4½-year cycle lows.

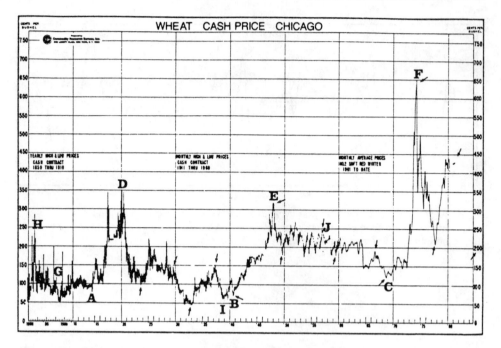

Figure 2.13 Cash price and cycle turns in Chicago wheat. Letters mark approximate 26-year highs and lows; arrows = 9-year cycle highs and lows.

effective profit-making tools for the speculator, investor, or producer. Do not ignore the corn market, particularly if you're a conservative trader or a newcomer to the futures markets.

SOYBEAN COMPLEX

By far the largest export crop of the United States, this market holds a near and dear spot in the hearts and pocketbooks of many traders. Although trading volume in the 1980's experienced a decline in the entire bean complex, this has not, in any way, altered the reliability of the cycles in beans, meal, or soybean oil. Figures 2.17 through 2.23 illustrate cycles, provide comments, and projections based on the various cycles. In terms of trading volume, the soybean complex in 1986 is not even a shadow of what it once was, yet I suspect that this will change dramatically in the years ahead as the world's food needs increase.

Take a close look at Figure 2.21, and observe the following:

1. Approximate 27-year cycle: One half the 54-year cycle is about 27 years, low to low. Based on this cycle, a low was made at #1, another low at #8, and low due at point A, with major tops at #'s 7 and 9. The next projected top is at time frame B. This cycle suggests that major lows could now be in the making, but remember that long-term cycles can and will be off in their actual count.
2. Approximate 10-year cycle: There have been four full repetitions of the cycle, which is ideally due to bottom in 1989. The next top should, therefore, come in 1994-1995, followed by a projected 1999 low.

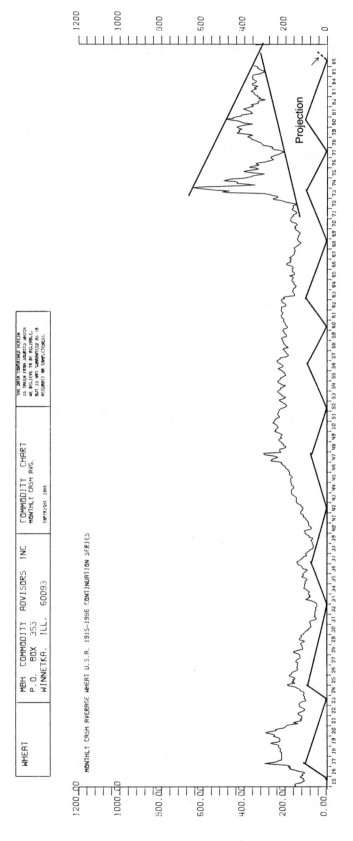

Figure 2.14 The approximate 9-year cycle in cash wheat prices 1915-1986. Note support and resistance since 1972.

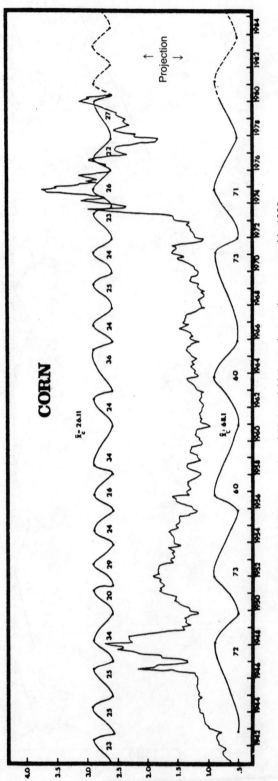

Figure 2.15   Cash corn cycles of 68.1 and 26.1 months, as they appeared in 1980.

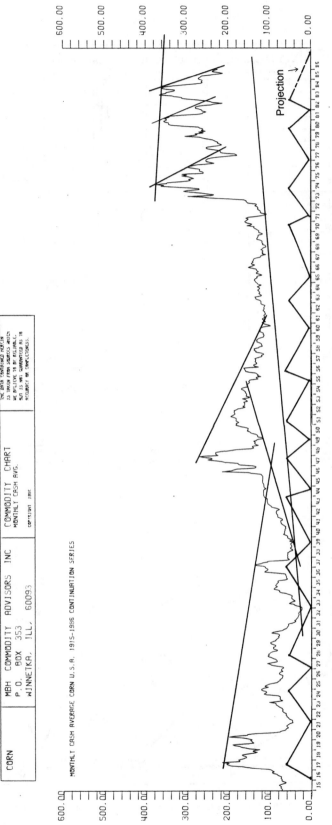

Figure 2.16 The approximate 5–6-year cycle in cash corn 1915-1986 showing long-term support and resistance trendlines.

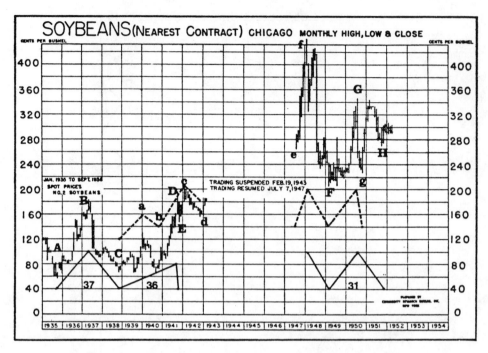

Figure 2.17   The 36- and 24-month cash soybean cycle, 1935-1951.

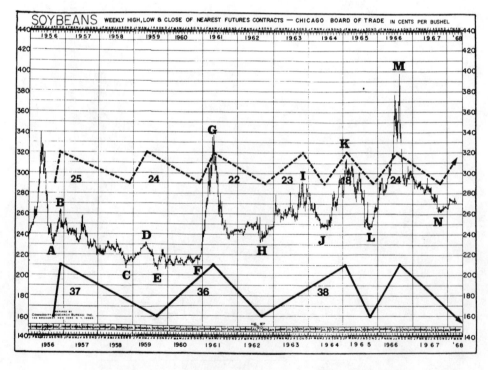

Figure 2.18   The 24- and 36-month cycles in soybeans, 1956-1968.

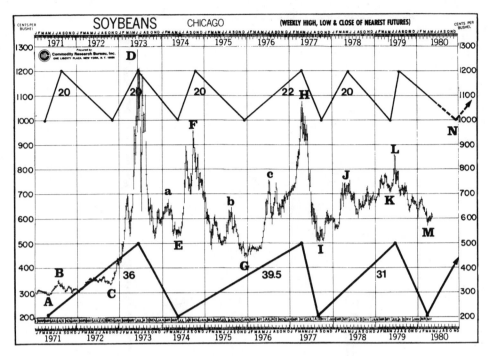

Figure 2.19   The 24- and 36-month cycles in soybeans, 1971-1980.

3. Approximate 34.7-month cycle is shown on the futures chart on 6, page 35. Recent lows of this cycle are shown on the cash chart as C, D, E, and F.

4. Approximate early decade low pattern is also shown on the cash chart. Note lows numbered 1 through 6. Observe that these tend to occur early in each decade and that a rally tends to follow. At times the rallies have been very large; at times, small. The next such pattern low is due in 1991-1993.

METALS

Metals, precious and otherwise, have enjoyed an avid following for many years, and so have their cycles. The charts accompanying this text highlight the numerous long-term cycles and their reliability. Bear in mind that the data history in gold is rather limited and, as a consequence, care must be taken lest we become too confident in the gold cycles. Silver and copper, on the other hand, have shown numerous cyclic tendencies, and their histories are lengthy. Note also that no charts have been included for platinum or palladium. In the case of palladium, the long-term data history is too limited for analysis, whereas in platinum the fixed producer price has obscured the cycles. As a final note, futures trading in precious metals on the basis of long-term cycles continues to be an effective and reliable strategy.

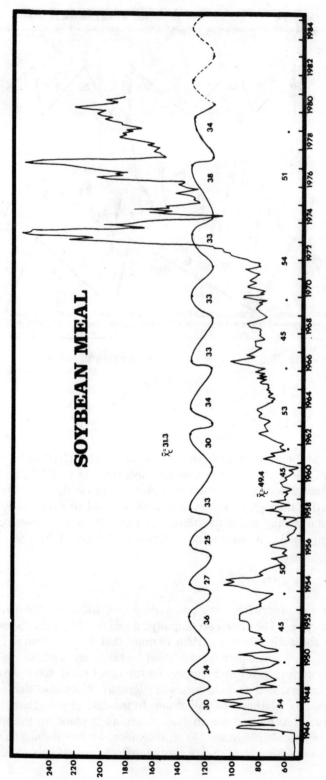

Figure 2.20   Cash soybean meal cycles of 31.3 and 49.4 months, 1946-1980.

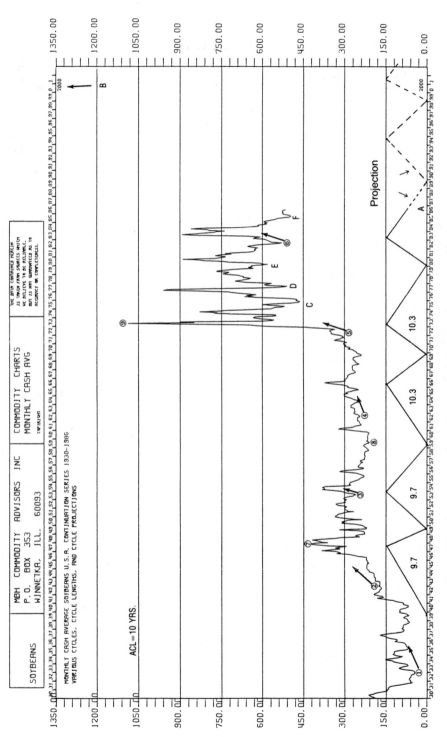

Figure 2.21 Long-term cycle analysis cash soybeans USA, with cycle projections.

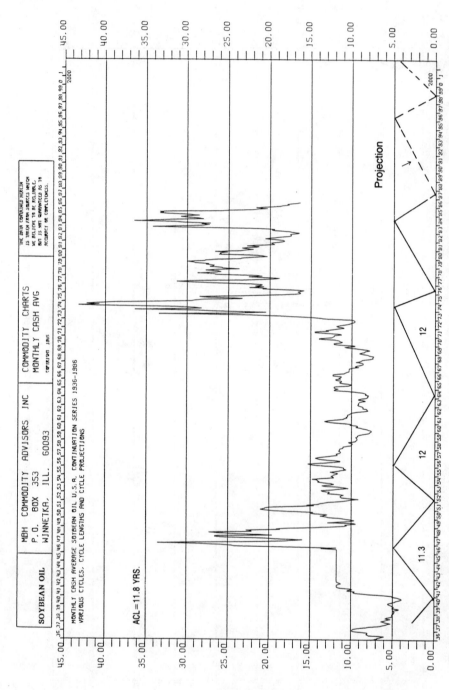

Figure 2.22 Soybean oil: approximate 11.8 year cycle. The last low based on the cash chart was made in 1976 with a low due in 1987.

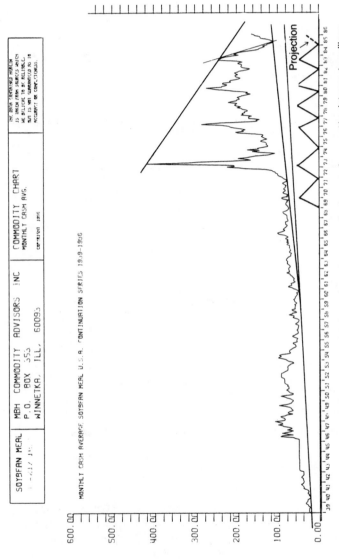

Figure 2.23   Recent 30—34-month cycles in cash soybean meal prices and support/resistance trendlines.

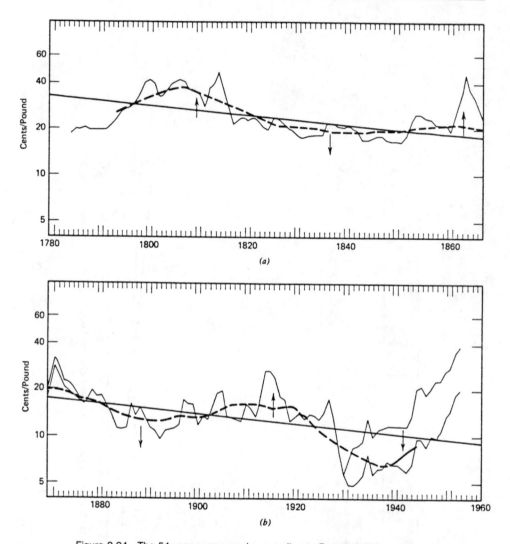

Figure 2.24   The 54-year copper cycle according to Dewey (1970, p. 578-9).

COPPER

Figures 2.24 and 2.25 show some previous studies of copper cycles. I'd like to call your attention particularly to Figure 2.26, which focuses on copper. Copper has had a long history of reliable cycles. The Foundation for the Study of Cycles and others have performed literally hundreds of studies on copper prices since there is a fairly continuous data history available. My conclusions and projections are as follows:

1. Approximate 12.8-year cycle lows and highs are shown. This cycle has been somewhat variable at times, but it is fairly reliable overall. It suggests that a low was made in 1984, yet a low even at this time would still be within reasonable bounds of the cycle length. A top is due in the early 1990's.

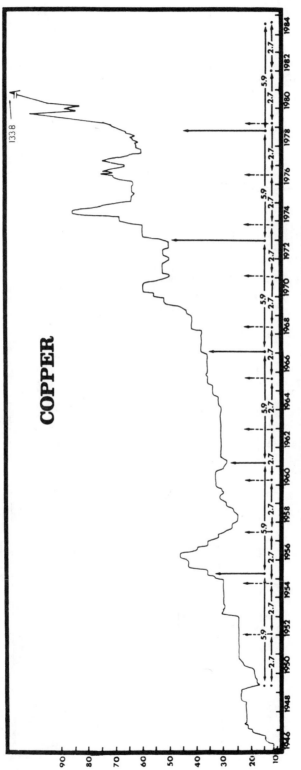

Figure 2.25   The 5.9- and 2.7-year cash copper cycles, 1946-1980.

39

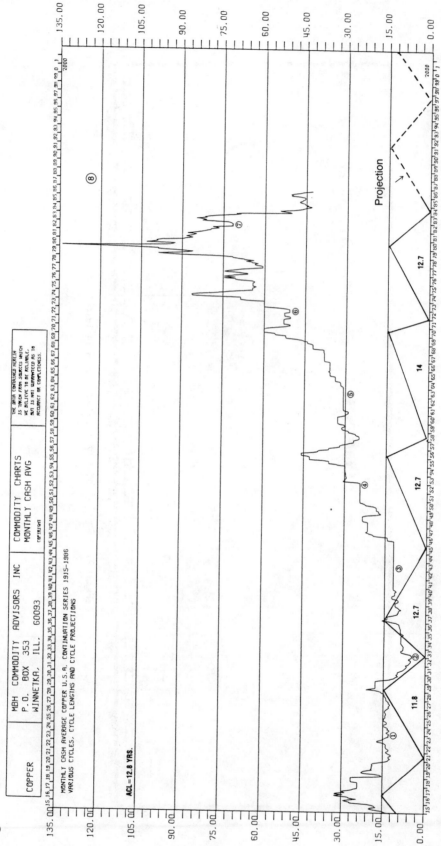

Figure 2.26 Copper: long-term cycle analysis and projections. Note that as we prepare to go to press, prices have staged a rally to approximately point #8, consistent with the projection made in 1986.

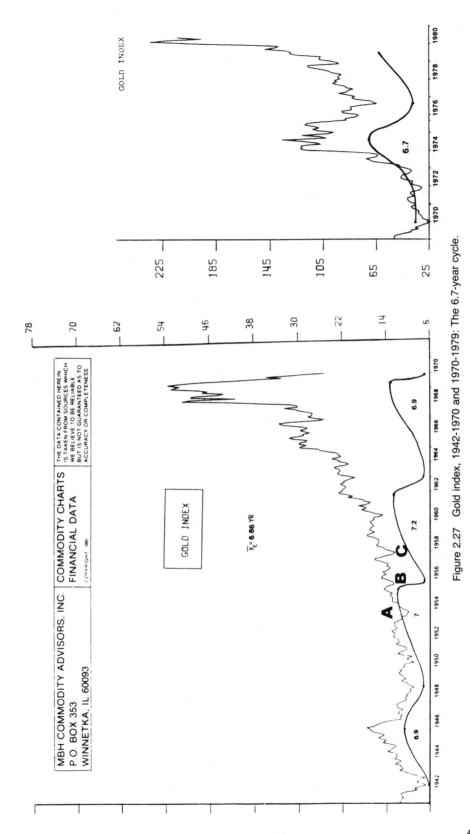

Figure 2.27 Gold index, 1942-1970 and 1970-1979: The 6.7-year cycle.

41

2. Early decade low pattern. Copper has shown a tendency to make lows early in each decade, most often in the years numbered 2 or 3. Though the subsequent upmove may at times be small, it does, nevertheless, appear to be consistent (lows marked 1-7 in Fig 2.26).

GOLD

Figure 2.27 shows some of my gold cycles work from 1980. Figure 2.28, dealing with gold, is another important study. The chart shows a combination of Gold Shares Index 1941-1974 and monthly cash average gold 1974-present.

There has been much discussion and controversy regarding the gold cycles. It appears that each faction sees a gold cycle consistent with its vested interest. Based on my work I show a rather unreliable cycle of 6.62 years, low to low. The next major low is projected for 1988-1989. A major peak is expected in 1991-1992 followed by what should be record highs in the 1997-1998 time frame.

SILVER

There are several important cycles in silver. The approximate 5.58 year cycle has been documented by The Foundation for the Study of Cycles. There is also an approximate 10 year cycle, low to low. The cycles in silver are not necessarily concomitant with those in the other precious metals. The cycles in silver will be examined more closely in later chapters. Figures 2.29 to 2.32 show some of the silver cycles.

COTTON

Because cotton prices have a long data history that has been readily available to researchers, cycles in cotton have received considerable attention and study. The Foundation for the Study of Cycles has devoted space to researching cotton cycles. Refer to their work for a more thorough analysis. My studies have revealed a number of reasonably reliable cycles, depicted in Figures 2.33 through 2.35. As a point of information, cotton has long been known as a trending market. Once a cycle tops or bottoms, the market has been prone to continue in the given direction with few significant interruptions. This makes cotton an ideal market for the cycles trader. Though trading activity has been down in recent years, this should not be a deterrent to the long-term trader.

COFFEE

Many traders tend to avoid the coffee market—this is understandable in view of the high degree of volatility in coffee futures. According to my studies, coffee cycles have run 6–7 years, low to low, and approximately 40–50 months, low to low. Both cycles are reliable and, provided one is willing to accept the risk of trading coffee futures, the cycles can be depended on for fairly reliable trends.

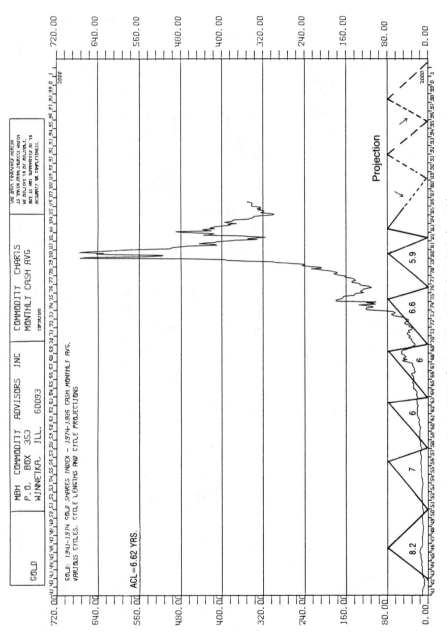

Figure 2.28 Cycle projection and analysis for gold.

43

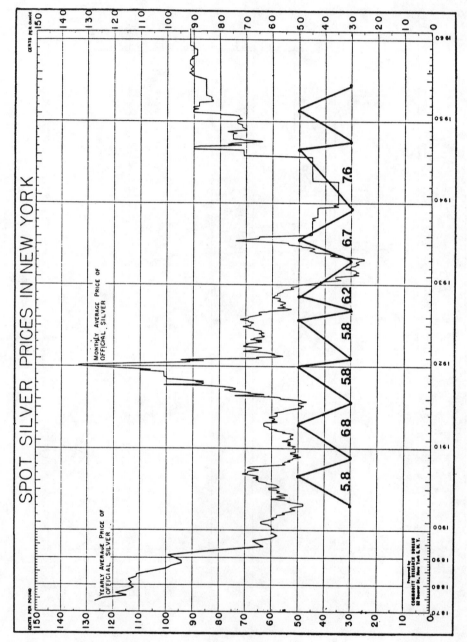

Figure 2.29 Cycles in cash silver, 1870-1960.

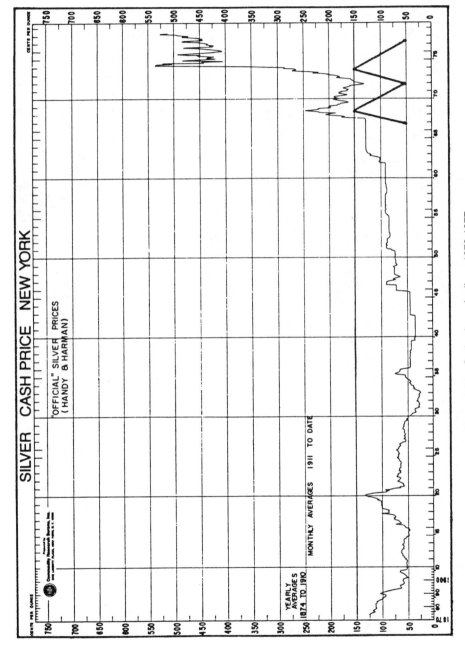

Figure 2.30 Cycles in cash silver, 1870-1977.

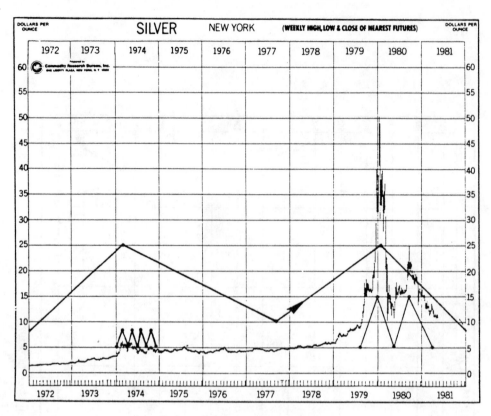

Figure 2.31   Several silver cycles.

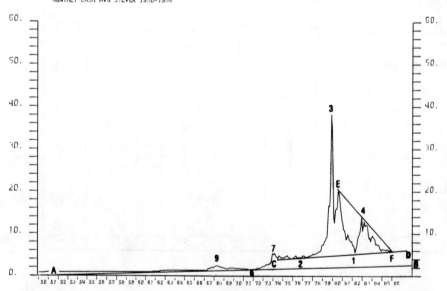

Figure 2.32   Long-term cycle in silver. Note cycle lows at 6, 2, 1 and highs at 9, 7, 3, and 4. Support at A-B, C-D and resistance at E-F.

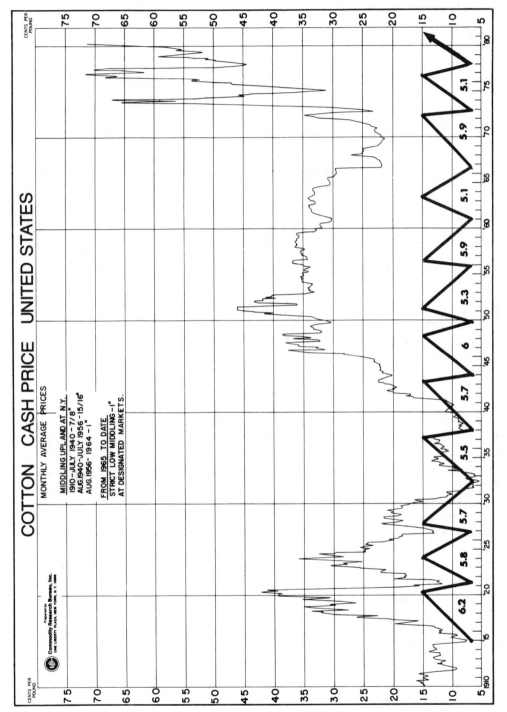

Figure 2.33   The long-term cycle in cotton. 1915-1980.

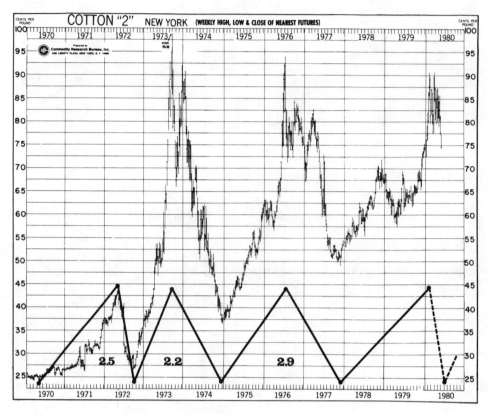

Figure 2.34   The 2.6-year cycle in cotton futures, 1970-1980.

Take a moment to study Figures 2.36 and 2.37. The coffee chart has, due to the nature and history of this market, required a few adjustments. During the early to mid-1940's the exchange was closed and no prices were available. The price during exchange closing is continued as a straight line plot through the reopening. Furthermore, prices during the 1970's were disrupted by the action of various coffee cartels, weather, etc., and several futures prices were used in place of cash prices during the spike of the early 1970's. The sharp runup during this period was primarily the result of frost in the growing regions, yet the cash market was severely disrupted and no consistent data source was readily available.

The approximate 6.44-year cycle is the major cycle in coffee prices and it has had a history of fairly good reliability. The next low is due in 1987. As a point of information, some of the major highs and lows in coffee correlate well with the major highs and lows in soybeans, reflecting the influence of Latin America's weather on both markets. The next low is projected to fall in late 1987 with a high due in 1990–1991. The subsequent cycles are shown by the dashed line.

SUGAR

Sugar has a long history of extremely quiet periods followed by periods of intense price volatility. Not only does sugar show a 54-year cycle but it has also shown a

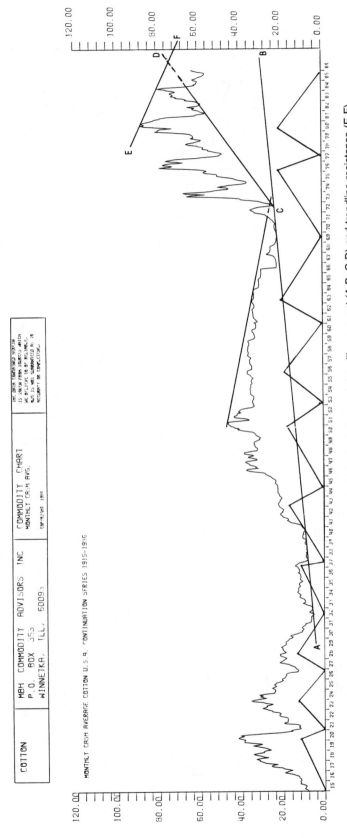

Figure 2.35 Long-term cycle in cotton, 1915-1985, alternate count, trendline support (A-B, C-D) and trendline resistance (E-F).

49

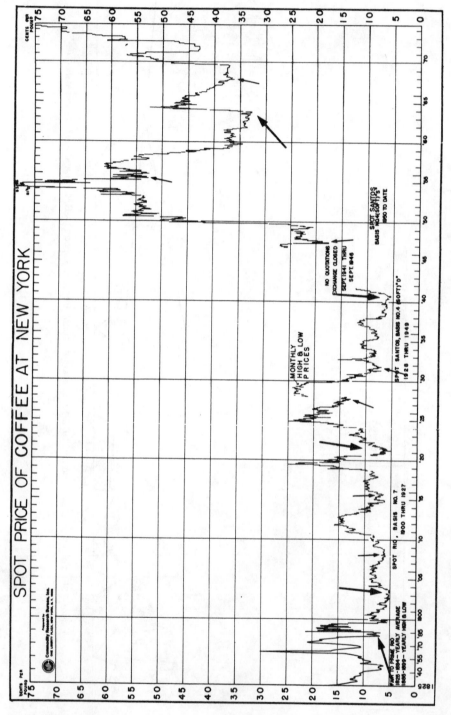

Figure 2.36 Long-term cycles in cash coffee. Large arrows show 18–20-year cycles.

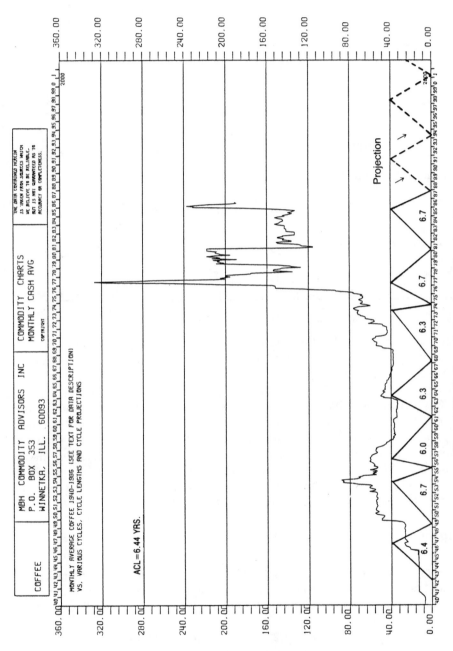

Figure 2.37 Cycle analysis and projections in coffee.

51

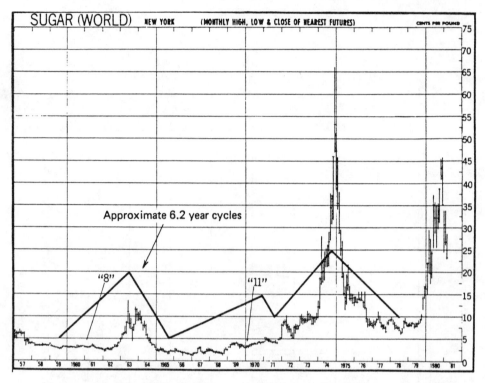

Figure 2.38   The approximate 6.2-year sugar cycle.

fairly reliable cycle of about 6–8 years (Figs. 2.38 and 2.40). As can be seen from the accompanying charts, the cycle has lengthened in recent years but still remains fairly reliable.

The cycle shown in Figure 2.39 has averaged 7.63 years, low to low. The last low was made in mid-1985 both in cash and futures. The trend has been up until the recent correction. The next top is projected for late 1987 to early 1988. Thereafter the next 7.63-year low should be seen in 1992–1993. The chart shows the balance of the cyclic projections. It should also be noted that sugar has had an approximate 54-year cycle, which, according to my research, last bottomed in the 1932–1934 time frame. If the cycle is on target, we could now be in the very early stages of a major new long-term bull market in sugar.

CURRENCIES

Currency futures do not have a lengthy trading history, but their cash markets do. My studies in cash-market cycles date back many years. They reveal a number of interesting cycles. In particular, the Canadian dollar has shown 11- and 22-year approximate cycles; the Swiss and D-Mark cycles of 3–4 years in length; and the Japanese yen, cycles of about 2 1/2 and 5 1/2 years in length. A selection of these cycles is shown in Figures 2.41 through 2.46. As a rule, trading in currencies has been fairly active, particularly in the Swiss and Yen. The markets have also shown fairly reliable intermediate-term cycles and should, therefore, be considered for inclusion in a cyclic trading programs.

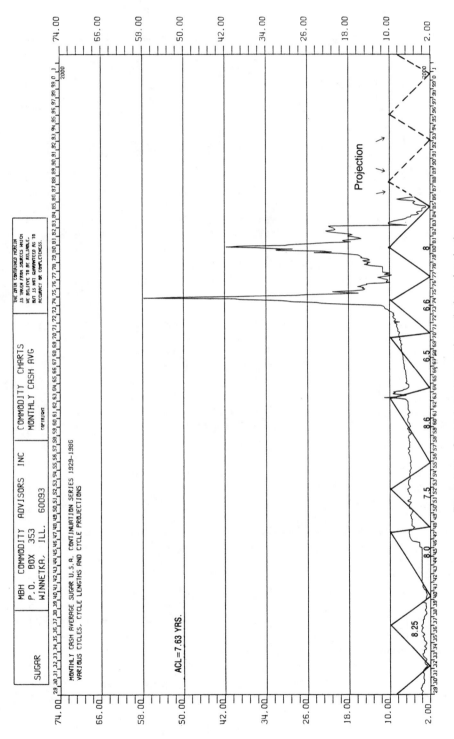

Figure 2.39   Sugar: Long-term cycle analysis and projection.

53

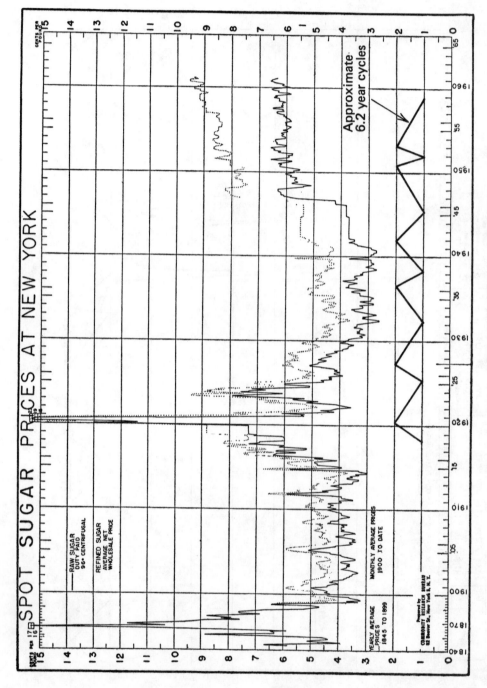

Figure 2.40   The long-term cycle in sugar, 1917-1959.

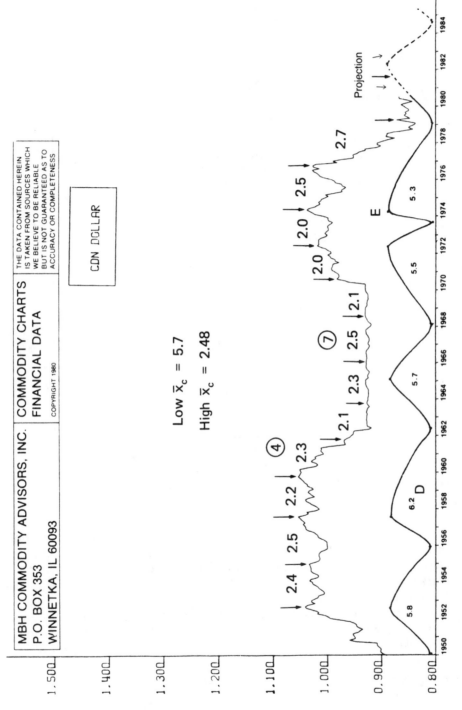

Figure 2.41   Cash cycles of 5.7 and 2.

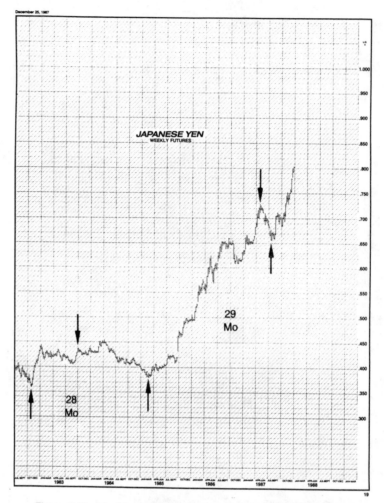

Figure 2.42   Monthly cycles in Japanese yen futures, 1983-1987.

Here are some comments that relate directly to Figure 2.45, which focuses on the Canadian dollar.

1. Approximate 22.23-year cycle. Though there have been only three repetitions of this cycle since 1915, I suspect that the cycle will prove to be a valid one. Based on this cycle we are now at what should be the start of a major bull market in the Canadian dollar that is likely to take the market to new all-time highs and a peak in the mid-1990's.
2. Approximate 7.41-year cycle. This cycle is part of the approximate 22.23-year cycle. It is shown as likely to bottom now as well, with a projected top in 1989−90.

STOCK INDICES

Perhaps the greatest marketing feat in commodities history was achieved when stock index futures were finally approved for trading in 1982. Since then, trading

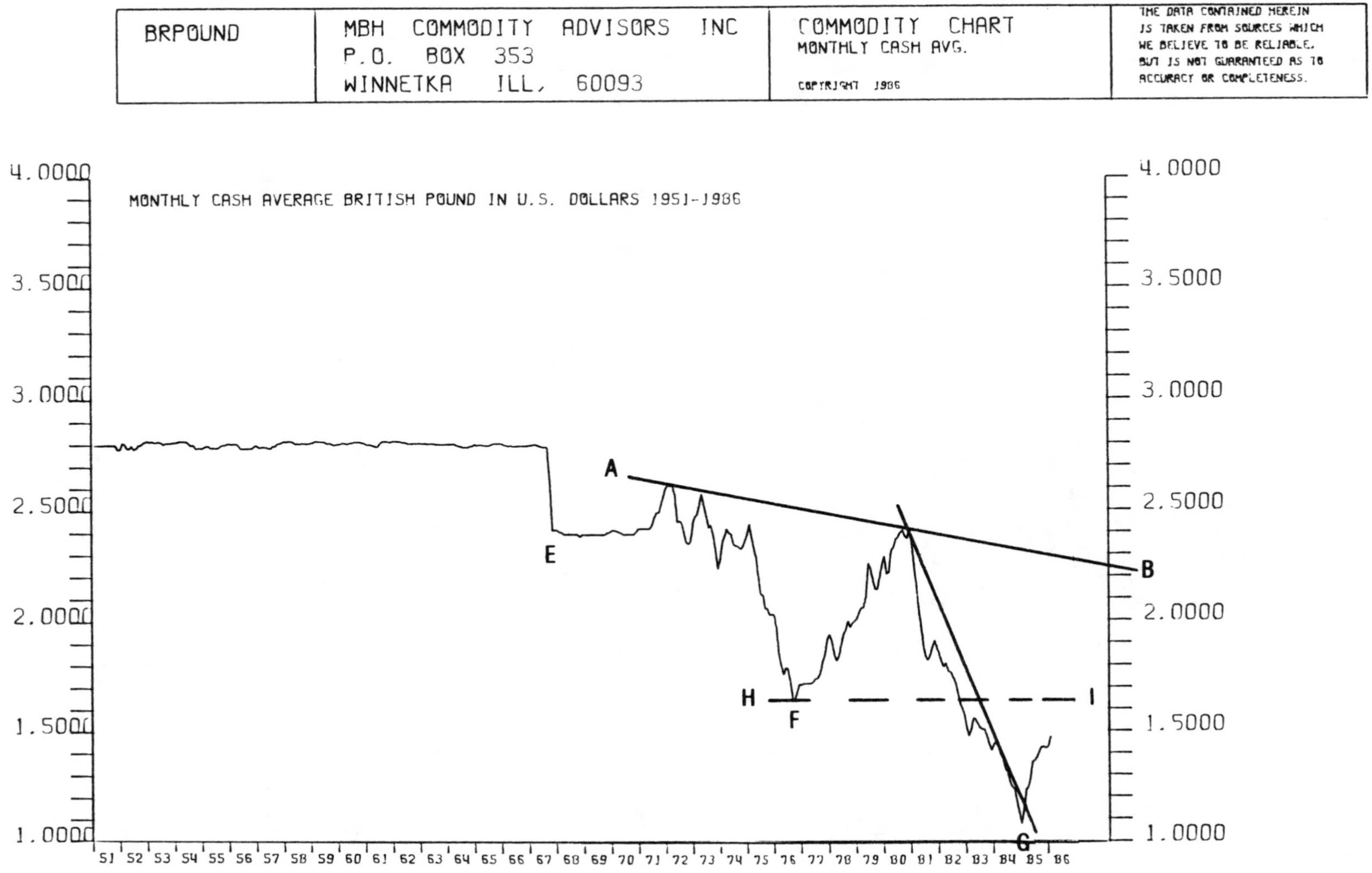

Figure 2.43 E, F, and G mark possible long-term cycle lows in British pound. Low G was an important low on the long-term cycle.

BRPOUND

MBH COMMODITY ADVISORS INC
P.O. BOX 353
WINNETKA ILL, 60093

COMMODITY CHART
MONTHLY CASH AVG.

COPYRIGHT 1986

MONTHLY CASH AVERAGE BRITISH POUND IN U.S. DOLLARS 1951-1986

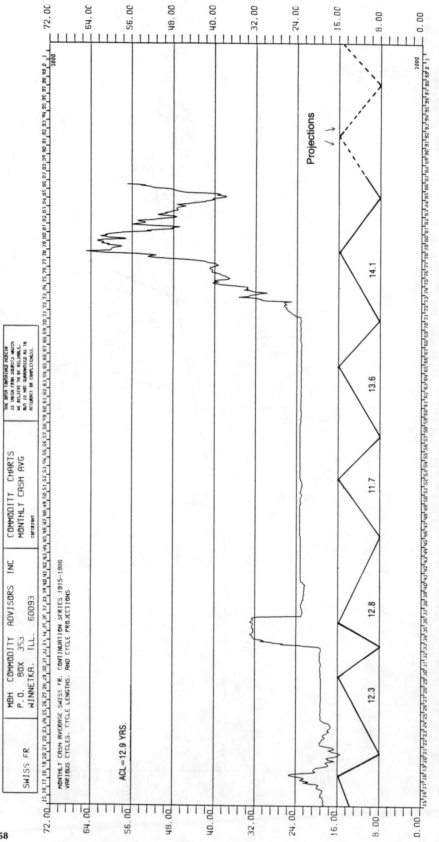

58

Figure 2.44 Long-term cycles and projection: Swiss franc. Note that Swiss franc has moved much higher since this chart and projections were made in 1986.

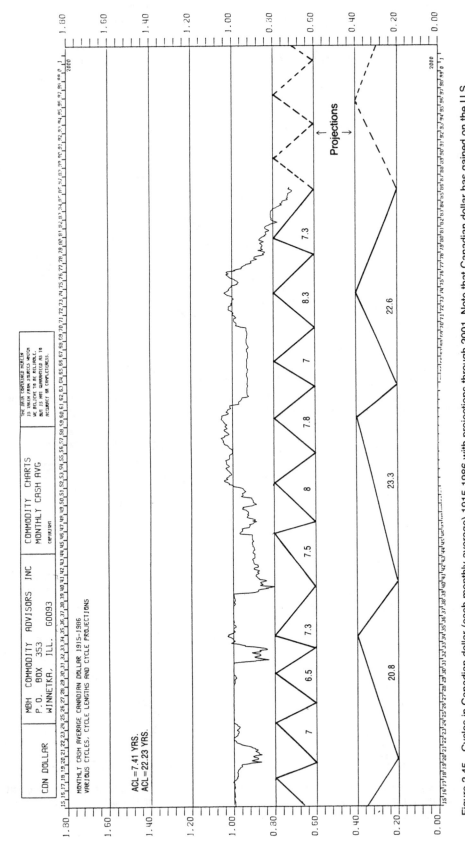

Figure 2.45　Cycles in Canadian dollar (cash monthly average) 1915-1986 with projections through 2001. Note that Canadian dollar has gained on the U.S. dollar since these projections were first published in 1986.

59

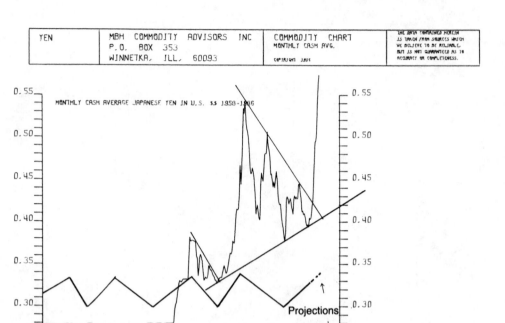

| YEN | MBH COMMODITY ADVISORS INC
P.O. BOX 353
WINNETKA, ILL, 60093 | COMMODITY CHART
MONTHLY CASH AVG.
COPYRIGHT 1985 | THE DATA CONTAINED HEREIN
IS TAKEN FROM SOURCES WHICH
WE BELIEVE TO BE RELIABLE,
BUT IS NOT GUARANTEED AS TO
ACCURACY OR COMPLETENESS. |

MONTHLY CASH AVERAGE JAPANESE YEN IN U.S. $$ 1958-1986

Projections

Figure 2.46 Various cycles, support and resistance in monthly cash average Japanese yen 1958-1986. Dashed lines show projections.

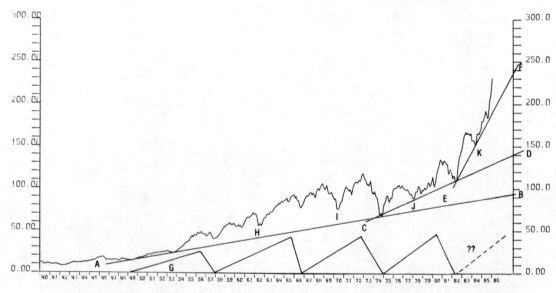

| S&P COMP | MBH COMMODITY ADVISORS INC
P.O. BOX 353
WINNETKA, ILL, 60093 | COMMODITY CHART
MONTHLY CASH AVG.
COPYRIGHT 1985 | THE DATA CONTAINED HEREIN
IS TAKEN FROM SOURCES WHICH
WE BELIEVE TO BE RELIABLE,
BUT IS NOT GUARANTEED AS TO
ACCURACY OR COMPLETENESS. |

Figure 2.47 Monthly cash average S&P stock average. A-B, C-D, E-F indicate long-term support trendlines. Zig zag marks approximate 8−9-year cycles. G-K mark approximate 4.2-year cycle lows.

volume has grown dramatically, along with record trading volume in the stock and bond markets. By formulating the contract specifications and making stock index futures viable, the exchanges have bridged the old gap between futures and stocks, attracting many new players to the markets. There could not have been a better vehicle to attract the public, inasmuch as stock price trends have been studied more often by more analysts and cyclic researchers than has any other market. Based on the Standard and Poor's average, Figure 2.47 shows two of the most important cycles in stocks. They are approximately 4.3 years and 8−9 years, low to low, in length. Many other cycles in stock prices exist, longer and shorter than the ones mentioned, yet the two included here are the most viable for long-term traders in stock index futures.

LUMBER

Though the market has historically been a quiet one on the futures side, the cycles in lumber, seasonal, long-term, and short-term have been very reliable. Figures 2.48 and 2.49 illustrate the long term cycles. The approximate 51−54-month cycle is not coincidentally in the same length range as is one of the stock market cycles. The approximate 8−9-year cycle is a multiple of the 51−54 month cycle, and has also been highly valid. Historically, lumber prices have made large price swings. This is an ideal market for the cycles trader, in spite of relatively light trading volume.

PETROLEUM

With the continued mid East crisis and efforts at price manipulation by OPEC, the petroleum market has attracted much attention and trading volume. Hence, examination of some of the long-term cyclic patterns is essential. Since the most continuous source of data available was the fuel-oil monthly cash average price, my research is based on this segment of the petroleum market. Initial studies suggest a possible 3−4-year cycle and 10-year cycles. See Figure 2.50 for an illustration of the cyclic patterns.

INTEREST RATES

The advent of trading in T-Bond futures has revolutionized the futures industry. In addition, it has attracted trading from all corners of the world. This has contributed to the record growth of T-Bond futures volume at the Chicago Board of Trade. In 1986, T-Bond futures were the single most actively traded futures contract. T-Bonds are an excellent market for the long-term trader who is familiar with the cycles. As you can see from Figures 2.52 and 2.53, there are several reliable cycles and tendencies in interest rates (short-term and long-term). Today, the banker, capital intensive business, speculator, or money manager who is not familiar with the reliable cycles in interest-rate futures is missing many opportunities.

There are several important patterns and cycles in short-term interest rates, as shown in Figures 2.51 and 2.53. These are as follows:

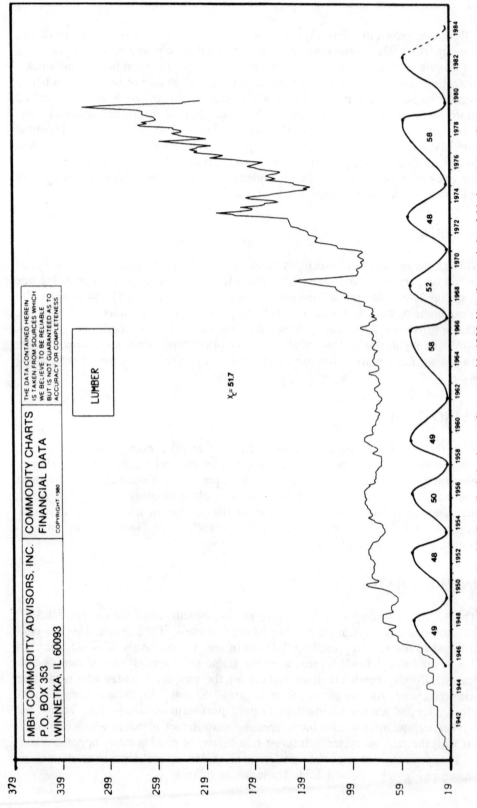

Figure 2.48 Cash cycle of 51.7 months in lumber, as it appeared in 1980. Note the regularity of this long-term cycle.

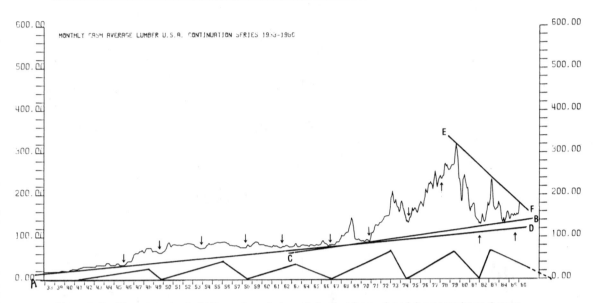

| LUMBER | MBH COMMODITY ADVISORS INC
P.O. BOX 353
WINNETKA, ILL, 60093 | COMMODITY CHART
MONTHLY CASH AVG.
COPYRIGHT 1987 | THE DATA CONTAINED HEREIN
IS TAKEN FROM SOURCES WHICH
WE BELIEVE TO BE RELIABLE,
BUT IS NOT GUARANTEED AS TO
ACCURACY OR COMPLETENESS. |

Figure 2.49 The approximate 51.7-month cycle in cash lumber (arrows) and the approximate 8-year cycle in cash lumber (zig zag), including long-term support and resistance (A-F), 1938-1986.

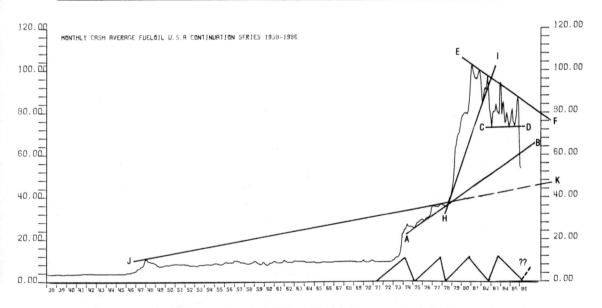

| FUEL OIL | MBH COMMODITY ADVISORS INC
P.O. BOX 353
WINNETKA, ILL, 60093 | COMMODITY CHART
MONTHLY CASH AVG.
COPYRIGHT 1986 | THE DATA CONTAINED HEREIN
IS TAKEN FROM SOURCES WHICH
WE BELIEVE TO BE RELIABLE,
BUT IS NOT GUARANTEED AS TO
ACCURACY OR COMPLETENESS. |

Figure 2.50 Monthly cash average fuel oil 1938-1985, showing approximate 3–4-year cycles and trendlines A-K. Note the cycle low projected for 1986.

63

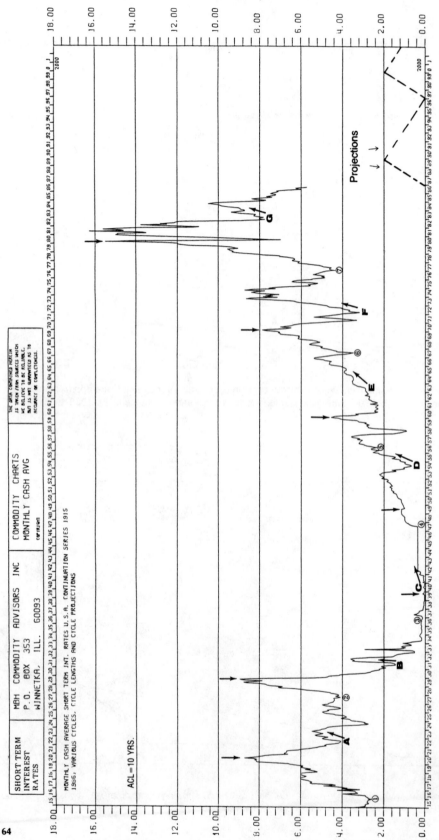

Figure 2.51 Cycles in short-term interest rates, 1915–1986.

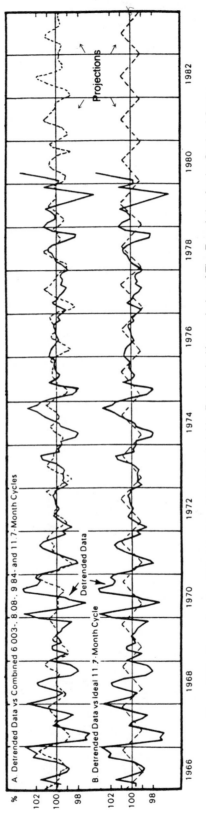

Figure 2.52 Several cycles (detrended) in railroad bond yields. Reprinted with permission of The Foundation for the Study of Cycles.

65

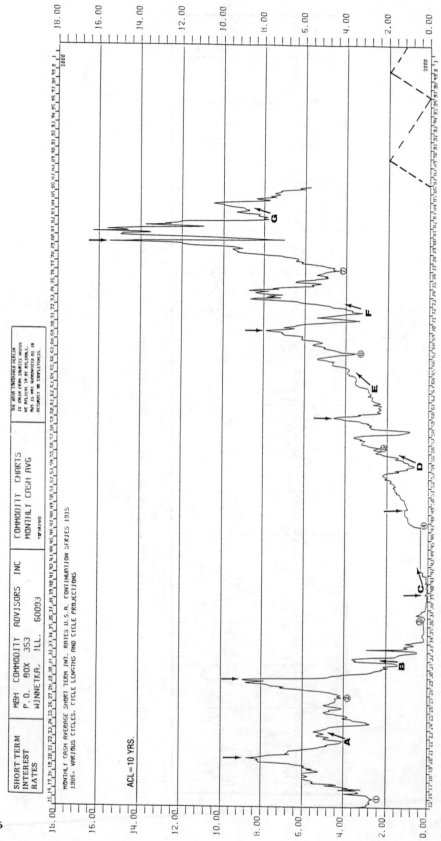

Figure 2.53 Cycle analysis and projection: short-term interest rates USA. Note the projected cycles (dashed lines).

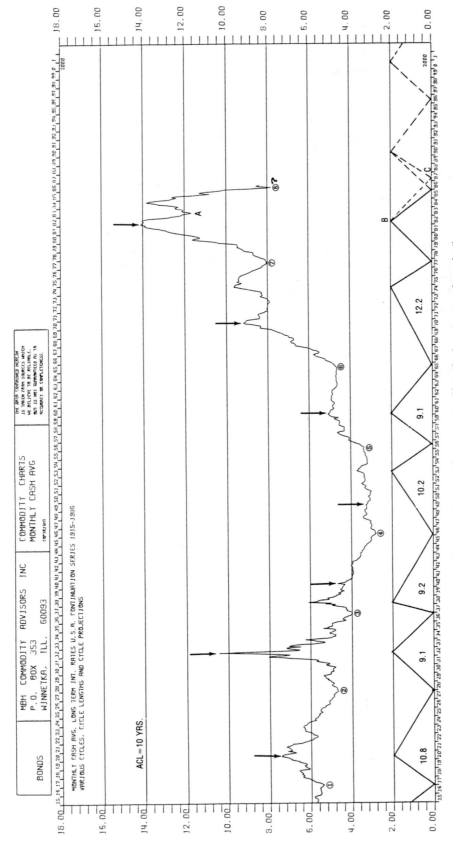

Figure 2.54 Cycles in long-term interest rates. Note the long-term cycle projections.

1. Approximate 10-year cycle. This cycle suggests that a low is being made to be followed by a top in the 1989 time frame and another low in the 1996–1997 time frame.
2. Early decade low pattern is shown by arrows and letters. Note that there has been a tendency for prices to bottom early in each decade.
3. Late decade high pattern is shown by arrows at the tops. Note that there has been a tendency for highs to be seen toward the latter part of each decade.

There are also several patterns to observe in long-term interest rates (see Figure 2.54). In particular, note:

1. Approximate 10-year cycle lows and highs are shown and projected. Note that an alternate count for the current cycle is possible, projecting a low in early 1987 as opposed to a low in the current time frame (see B,C). Low A was the bottom of a shorter term cycle.
2. Mid-decade low pattern is shown as lows numbered 1–8. Note how accurate this pattern has been and note its recent position (#8).
3. Late decade high pattern is shown by arrows marking the tops. Note also the repetitiveness of this pattern. See also short-term interest rate discussion.

There are many other long-term cycles. In fact, an analysis of all important long-term cycles in futures, and cash markets, as well as in the economy, could fill an entire book. I encourage you to do your own research, or to keep in touch with my up-to-date studies which are published by my office at irregular intervals.

3
Some Intermediate-Term Patterns

Intermediate-term cycles in the cash and futures markets provide the most reliable trading opportunities, though certainly not the most frequent. Typically, such cycles as the approximate 14- to 19-week cycles in Stock Index Futures and the approximate 36- to 48-week cycles in most of the other markets have frequently provided some of the most profitable and dependable opportunities in the futures markets. In addition, these cycles are important to producers and hedgers seeking market entries for their particular needs. The 9- to 11-month cycle, another of the intermediate-term cycle, will be given individual attention, in the next chapter due to its pervasive nature. The present chapter also discusses intermediate-term cycles too long to be termed short-term cycles, or too long to fall within the limits of the typical 9- to 11-month patterns (but too short to be called "long-term cycles").

WHY INTERMEDIATE-TERM CYCLES ARE IMPORTANT

A good majority of futures traders are not professional traders. Professional traders are those who have no employment other than investing or speculation in the futures markets. Most individuals cannot monitor markets very closely and, as a consequence, are more concerned with long-term and intermediate-term price movements in the markets. Short-term, or day trading, is generally not acceptable to many people because of their time commitments. The intermediate-term cycles lend themselves to a more leisurely program of study and implementation. Timeliness (in the sense of market entry) is just as important for intermediate term trading as it is for short-term positions, yet the decision-making process can take more time.

In addition to the attraction they hold to investors and the public in general, intermediate-term cycles are important to hedgers and commercial interests. For various reasons, these groups or individuals wish to either buy or sell hedge for an intermediate time period. By having cyclic information at their disposal, they can time market entry to protect their special interests.

A third (and growing) area of application for intermediate-term cycles is in the area of futures options. Though most options-trading programs concentrate on the interrelationships between futures and options, the use of intermediate-term cycles can be a significant addition to a program of options trading. All three aspects will be discussed later in this book.

EXAMINING THE INTERMEDIATE-TERM PATTERNS

The balance of this chapter is dedicated to a visual presentation of intermediate-term cycles (not necessarily including the 9- to 11-month cycles) and their recent status. Borrowing from *The Handbook of Commodity Cycles*, the history of these cycles is examined from approximately 1973 to 1980. A current weekly futures chart is included, which updates the cycles from approximately 1981 to 1986. The emphasis of this analysis is threefold as follows:

1. <u>The cycles are reviewed for reliability.</u> Has the given cycle continued to behave as it did when previously discussed in *The Handbook of Commodity Cycles?* Has it varied? If so, is it now unreliable? Has it become more reliable? Is it a viable cycle in terms of trading? Has the nature of the given market changed (in some cases, trading volume in the given market has declined to the point of virtual nonactivity)?
2. <u>As a reference, some of the timing signals originally explained in *The Handbook of Commodity Cycles* are illustrated at cycle tops and bottoms.</u> Those who are not yet familiar with these signals need not be concerned. Later on in the book, when these signals are reviewed, you may return to and reread this chapters.
3. <u>Evaluation of the intermediate-term cycles is provided from the standpoint of real time trading.</u> Brief comments are provided on given cycles and how they have been performing recently in the markets, both in terms of timing indicators and potential risk and reward.

LIVE CATTLE

Figure 3.1 shows the approximate 30-week cycle in live cattle futures from 1975 through 1980. When this chart was first published, the longest cycle had run about 34 weeks, low to low, and the shortest about 25 weeks, low to low, yielding an average cycle length of 29.67 weeks, low to low. Examine the current chart, Figure 3.2. The current update reveals that the cycle of preference in live cattle futures is the approximate 40- to 50-week cycle. The cycle that appeared in the 1975–1980 data probably still exists as a one-half cycle of this more important intermediate-term pattern. The original chart has been reworked, with arrows on the approximate 40- to 50-week cycle highs and lows, which, of course, is the 9- to 11-month cycle. Also shown are a few of the timing signals.

With the addition of five repetitions of the 40- to 50-week cattle cycles, this is clearly the most useful intermediate-term cycle in cattle futures. In addition, the timing signals (as illustrated) appear to have been quite reliable at tops and bottoms. This is the single best cycle for intermediate-term trading in cattle futures, particularly when combined with effective timing tools. Remember, cycles can and do change in length. Therefore, continuous monitoring of cycles is recommended to determine if their length has changed significantly.

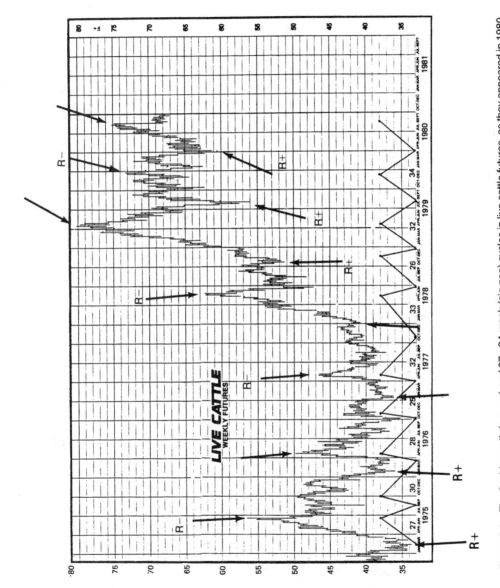

Figure 3.1 The 9–11-month (arrows) and 27–34-week (zig zag) cycles in live cattle futures, as they appeared in 1980. Some of the weekly timing signals are also shown (R+ = weekly upside reversal; R− = weekly downside reversal).

71

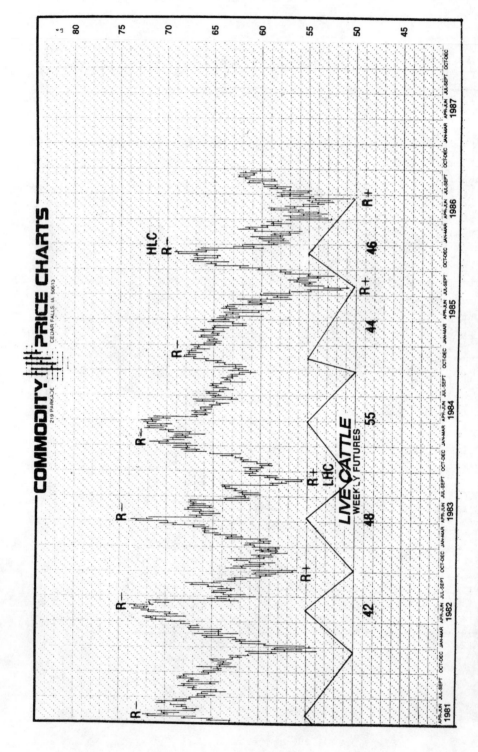

Figure 3.2 The approximate 9–11-month cycles in cattle futures and timing signals at cycle turns. (R+ = weekly upside reversal; R− = weekly downside reversal; HLC = High/Low close signal; LHC = Low/High close signal).

PORK BELLIES

The pork bellie market, a favorite of old-time futures speculators, has fallen on hard times (in regard to volume) in recent years. Though the intermediate-term cycle from 1971 through 1980 was rather variable in length with a count as short as 32 weeks, low to low, and as long as 50 weeks, low to low, it was, nevertheless, a reasonably reliable pattern. The approximate one-half cycle was, as in the case of live cattle futures, present, but not as reliable. Continuation of this cycle for the 1981–1986 data is shown in Figure 3.4 along with some of the timing indicators at tops and bottoms. As a point of information, the tops and bottoms A through F (Figure 3.3) are tops and bottoms of the approximate 3.7-year long-term cycle.

Based on its current status, the pork bellie cycle has stabilized within the 40- to 50-week time span parameters, given a reasonable degree of variation. Longer cycle counts have, indeed, been seen, but the cycles have become relatively more symmetrical and, hence, predictable. The last cycle is shown with a possible count of 34 weeks, low to low, which would be a short count. There may be a more likely count of about 57 weeks, low to low, which would be a bit longer than usual. Time will tell about the resolution of this pattern. The timing signals as shown have been very reliable. The cycles and timing indicators in pork bellie futures are very reliable for the speculator, provided that the reduced trading volume and very high volatility are taken into consideration. Pork bellie trading is still something reserved for higher risk traders, in spite of the fairly reliable cycles this market has shown.

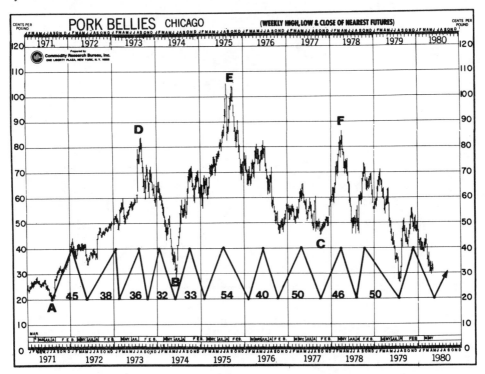

Figure 3.3   Intermediate-term cycle in pork bellies (zig zag), and approximate 3.6-year cycles A–F.

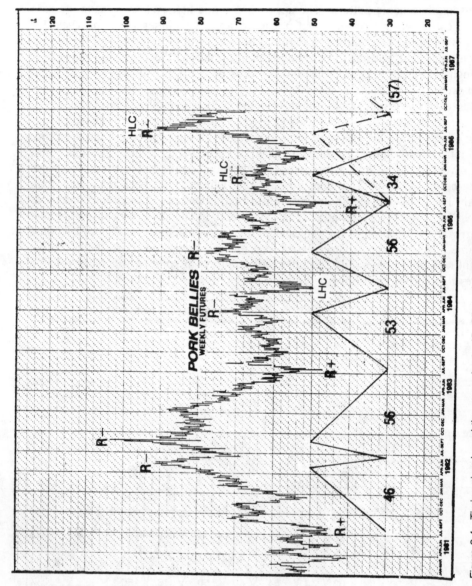

Figure 3.4 Timing signals and the approximate 45–55-week cycle in pork bellie futures (note alternate cycle count as dashed line). (Timing signal abbreviations explained on previous figures).

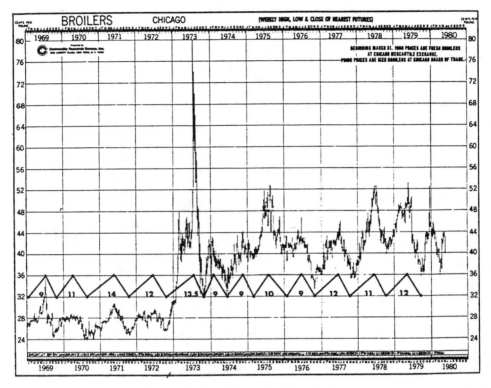

Figure 3.5 The 11.5-month cycle in broilers.

BROILERS

A steady decline in trading volume both in broilers has made this market a thing of the past. Hence, no new information on broilers is available. This is unfortunate, since its cycles were extremely reliable from a seasonal standpoint, as well as from the perspective of intermediate-term trading. In the future, interest in this market (as well as in shell egg futures) may be revived. If this is the case, then cycle trends may be expected to continue along the same basic patterns as they have in the past. (See Figure 3.5.)

EGGS

For many years, one of the most reliable seasonal markets was shell egg futures. That the trading volume in shell eggs has declined to a virtual standstill is, indeed, a loss to those who trade by cycles. In the event that trading may one day be revived, two charts are included from *The Handbook of Commodity Cycles* (Figures 3.6 and 3.7). Note from the cash monthly egg chart (Figure 3.8) that the cash egg market has certainly not been tame by any standards. In the cash chart there are clear indications that the approximate 11 1/2- to 13-month cycle is still reliable. But lack of trading volume should keep speculators away.

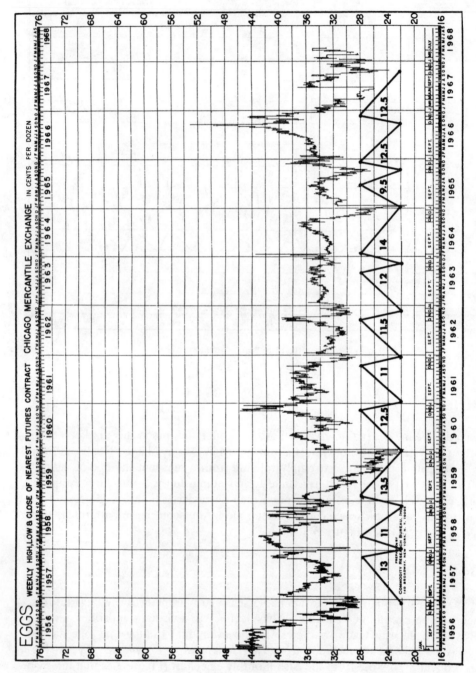

Figure 3.6 Intermediate-term cycle in egg futures, 1956-1967.

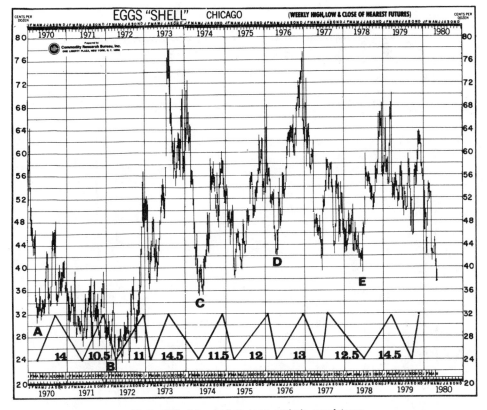

Figure 3.7   Intermediate-term cycle in egg futures.

POTATOES

The potato market has ceased to be a viable trading entity due to a variety of problems. This is unfortunate, since for many years the potato market exhibited highly reliable cycles and seasonals. The weekly charts (Figures 3.9 and 3.10) show a pattern running from approximately 29 to 36 months, low to low. The updated chart (Figure 3.11) shows the continuation of this cycle. Technically speaking, the length of this cycle (about 3 years) would qualify as a borderline long-term cycle; however, it has been included as an intermediate-term pattern. This is a moot point, since futures trading in potatoes is no longer active. If futures trading in potatoes revives, this market may make a good candidate for cyclic and seasonal trading in view of its historically high reliability.

ORANGE JUICE

The history of orange-juice futures has been one of high volatility and relatively thin trading volume. In spite of these limitations, the cycles have been fairly regular. An examination of Figures 3.12 through 3.14 shows an approximate 56-week cycle that has run as short as 43 weeks and as long as 61 weeks, low to low. The

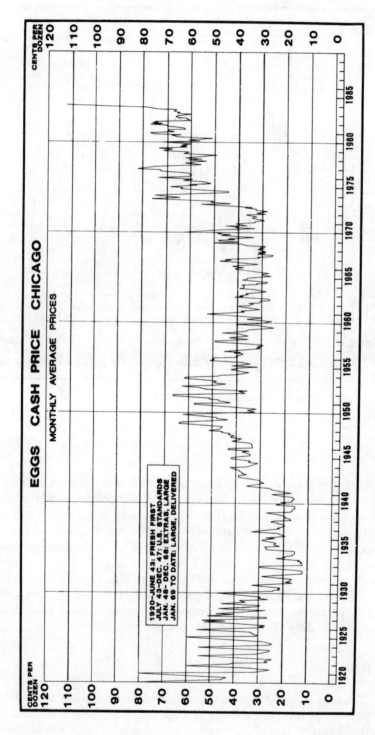

Figure 3.8   Monthly cash average eggs. Note highly volatile price history.

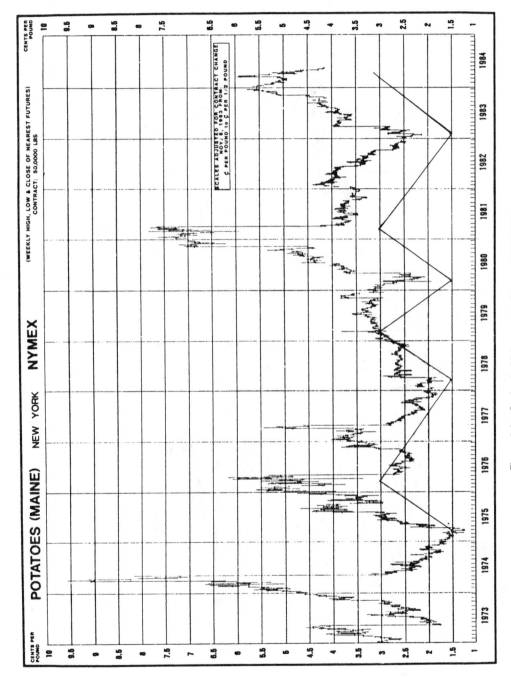

Figure 3.9   Cycles in Maine potato futures, 1973-1984.

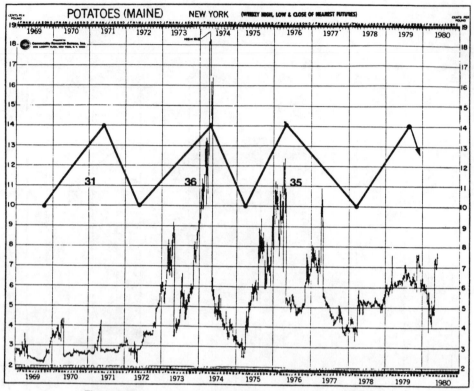

Figure 3.10   Intermediate-term cycle in potato futures, 1969-1980.

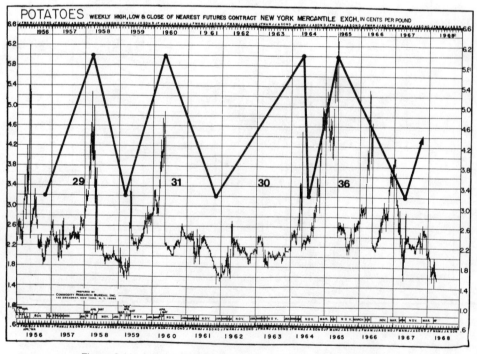

Figure 3.11   Intermediate-term cycle in potato futures, 1956-1967.

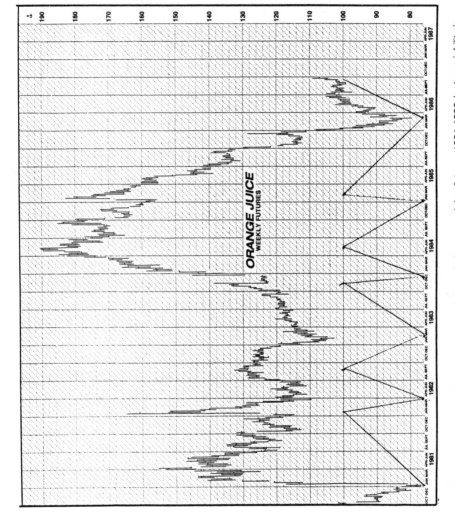

Figure 3.12   The approximate 10–15-month cycle in orange juice futures 1981-1986 (note variability in cycle length).

Weekly High, Low—Friday Close

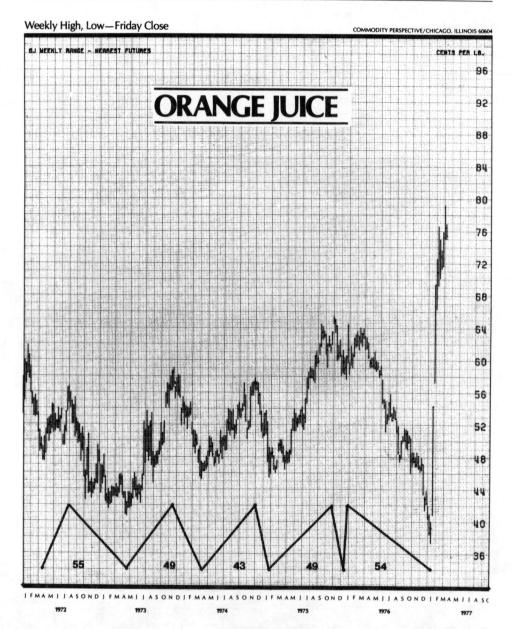

Figure 3.13   Intermediate-term cycle in orange juice futures, 1972-1977 (note variability in cycle length).

seasonal factor in this market is, indeed, an important one, as most of the bullish moves of substance have had their roots in frost and freeze scares. This is likely the cause of an approximate 12-month cycle as opposed to a 9- to 11-month cycle. Timing signals and indicators appear to be reasonably valid. For the strong and the brave, orange juice might prove a good market to trade both from a seasonal and cyclical standpoint.

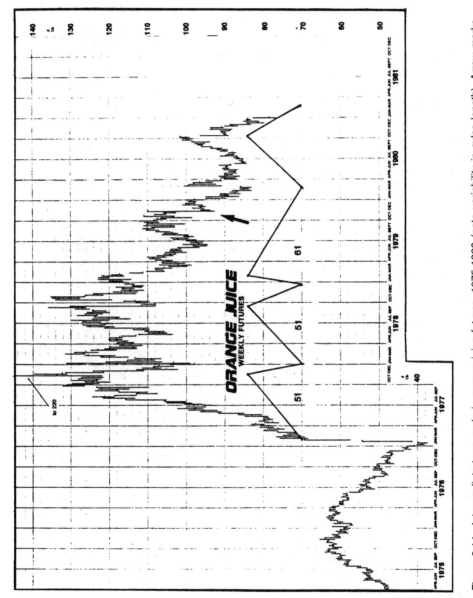

Figure 3.14 Intermediate-term cycle in orange juice futures, 1975-1980 (note variability in cylce length). Arrow marks alternate low.

SUGAR

The cycles in sugar have been rather erratic, not only during the 1970's but into the 1980's as well. (See Figures 3.15-3.16). Because the intermediate-term cycles in sugar have not been particularly reliable in recent years. Avoiding the market on the basis of these cycles for net long or short intermediate-term positions is, therefore, recommended. However, now that futures options in sugar are traded, withstanding the deviation in cycle lengths (by buying time through the use of a futures option) might well be possible. Seasonal and short term cycles, however, do have potential.

PLYWOOD

Since publication of *The Handbook of Commodity Cycles*, the plywood market has ceased to be a viable trading entity due to a significant drop in volume. However, lumber futures are still trading in sufficient volume to permit reasonably good price executions. Both the lumber and plywood markets continue to exhibit

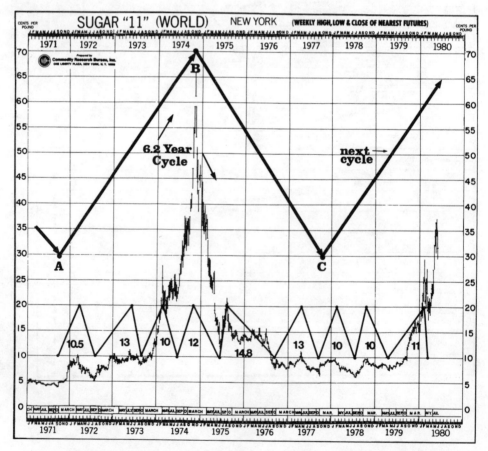

Figure 3.15   The approximate 12.5-month sugar futures cycle (1971-1980).

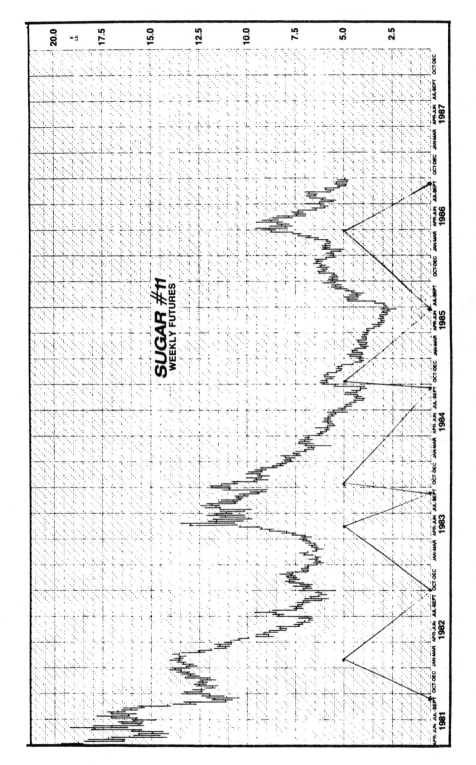

Figure 3.16   The approximate 12.5-month cycle in sugar futures 1981-1986.

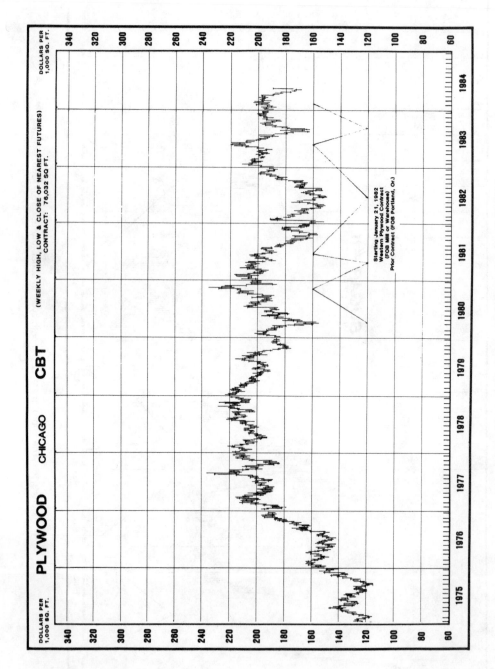

Figure 3.17 Plywood futures intermediate-term cycles 1980-1984.

Weekly High, Low—Friday Close COMMODITY PERSPECTIVE/CHICAGO, ILLINOIS 60604

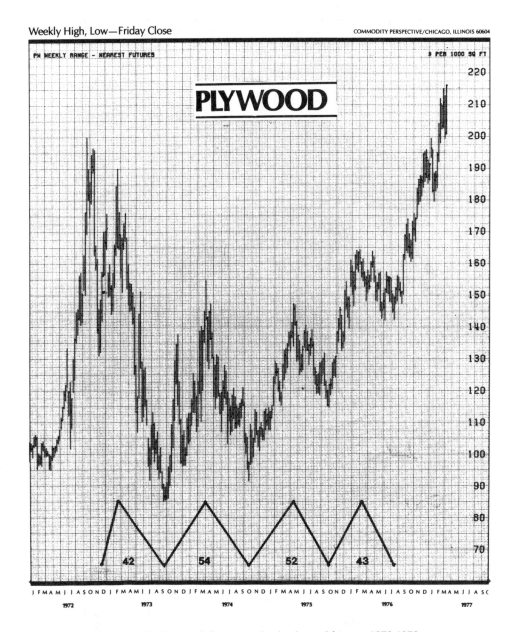

Figure 3.18 Intermediate-term cycles in plywood futures, 1972-1976.

reliable seasonal price tendencies. Figures 3.17 and 3.18 show the weekly plywood charts covering 1972 through 1980. Figure 3.19 shows the 1975 through 1980 time span along with the cycles. Note that the approximate 42- to 61-week cycle has continued valid; however, trading lumber is a much better alternative to plywood futures. See the following lumber analysis.

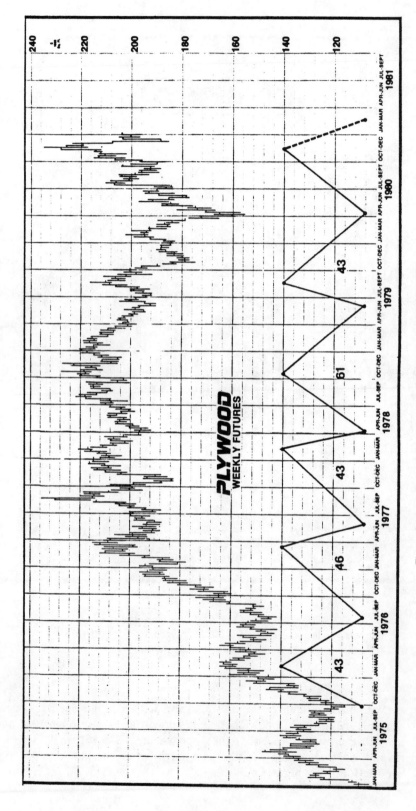

Figure 3.19   Intermediate-term cycles in plywood futures, 1975-1980.

LUMBER

The lumber cycles are shown in Figure 3.20. Four repetitions of an approximate 26- to 32-month cycle are apparent. Though not symmetrical, the cycle has been fairly reliable, and the cycle turns typically come in advance of large moves. Figure 3.21 shows the most recent cycle (1984-1986). Lumber has not been especially active in recent years, however, it is still a reasonably liquid market. Given the reliable cycles and seasonal tendencies in lumber futures, lumber is a good vehicle for cyclic and seasonal trading, and is recommended without hesitation.

GOLD

The intermediate-term cycles in gold are essentially similar to those of silver; however, they have been somewhat more reliable. Figures 3.22 and 3.23 show the behavior of this cycle over many years. Note that since 1982 the cycles have been especially reliable. In addition, the timing indicators shown have had a good record of reliability. The gold market is actively traded, has excellent seasonal tendencies, and reliable cycles. In addition, the market has actively traded futures options, thereby making it a good all-around vehicle for those using cyclic trading methods.

SILVER

The history of silver cycles has been rather erratic; however, some salvation can be taken in the approximate 20- to 25-week cycles. Figure 3.24 shows how these cycles behaved during the 1972−1976 time frame. Figure 3.25 shows their behavior in recent years.

Figure 3.26 shows that the cycles have not only been fairly regular as measured across the lows but that they have also been prone to early tops. Figure 3.26 also shows some of the traditional timing indicators and their incidence at cycle tops and bottoms.

PLATINUM

The platinum market has shown a fairly good cycle of approximately 7 to 8 months, low to low. Figure 3.27 shows how the cycles have looked from 1981 to 1986. The cycle was most likely present previous to the 1981 time frame. Interested parties should examine the charts for indications of this cycle. The signals, also shown on Figure 3.27, are also quite reliable. The recent cyclic behavior of platinum is reliable. Within the ability of traders to accept the extreme volatility and relatively thin volume of trading, I believe that platinum can be traded from a cyclical perspective.

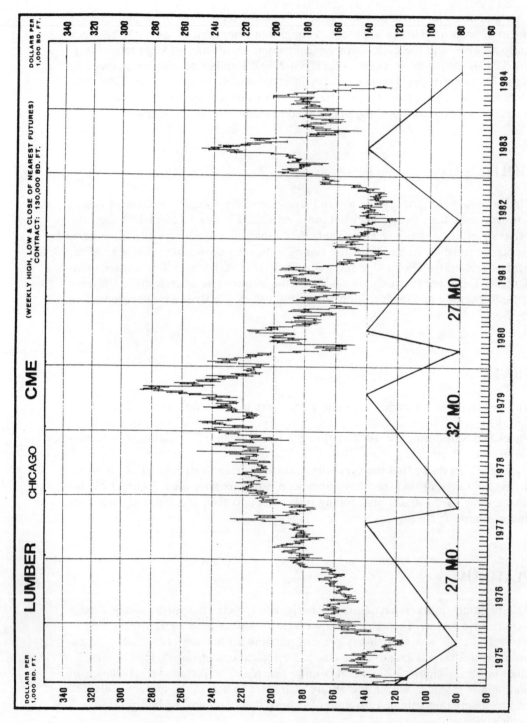

Figure 3.20   The approximate 26½–30-month cycle in lumber futures 1975-1984.

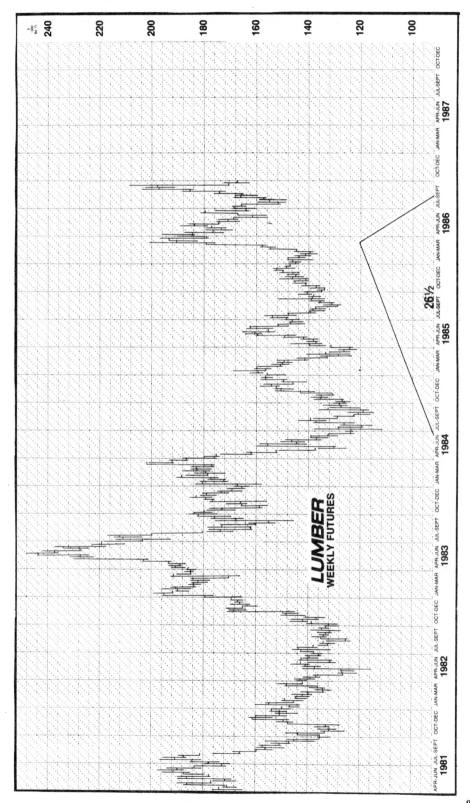

Figure 3.21   The approximate 26½–30-month cycle in lumber futures 1984-1986.

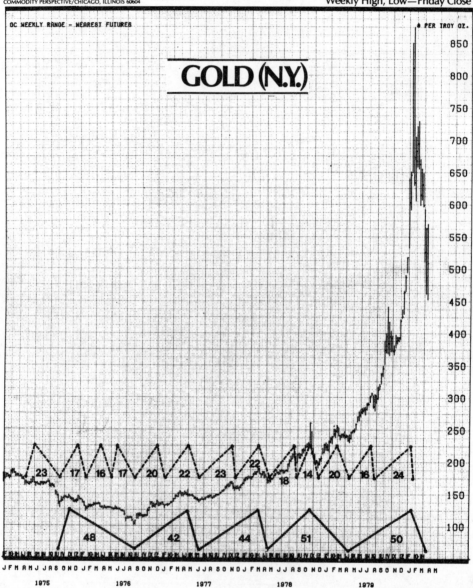

Figure 3.22   Intermediate-term cycles in gold futures, 1975-1980.

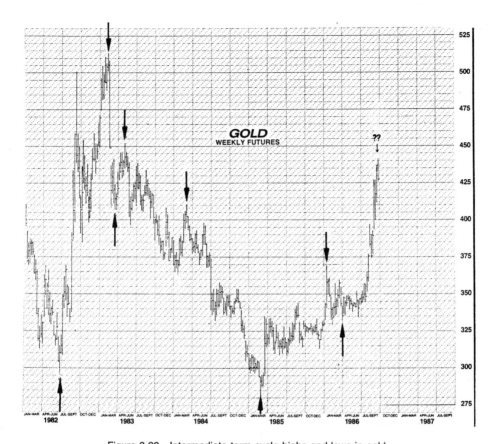

Figure 3.23   Intermediate-term cycle highs and lows in gold.

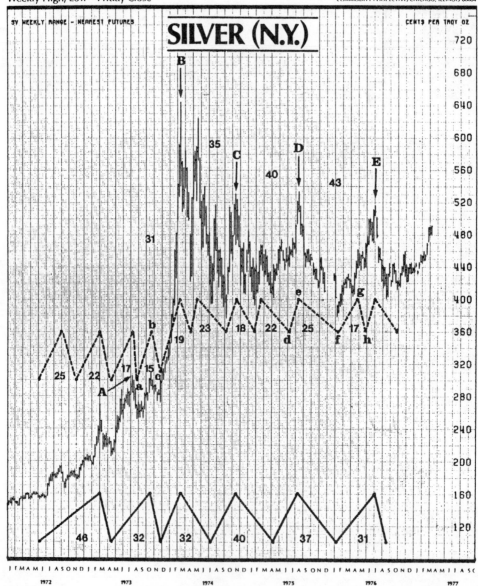

Figure 3.24　Intermediate-term cycles in silver futures, 1972-1976.

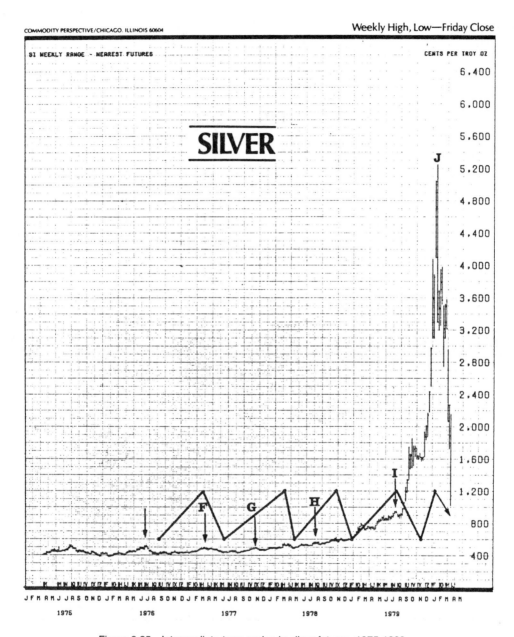

Figure 3.25   Intermediate-term cycles in silver futures, 1975-1980.

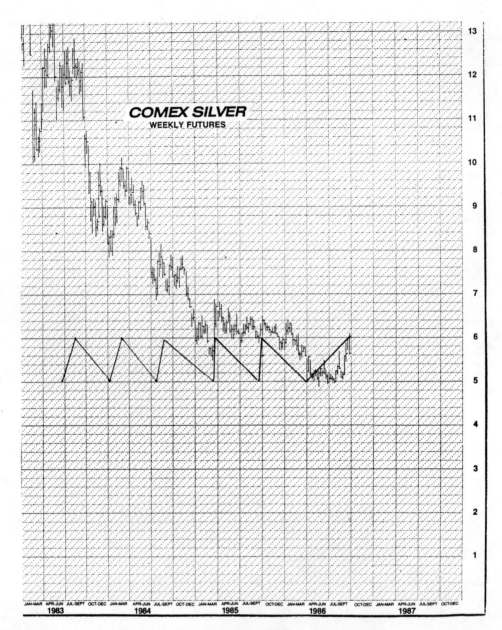

Figure 3.26 Intermediate-term cycles in silver, 1983-1986.

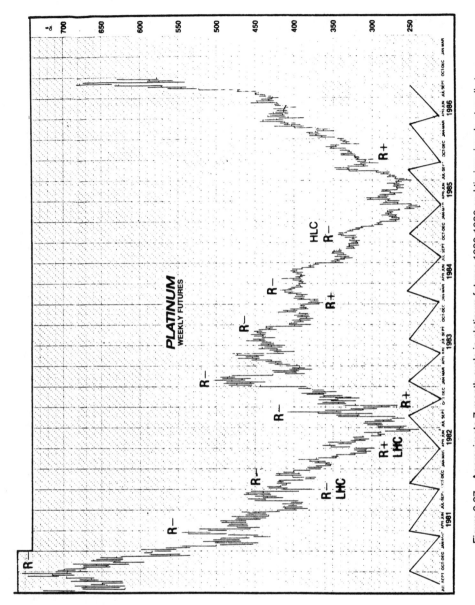

Figure 3.27   Approximate 7-month cycle in platinum futures 1980-1986 and timing signals at cyclic turns.

97

COTTON

A number of cycles in cotton futures exist. The approximate 2.5-year (30-month) cycle shown in Figure 3.28 and in Figures 3.29 and 3.30 (ABC, CDE, and EFG) is more of a long-term cycle; however, its direction is critically important to the approximate 20-week cycle shown in Figures 3.30 and 3.31. As a rule, cotton cycles have not been as reliable as have cycles in other markets. The circled numbers 1, 2, and 3 refer to items discussed in *The Handbook of Commodity Cycles*.

In updating work on the approximate 20-week cycles for the period 1981–1986, the following items were observed:

1. The approximate 20-week cycle most likely has lengthened to an average of 23 weeks, low to low.
2. The cycle appears to have become more reliable. With the exception of one cycle, ABC (See Figure 3.31), the 23-week cycle appears to have called a majority of the turns since 1981.
3. The ability of the cycle to call D (Figure 3.31), an important low, further attests to its validity.
4. Timing signals shown on Figure 3.31 have been quite reliable.

Figure 3.28   2.5-year cotton cycle, 1935-1951.

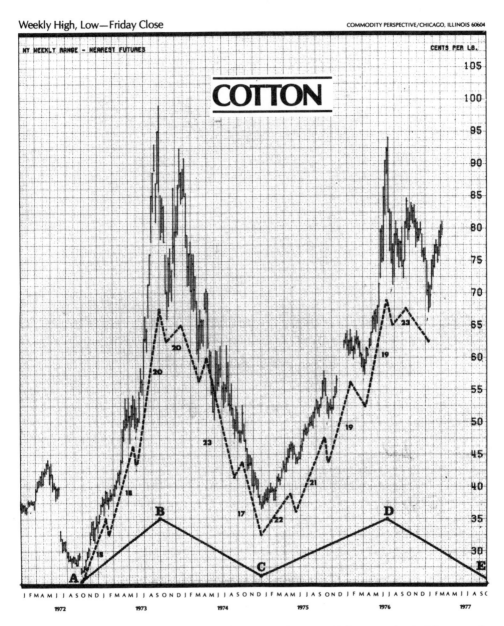

Figure 3.29 The approximate 20-week cycle in cotton futures and the approximate 2.5-year cycle A-E, 1972-1977.

Note that the apparent large drop on the chart in 1986 was due to a contract switch on the weekly charts. The decline is real; however, it appears as a switch in contracts as opposed to a gradual drop. Various fundamental factors were responsible for this situation.

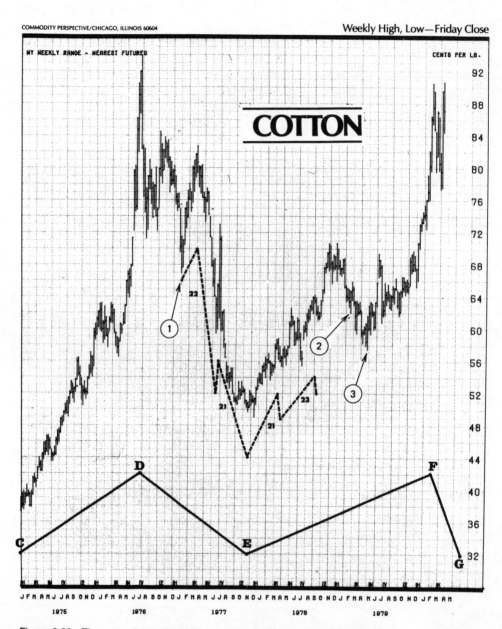

NY WEEKLY RANGE - NEAREST FUTURES

CENTS PER LB.

COTTON

Figure 3.30 The approximate 20-week cycle in cotton futures, and the approximate 2.5-year cycle C-G 1976-1979. ①, ② and ③, point out timing signals at possible cycle lows. ② & ③ are alternate laws.

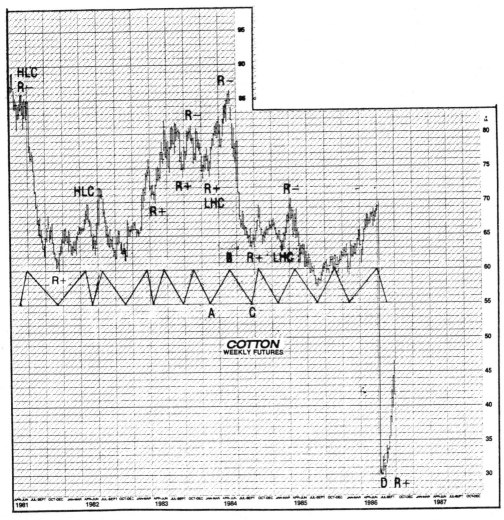

Figure 3.31 Approximate 20-week cycles in cotton 1981-1986 and timing signals at cycle turns. Note that the approximate 20−23-week low was made at "D".

WHEAT

The approximate 12-month cycle in wheat is one of the most reliable and certainly one of the most well researched cycles in the futures markets. Typically, a cycle that runs about 12 months is most likely a seasonal cycle. Because wheat is also one of the most reliable seasonal markets, the approximate 12-month cycle is probably another representation of the seasonal pattern. Figures 3.32 through 3.34 show the cycle lows, highs, and cycle lengths from 1935 through 1980, but not continuously. Figure 3.5 updates the cycles through 1986. This is readily seen as

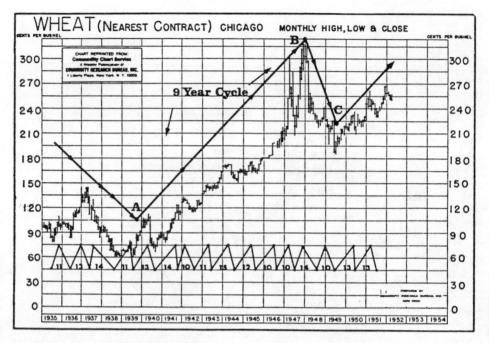

Figure 3.32 The 12.2-month cycle in wheat futures, 1935-1951, and the approximate 9-year cycle A, B, C.

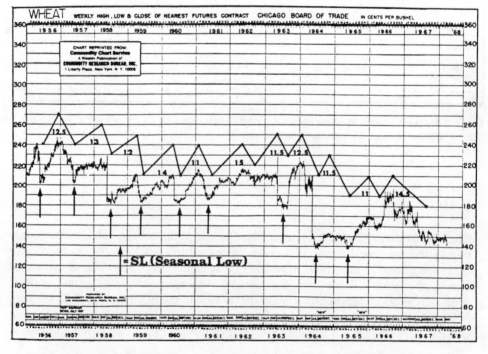

Figure 3.33 The 12.2-month cycle in wheat futures, 1956-1968. Arrows mark seasonal lows.

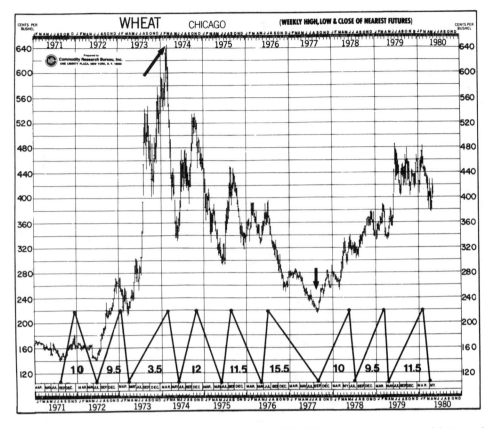

Figure 3.34   The 12.2-month cycle in wheat futures, 1971-1980. Arrows mark top and bottom of approximate 9-year cycle.

one of the premier cycles in wheat futures. Updating the cycle from 1981 to 1986, the following conclusions are reached:

1. The approximate 12-month cycle remains valid and reliable.
2. The timing signals shown have continued to be reliable correlates of tops and bottoms.
3. The seasonal cycle in wheat is still valid.

SOYBEANS

For many years, soybean complex prices have been significantly affected by seasonal factors. However, they have also shown several fairly distinct and reliable cycles. In addition to the approximate 30- to 34-month cycles, the approximate 19- to 25-month cycles have also been reliable. The Foundation for the Study of Cycles has done considerable research on the many cycles in soybean prices. In addition to the approximate 9- to 11-month cycles and the longer cycles mentioned above, indications of a cycle running approximately 17 to 22 weeks in length, low to low, also exist. The 9- to 11-month cycle is shown in Figures 3.36, 3.37, and 3.38. In terms of reliability, the shorter term cycle (marked by arrows at tops

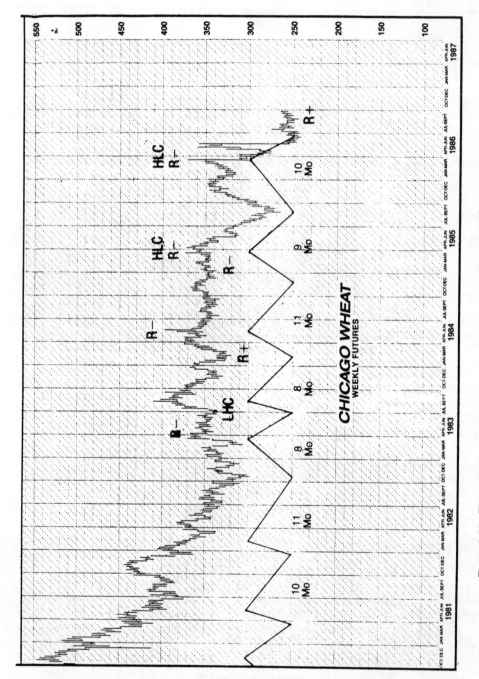

Figure 3.35   The approximate 12.2-month cycle in wheat futures and timing signals at cycle turns.

SOYBEANS

Chicago Board of Trade
Weekly High, Low—Friday Close

COMMODITY PERSPECTIVE/CHICAGO, ILLINOIS 60604

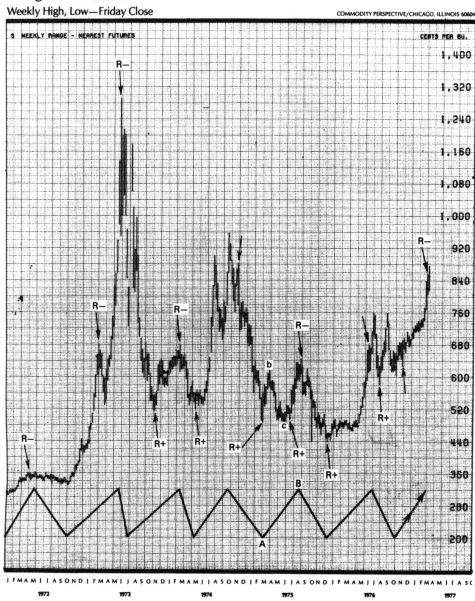

Figure 3.36 Intermediate-term cycle in soybean futures, 1972-1976, and timing signals at cycle turns.

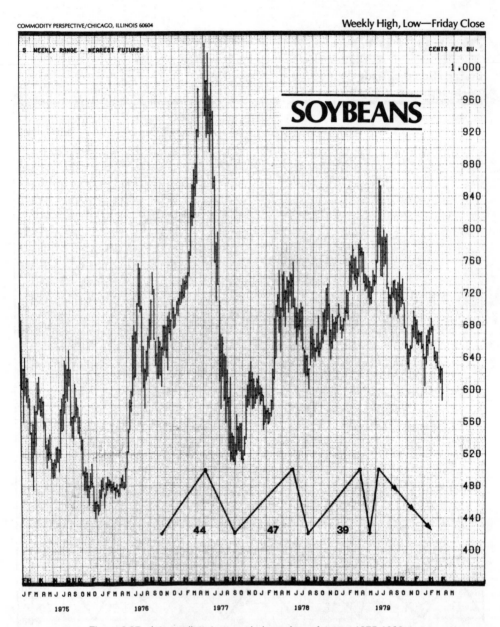

Figure 3.37   Intermediate-term cycle in soybean futures, 1975-1980.

and bottoms) has been reasonably stable across its lows; however, it has been quite erratic in terms of symmetry, often topping very early in the cycle or very late, depending on the underlying direction of seasonals and other cycles. My timing studies on the soybean complex commodities reveal weekly upside and downside reversals that are accurate between 65 percent and 85 percent of the time, with the highest timing reliability in soybean oil futures.

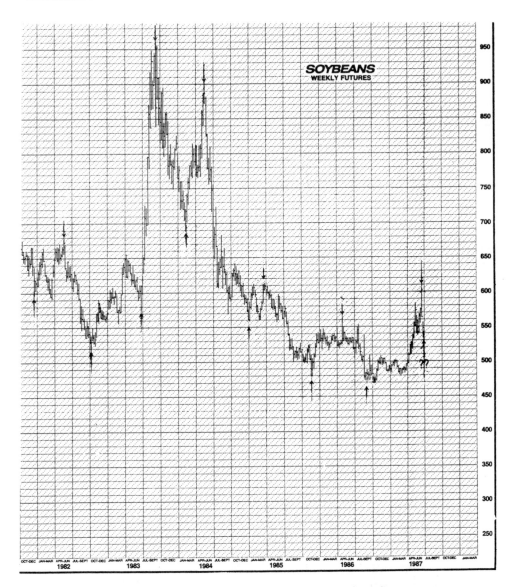

Figure 3.38   Approximate 9–11-month cycles in soybean futures.

CORN

The approximate 12.2-month cycles in corn futures has continued to be a relatively reliable pattern. As is true with wheat, the approximate 12-month pattern is most likely a seasonal pattern. The approximate 9- to 11-month cycle most likely will yield better results. This cycle is covered in the next chapter. In terms of stability, a comparison of the charts from the 1956 to 1968 and the 1981 through 1986 time frame shows that the cycles have continued to run about 12.2 months, low to low. Some of the timing indicators at cycle lows and highs are marked on the 1981–1986 weekly chart. They continue to be reliable as well. Because the

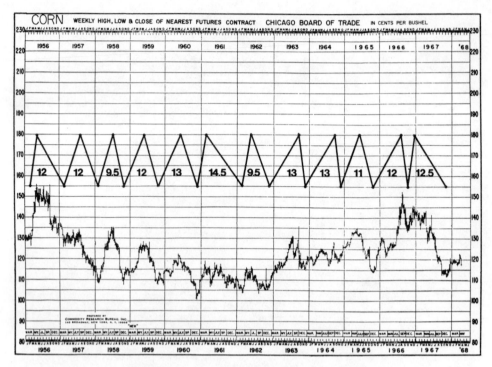

Figure 3.39   The 12.2-month cycle in corn futures.

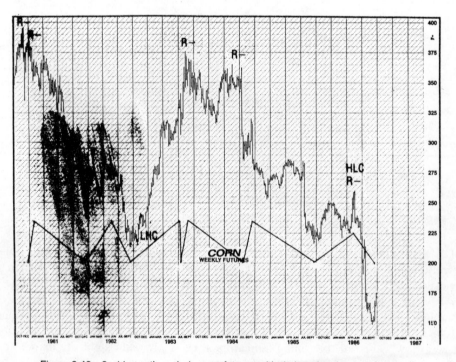

Figure 3.40   9–11-month cycle in corn futures with timing signals at cycle turns.

recent cycles have been considerably irregular in terms of the highs, the corn cycle is not an especially attractive one for traders. Should they become more symmetrical, I'll change my point of view. I'd rather trade the wheat cycles if the corn cycles continue to be skewed. As a viable alternative, consider the 9- to 11-month cycles in corn, covered in the next chapter. (See Figures 3.39 and 3.40.)

CANADIAN DOLLAR

Cycles in Canadian dollar futures have had a somewhat erratic history. In recent years the intermediate-term cycles have, to some degree, stabilized in the approximate 45- to 55-week, low to low, range. The cycles during the 1970's (Figure 3.41) were shorter. Now that futures trading has been in process for over 12 years, the cycles recently seen are probably more reliable. Note from Figure 3.42 that a short cycle of approximately 34 weeks, low to low, was seen in 1984–1985. Note that during periods of time that are likely to witness long-term cycle lows, intermediate-term cycles can become more volatile and less reliable. Though trading volume in Canadian dollar futures is still very thin, things may pick up considerably if long-term cycle lows are made. In terms of timing signals, the Canadian dollar is above average in reliability.

DEUTSCHE MARK

The D-mark has shown one of the most reliable intermediate-term cycles of all the currency futures. Figure 3.43 illustrates the behavior of the approximate 25- to 35-week cycle during the 1970's. In recent years the cycle has stabilized, most likely concurrent with an increase in trading volume, and now runs approximately 23 to 33 weeks, low to low. This is illustrated in Figure 3.44, with arrows marking the cycle lows and highs. In terms of timing signals and reliability, the D-mark weekly signals have been running 60 percent to 67 percent accurate. Though trading volume in the D-mark is not as active as it is in the Swiss franc, the cycles are reliable enough for cyclic trading.

SWISS FRANC

The Swiss franc cycles have been running somewhat shorter than those in the D-mark, though ideally little or no difference between the cycles should exist in these currencies since they are, to a certain extent, related. However, from the accompanying chart analyses, the cycles are indeed different and apparently more reliable in the D-mark than they have been in the Swiss franc. See Figures 3.45 and 3.46 for an examination of the approximate 26- to 35-week cycles. As far as timing indicators are concerned, the standard indicators such as weekly upside and downside reversals have, in recent years, been accurate between 61% and 75% of the time. As a result, a rather difficult situation exists, inasmuch as the cycles in the D-mark are more reliable, but the timing in Swiss francs appears more reliable. In either case, my work suggests that both markets are good vehicles for the cyclic trader, not only from the standpoint of cycles and timing but also from the perspective of large-size moves and good trends.

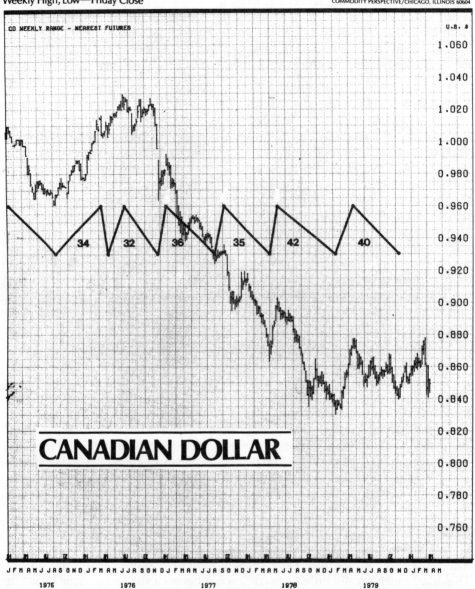

Figure 3.41   Cycles in Canadian dollar futures.

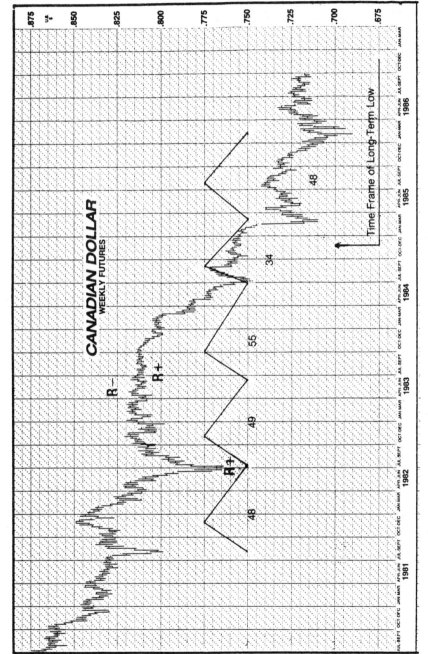

Figure 3.42   8–12-month cycle in Canadian dollar futures showing timing signals. Time frame of ideal long-term cycle low is also shown.

111

Figure 3.43　Intermediate-term cycle in D-mark futures, showing timing signals.

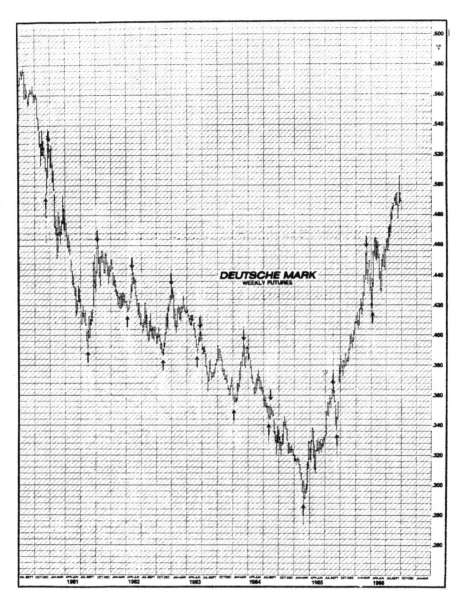

Figure 3.44   Intermediate-term cycle in D-mark futures (arrows mark highs and lows).

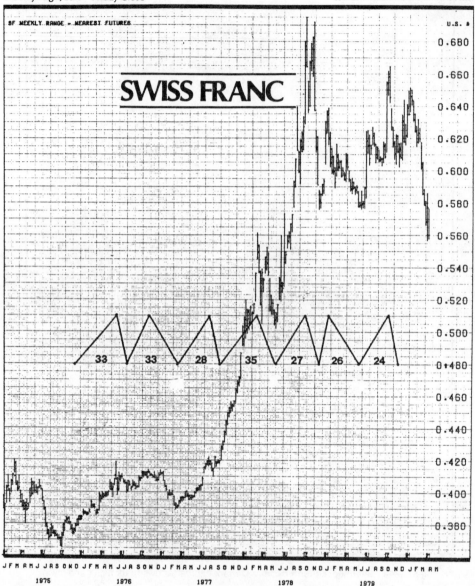

Figure 3.45　Intermediate-term cycle in Swiss franc futures.

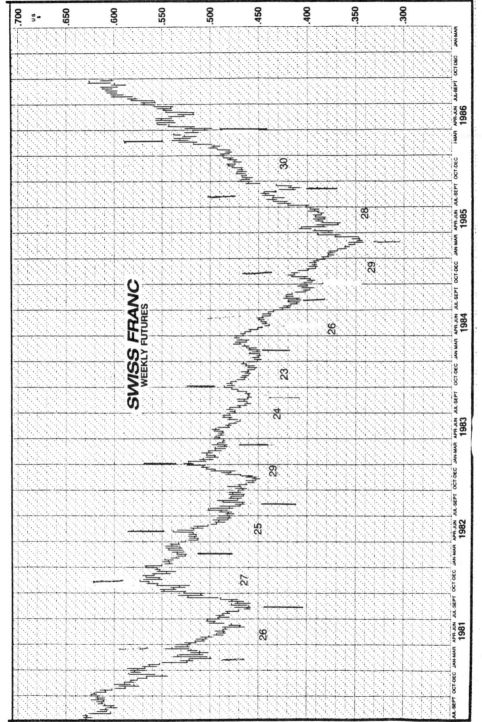

Figure 3.46   Intermediate-term cycle lows and highs in Swiss franc futures.

JAPANESE YEN

The yen has continued to be a reliable market with respect to cycles, as well as a market with exceptionally long and strong trends. The long-term uptrend followed by the long-term downtrend shown in Figure 3.47 revealed a fairly reliable cycle running from 19 to 25 weeks, low to low. The most recent chart (Figure 3.48) shows the same basic cycles persisting during the 1981–1986 time frame.

Weekly High, Low—Friday Close   COMMODITY PERSPECTIVE/CHICAGO, ILLINOIS 60604

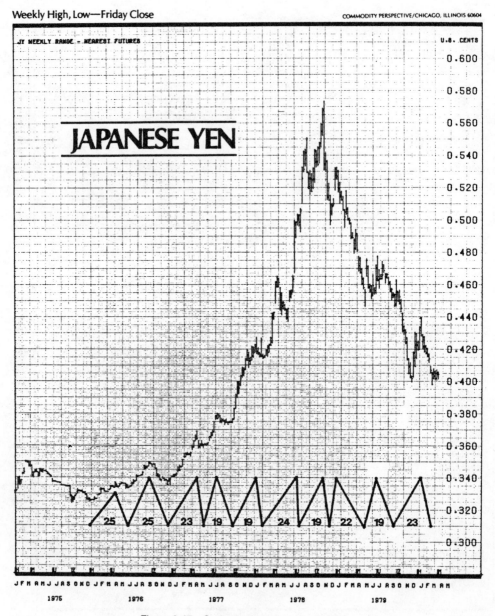

Figure 3.47   Cycles in Japanese yen futures.

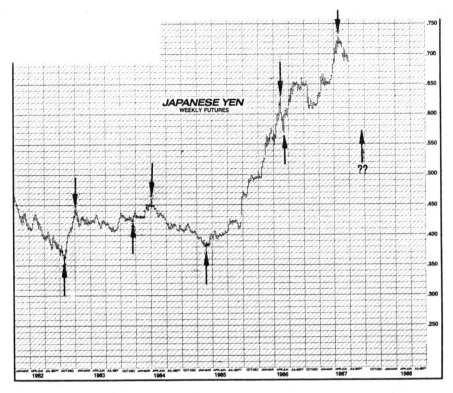

Figure 3.48   Weekly cycles Japanese yen futures 1982-1987.

This is a very positive testimonial to cycles as well as to the stability of the yen as a good market for cyclic trading. My work with standard timing signals (such as weekly up and downside reversals) at cyclic turning points indicates reliability of about 65 percent to 68 percent. This is a high level of reliability that, when combined with fairly stable cycles, can yield significant profits using the cyclic approach.

BRITISH POUND

Interestingly, the approximate 23- to 28-week cycle in British pound futures originally presented in *The Handbook of Commodity Cycles* has persisted in spite of the international currency turmoil of the 1980's. Figure 3.49 shows my original work with these cycles, and Figure 3.50 updates the cycles from 1981 through 1986. Granted, the cycles are not perfect, nor are they entirely symmetrical. However, as is discussed later, neither perfection nor symmetry is required of economic or futures market/cash market cycles. Timing is very important. My work with timing indicators such as weekly upside and weekly downside reversals during the ideal time frame of a cyclic turn suggests reliability of about 63 percent to 71 percent. These are good numbers, and they make the pound a reliable currency for futures trading. Remember, trading volume in the pound has not been very high, yet the market does show the important prerequisites of reliable cycles,

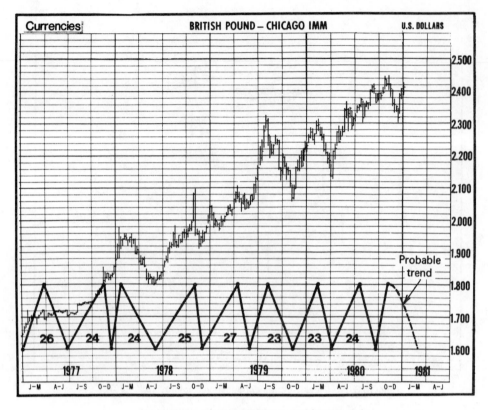

Figure 3.49   Cycles in British pound futures.

reliable timing, and good trends, and it also has futures options available for those who wish to employ options in a trading program.

TREASURY BILLS/TREASURY BONDS

In spite of a large trading volume in interest-rate futures, the intermediate term cycles have not been as reliable as expected. In the 1970's, trading in Treasury bill futures was very active; however, in the 1980's, Treasury bond futures have become the single most actively traded market in the world. The charts reveal that since the 1981 time frame, T-bond futures have had a cycle of approximately 22 weeks, low to low, and another cycle of approximately 12 to 16 weeks, low to low. This cycle is also found in T-bill futures (see Figures 3.51 and 3.52). The timing signals have been moderately reliable in T-bonds, yet they have been over 65 percent accurate in T-bill futures. This is disappointing, inasmuch as T-bonds futures are more actively traded and have had some large price swings. But other timing indicators discussed later in this book have good potential in T-bonds, and the market should not be ignored as a cyclic trading vehicle. Although T-bill futures have declined considerably in activity, they should still be considered seriously by most traders, particularly for short term and intermediate-term price swings as an alternative to higher risk trades in T-bond futures.

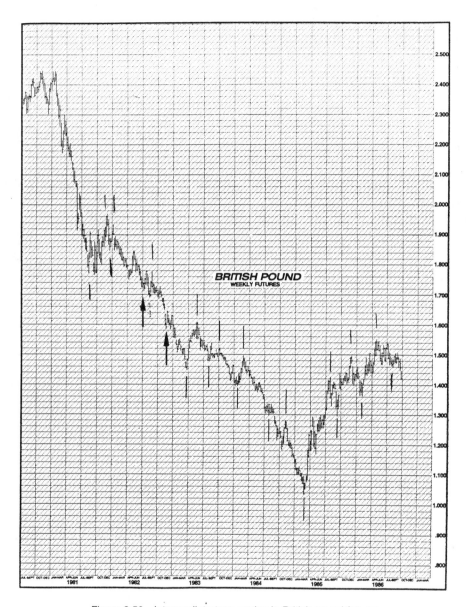

Figure 3.50 Intermediate-term cycles in British pound futures.

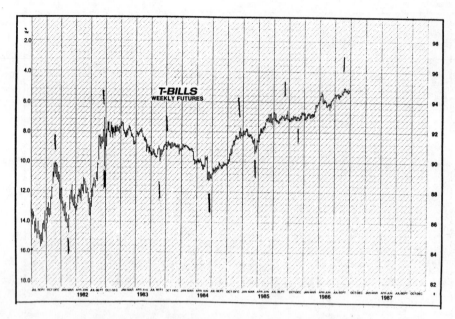

Figure 3.51   9–11-month cycle in T-bill futures 1982-1986.

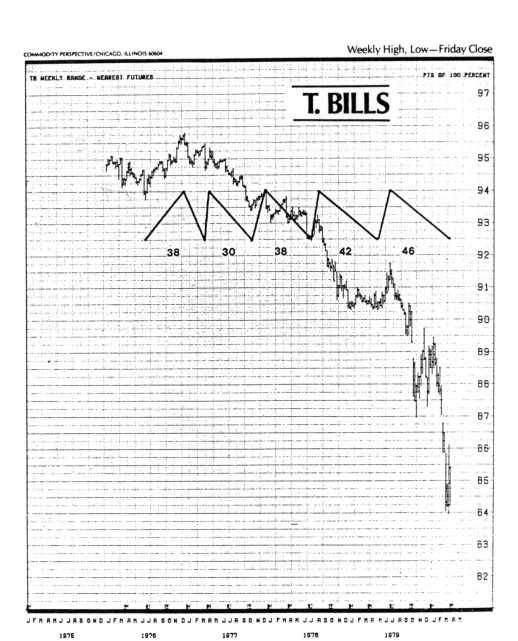

Figure 3.52   9—11-month (40-50 week average) cycle in T-bill futures 1976-1979.

4
The 9- to 11-Month Cycle

One of the most pervasive cycles in cash and futures commodity markets is the approximate 9- to 11-month cycle. This is the single most important cycle in the futures markets. As an illustration of its reliability, examine Figure 4.1. It shows the Commodity Research Bureau Futures Price Index from 1968 through 1980. The CRB (Commodity Research Bureau) futures index is comprised of approximately 27 different markets. When combined, these markets in aggregate represent the overall trend of futures prices. In examining Figure 4.1, many repetitions of the 9- to 11-month cycle are observed with only a few cycles running longer or shorter than the norm. Some extremely large up and down moves have taken place during the 9- to 11-month up and down phases. Figure 4.2 updates the 9- to 11-month cycles. Note that the reliability of the cycles has not changed appreciably. In fact, the CRB index continues to represent these cycles exceptionally well. Finally, note that CRB index futures are now traded in New York. This makes participation in a broad basket of markets a relatively simple matter. The CRB futures index is an ideal way to trade the intermediate term swings in the rate of inflation inasmuch as inflation tends to be reflected in commodity price movement.

Another reason for the importance of 9- to 11-month cycles in futures trading (in addition to the accuracy of the cycles and the ability to trade CRB index futures) is that a majority of traders and producers are most interested in price swings of 4 to 5 months duration (i.e., about half the 9- to 11-month cycles). From the producer's standpoint, 4- to 5-month time segments are important for planning and hedging purposes. A crop planted in May comes out of the ground in September to October. The typical speculator tends to shy away from ultrashort-term trading, yet does not have the discipline for ultralong-term trading. Hence, the 4- to 5-month average time swings of the 9- to 11-month cycles are ideal for many speculators. Finally, the advent of futures options with defined risk and limited life span fits almost hand in glove with the 9- to 11-month cycles, thereby opening new avenues of trading using cyclic patterns derived from the 9- to 11-month tendencies.

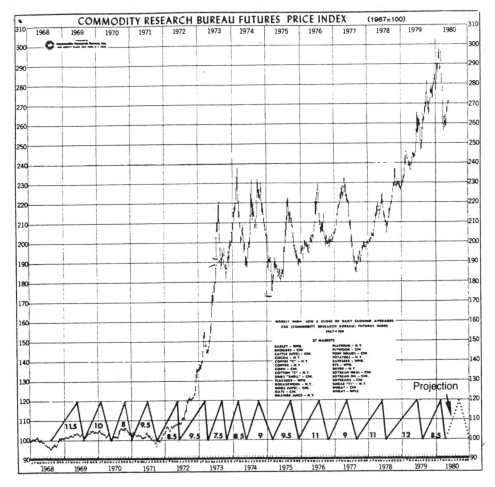

Figure 4.1   The 9—11-month CRB futures index cycle, 1968-1980.

GENERAL APPLICATION

A simplified application of the 9- to 11-month cycles (yet one that can yield significant opportunities and profits for the position trader) is to buy in the time frame
of an expected 9- to 11-month cycle low liquidating longs and going short when
the approximate 9- to 11-month cycles are due to peak or have peaks. When
combined with money management techniques to limit losses, and precise timing
indicators to optimize entry, this can be an effective practical application of the
9—11-month cycles, one which is both simple and definitive at the same time.
Figures 4.3 through 4.6 provide some historical examples on daily closing price
charts of this elementary but effective strategy.

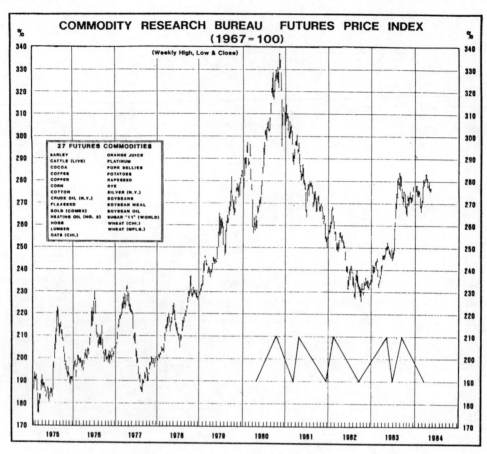

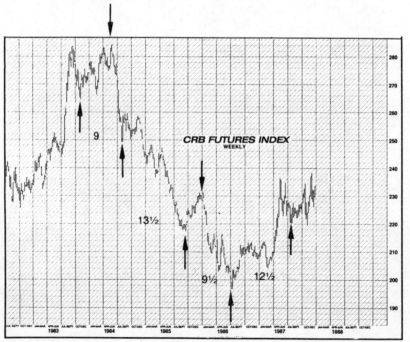

Figure 4.2   Continuation of the 9–11-month CRB cycle.

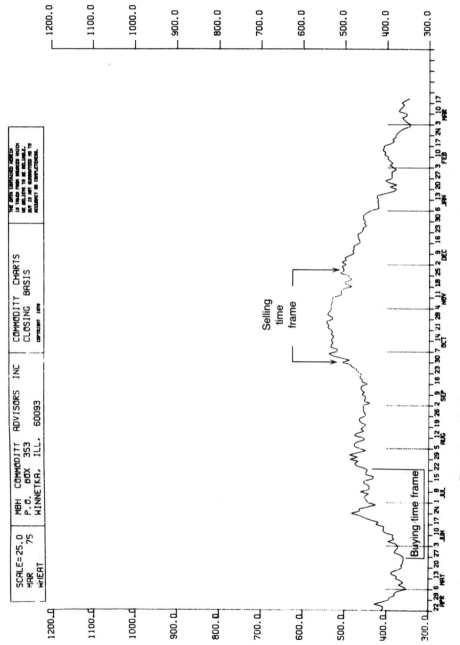

Figure 4.3   March 1975 wheat; 9–11-month cycle entry and exit.

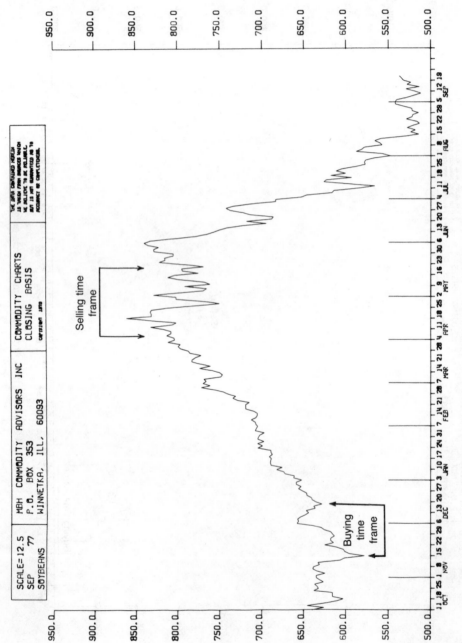

Figure 4.4   September 1977 soybeans: 9–11-month cycle entry and exit.

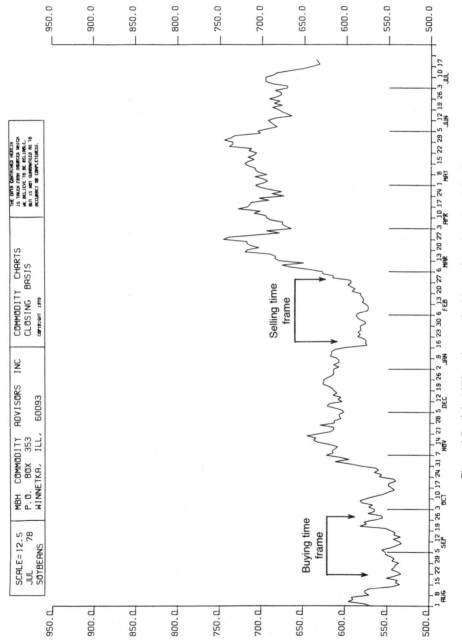

Figure 4.5 July 1978 soybeans: 9–11-month cycle entry and exit.

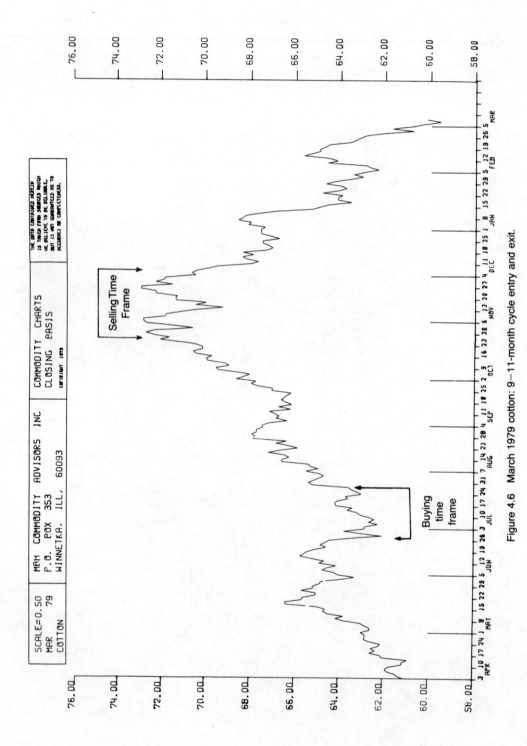

Figure 4.6 March 1979 cotton: 9–11-month cycle entry and exit.

TIMING CONSIDERATIONS WITH THE 9- to 11-MONTH CYCLES

Timing is an important consideration when trading with the 9- to 11-month cycles (or, for that matter, with any cycles). Though timing is not the focus of this chapter, a few words about this topic are relevant prior to a later extensive examination of the subject.

In spite of the historical validity of 9- to 11-month cycles in a majority of the futures markets, timing is still of the essence. Timing compensates for the variability of cycles. When a 9- to 11-month cycle bottoms late, entry at too early a point might result in one loss or several losses in succession. When a cycle tops too early or too late, the same negative consequences can occur. Timing indicators are used in order to compensate for variation in cycle length. Therefore, I caution you against such rigid adherence to the 9- to 11-month cycles (or to any cycle) that you permit good sense and timing to fall by the wayside. Even futures options (which are designed to "buy time") cannot be of value if timing is off by a considerable amount. I urge you to put the 9- to 11-month cycle work *together with the timing indicators described later in this book*. The two are inseparable for trading purposes.

LOOKING AT A FEW OF THE MARKETS

Figures 4.7 through 4.21 illustrate the 9- to 11-month cycles in a variety of markets. The cycle lengths are specifically illustrated, along with the low to low count. Note their reliability and persistence through the years! Also note the text accompanying each chart.

Figure 4.7   9–11-month cycles in corn futures. Lows have, as in most cycles, been more regular than highs.

Figure 4.8 9–11-month cycles in soybean futures.

Figure 4.9 9–11-month cycles in wheat futures. Note that wheat cycles have not been as reliable as those in soybeans.

Figure 4.10 9−11-month cycles in soybean oil futures. Only one cycle has been out of the time window since 1976.

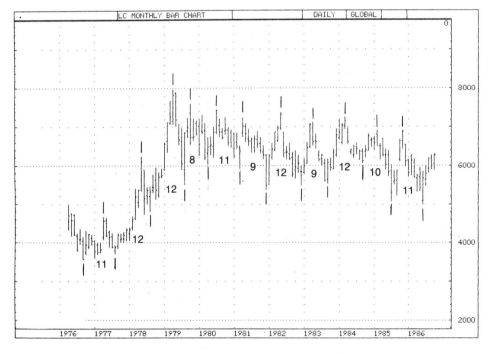

Figure 4.11 9−11-month cycles in live cattle futures.

Figure 4.12   9–11-month cycles in hog futures.

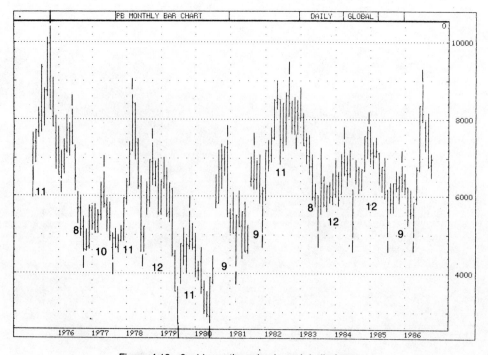

Figure 4.13   9–11-month cycles in pork belly futures.

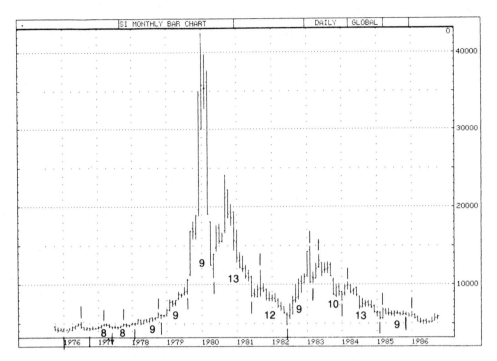

Figure 4.14 9−11-month cycles in silver futures.

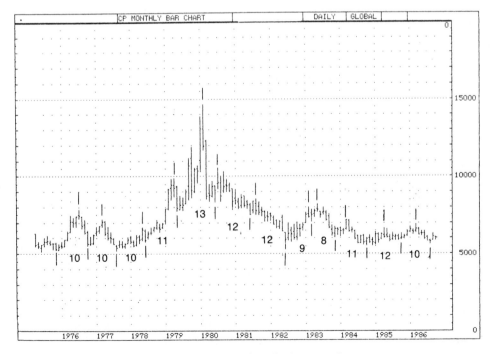

Figure 4.15 9−11-month cycles in copper futures.

Figure 4.16 9−11-month cycles in Treasury bill futures. The cycles have not been very reliable.

Figure 4.17 9−11-month cycles in British pound futures. The cycles have been quite reliable.

Figure 4.18 9−11-month cycles in coffee futures.

Figure 4.19 9−11-month cycles in Canadian dollar futures.

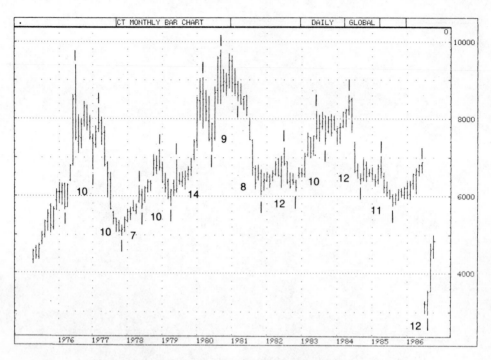

Figure 4.20   9−11-month cycles in cotton futures.

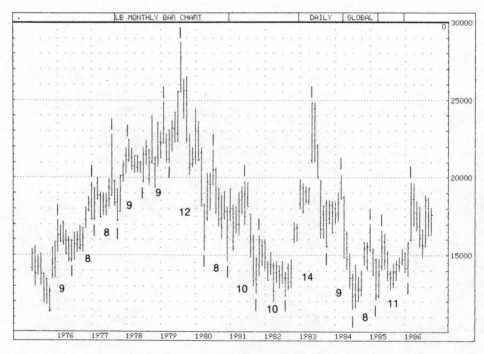

Figure 4.21   9−11-month cycles in lumber futures.

CLOSING COMMENTS ABOUT THE 9- to 11-MONTH CYCLES

In closing, note that currency futures markets (with the possible exception of the British pound and Canadian dollar) have not shown a 9- to 11-month cycle. In addition, the 9- to 11-month cycles have been rather variable in interest rate futures, although a number of very good 9- to 11-month cycle repetitions have occurred in T-bond and T-bill futures. For those just getting started either in futures trading or in the cyclic approach to market analysis and trading, the 9- to 11-month cycles are recommended as an excellent beginning, not only for analytical studies and application of concepts but for trading as well.

5
Some Short-Term Cycles

The short-term approach to futures trading has been a favorite topic of traders for many years. There has been persistent debate about the reliability and desirability of using short-term cycles for speculation in futures. My work continues to suggest that short-term cycles do indeed exist, and they are valid for speculation in futures. *The Handbook of Commodity Cycles* provides extensive coverage of short-term cycles. My beginning topic at that time was based on the Burton Pugh's assertion of lunar influences on price. Pugh claimed that during a full moon phase the price of wheat tends to move higher, and in the new moon phase wheat prices tend to move lower. Some of the illustrations provided by Pugh are shown in Figures 5.1 through 5.3. As a point of information, note the more recent wheat example showing the full moon/new moon market behavior.

Understandably, the lunar phase idea remains controversial; however, when seen in the sense of correlation as opposed to causality, the concept becomes more palatable even to the most conservative traders. Many cycles (both in the markets and in nature) run concurrently, either by chance or cause. Yet, regardless of whether their commonality is attributed to cause and effect or coincidence, a majority of markets exhibit short-term cycles of approximately 24 to 34 days in length. Most of these cycles run about 28 trading days in length, low to low. In addition, short-term cycles tend to cluster in fractions and multiples of the approximate 28-day period. Hence, we expect to find cycles of about 14 days, 7 days, 21 days, and 56 days in average length.

This chapter pinpoints numerous short-term cycles and their current status. Charts from *The Handbook of Commodity Cycles* are referred to, and updated, noting any significant differences from the original findings. In addition, I comment on the reliability of timing indicators, cycle length, and other remarks relevant to short-term speculation with cycles.

WHAT IS A SHORT-TERM CYCLE?

For the purpose of this book, a short-term cycle is defined as running from approximately 7 to 65 days in length, as measured across the lows. Cycles of 7 days or less are also short-term; however, they must be studied using intraday data as

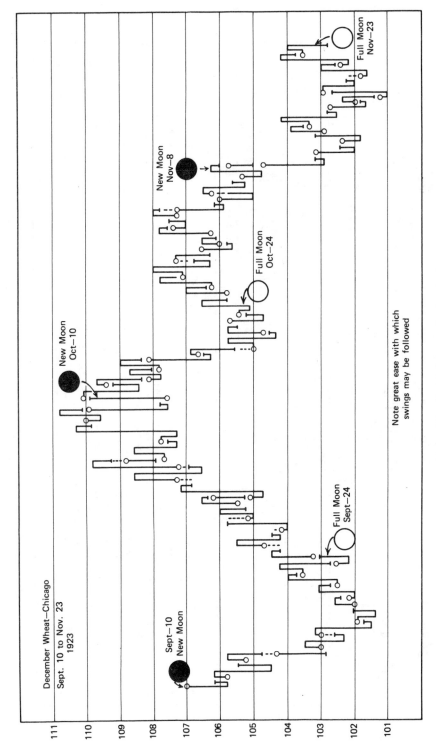

Figure 5.1 Pugh's lunar cycle signals.

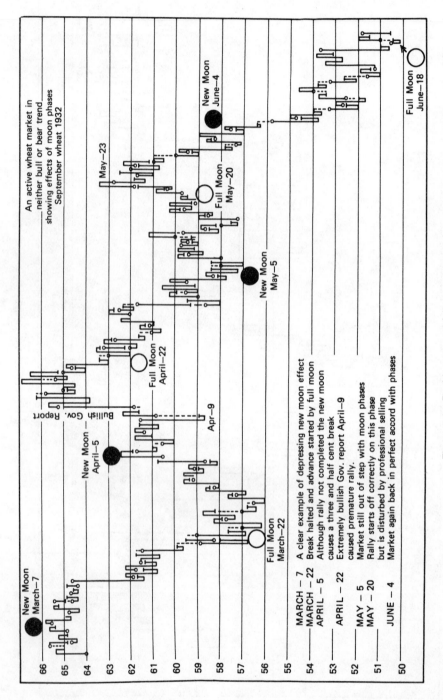

Figure 5.2 Pugh's new and full moon signals.

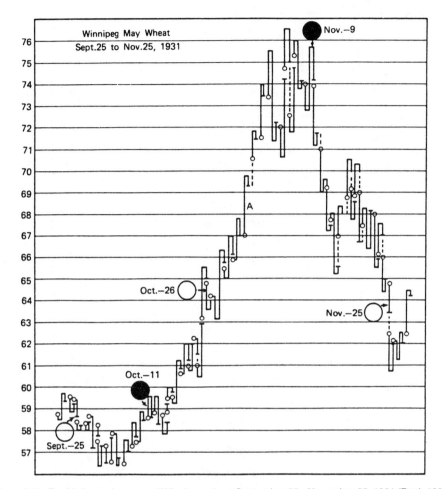

Figure 5.3   Pugh's lunar phases and Winnipeg wheat September 25–November 25, 1931 (Pugh 1933).

opposed to the daily prices used to analyze short-term cycles of 7 days and longer. Even cycles of 7 to 11 days might more easily be discerned on the basis of intra-day data.

As a variant of short-term cycles, the use of seasonal price tendencies is possible on a very short-term basis. There are many time periods during which a high probability of up or down turns has occurred historically, based on seasonal considerations. These short-term seasonal tendencies will be discussed later, when seasonality is explained and applied to the markets.

WHEAT

The short-term cycles in wheat have been approximately 28 days, low to low, and the double cycle has averaged approximately 56 days, low to low. Figures 5.5 through 5.7 illustrate these cycles in the 1970's and the 1980's. A high degree of

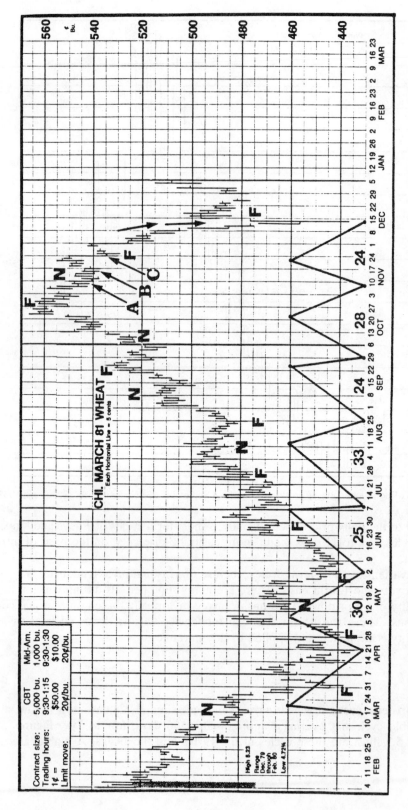

Figure 5.4 March 1981 Chicago wheat showing short-term cycle and new moon and full moon dates. N = new moon; F = full moon.

142

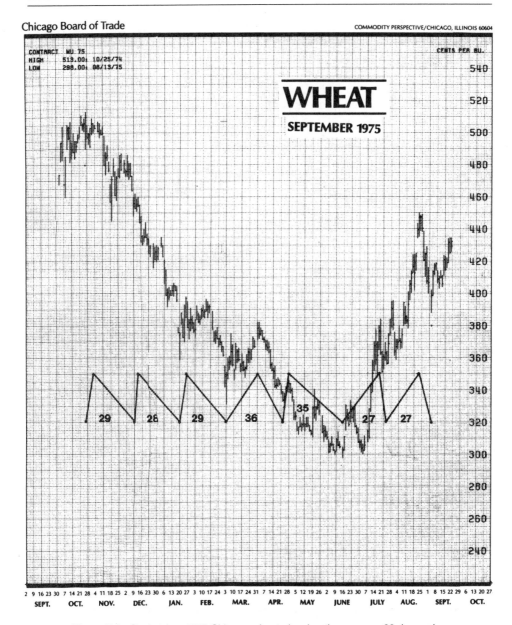

Chicago Board of Trade   COMMODITY PERSPECTIVE/CHICAGO, ILLINOIS 60604

Figure 5.5   September 1975 Chicago wheat showing the average 28-day cycles.

stability and reliability is apparent for this cycle, and both the approximate 28-day and 56-day cycles are recommended for short-term trading. Remember that timing indicators, to be discussed later, are designed to compensate for the time variance of cycles.

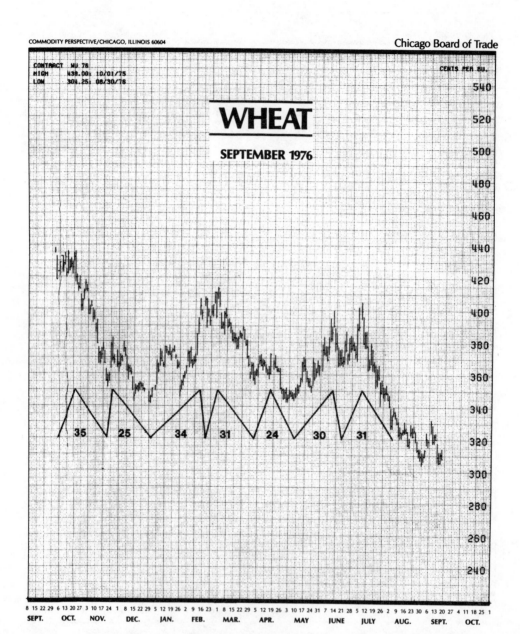

Figure 5.6   September 1976 Chicago wheat showing the average 28-day cycle lows and highs.

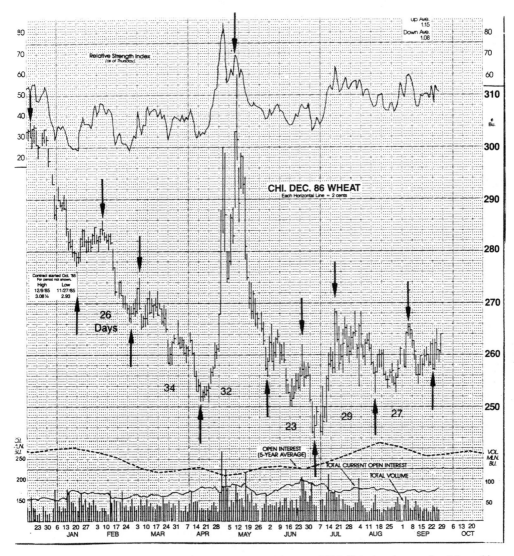

Figure 5.7   The approximate 28-day cycle in wheat futures, 1986. Note two long cycles followed by short cycle of 23 days as cycles attempt to "self correct."

SOYBEANS

The cycles in soybean futures have also shown a tendency toward approximate 28-day and 56-day lengths. Figures 5.8 and 5.9 illustrate both cycles as well as a number of timing indicators. Though the 1980's have witnessed a distinct reduction of trading volume in soybean and soybean complex futures, the cycles have, nevertheless, remained fairly reliable. Combined with the availability of futures options, the short-term cycles are viable for trading purposes. Note also the cycles in soybean oil and soybean meal.

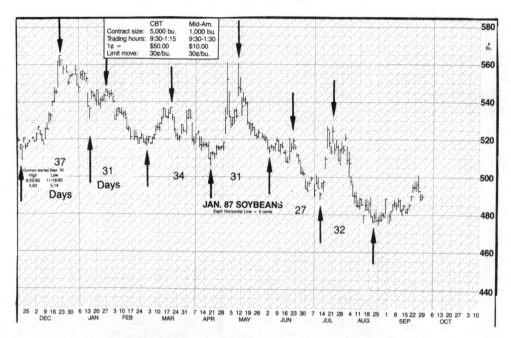

Figure 5.8   The approximate 28–34-day cycle in soybean futures, 1986.

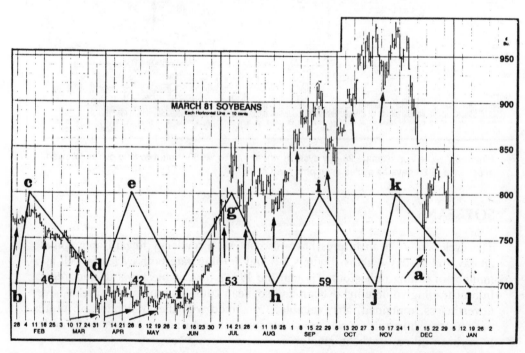

Figure 5.9   Cycles in March 1981 soybean futures (arrows show timing signals at or near turns of the 28-day cycles). The approximate 56-day cycles are shown.

GOLD

Gold futures have been a perennial favorite among short-term traders. Though there have been periods of thin volume, gold futures always seem to become revitalized in sufficient time to attract the continued following of many traders. The seasonal price tendencies in gold futures have been very reliable. The short-term cycles, however, have not been as reliable as gold traders would like them to be. Figures 5.10 and 5.11 show the cycles in 1981 and in 1986. Generally, the cycles have run approximately 28 days and 56 days in length, low to low. Timing indicators have been reliable. The availability of futures options makes this market ideal for speculators.

COPPER

Not only does the copper market have some of the most reliable seasonal trends of any of the futures markets but it also shows a number of reliable short-term cycles. Two important cycles have occurred here, one running approximately 10 to 12 weeks, low to low, and the other approximately 18 days on the average, low to low. Illustrations of these cycles are found in Figures 5.12 through 5.14. Timing work in copper suggests that the indicators are quite reliable. The most profitable times to trade copper for the short term are when seasonals are in a strong up or down period. This would mean that during the November through March time frame, the long side should be considered on short-term cycles lows as perhaps more reliable, whereas the period from early April through August should be considered one during which the short side and cyclic tops might prove more reliable.

LIVE CATTLE

The live cattle market has had reliable cycles for many years, in spite of relatively thin volume in the last decade. As readers will recall, the intermediate-term cycles in cattle futures have been very reliable. The short-term cycles have run from 14 days to 28 days on the average. Trading volume has been a bit low in the 1983–1986 time frame; however, no apparent reduction in cyclic accuracy has occurred. Currently, the cycles of approximately 14 and 28 days continue to enjoy a high degree of reliability, particularly when combined with seasons and timing indicators. Figures 5.15 and 5.16 show some history on these two cycles. From a cyclic standpoint, the cattle and feeder cattle markets, though rather thinly traded, are still reliable.

COCOA

When *The Handbook of Commodity Cycles* was published, cocoa cycles were not considered very reliable. Figure 5.17 shows a chart of the approximate 25-day cycle in December 1981 cocoa. Indeed, the short-term cycles have not been especially interesting. In fact, the market has, in recent years, shown a highly reliable pattern running from 30 to 40 trading days in length, from low to low. These

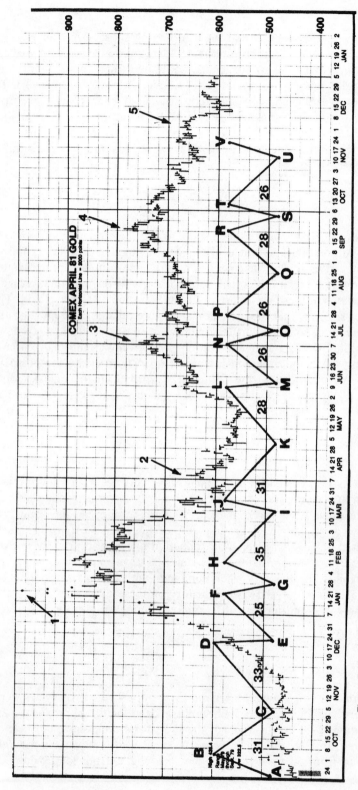

Figure 5.10　April 1981 gold futures cycles. Letters show 25–32-day cycles; numbers show "double cycle" highs. (i.e., = 56-day cycle)

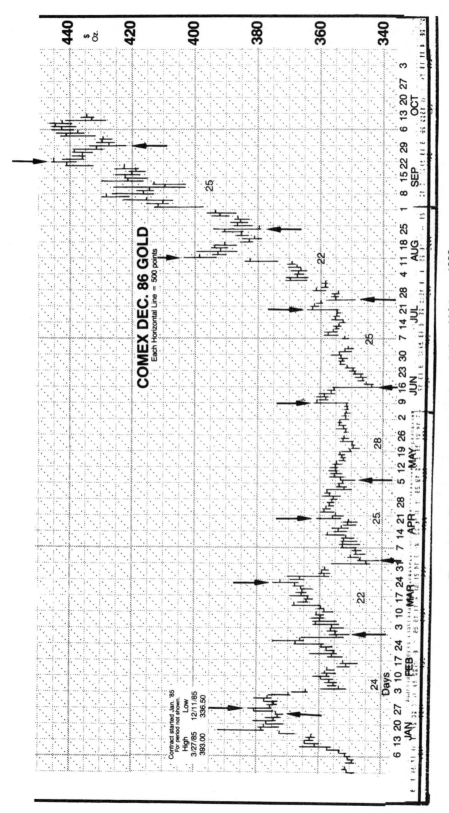

Figure 5.11   The approximate 25—30-day cycle in gold futures, 1986.

149

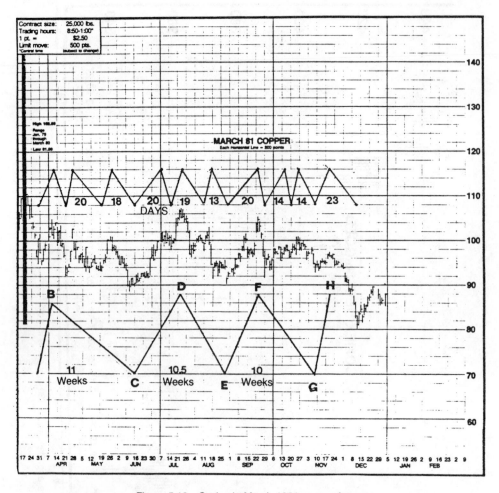

Figure 5.12   Cycles in March 1981 copper futures.

DECEMBER 1978

Commodity Exchange, Inc. N.Y.

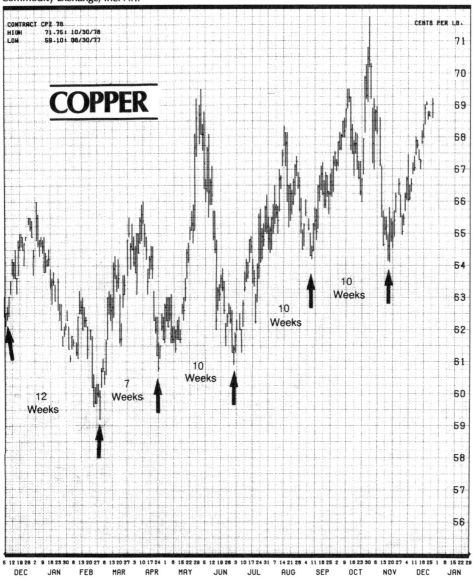

Figure 5.13   Cycle lows (arrows) in December 1978 copper futures.

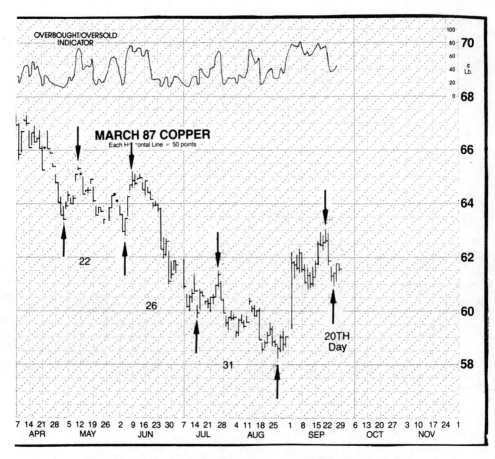

Figure 5.14 Approximate 25–30-day cycle in copper futures, 1986.

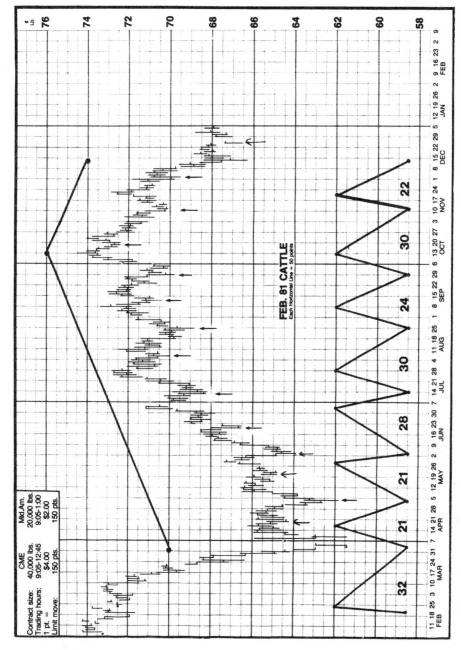

Figure 5.15 Cycles in February 1981 live cattle futures. Zig zags show approximate 28-day average cycles. Arrows mark approximate 14-day cycle lows. Large zig zag at top shows approximate 9–11 month cycle.

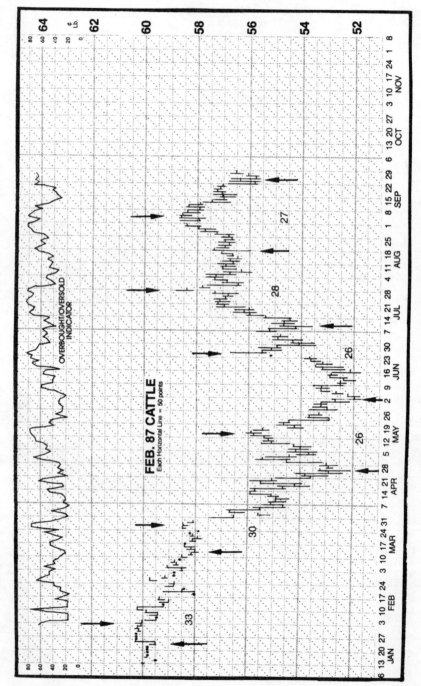

Figure 5.16 25–35-day cycle in cattle futures, 1986.

154

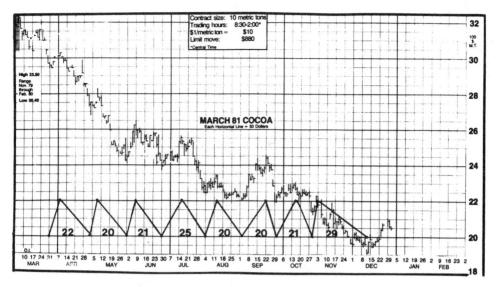

Figure 5.17   Cycles in March 1981 cocoa futures.

cycles are shown in Figure 5.18. Though trading volume has been very thin in cocoa futures, the cyclic reliability of the 30 to 40 day pattern makes this market particularly well suited for the short-term trader. However, I caution novices to be particularly careful when trading in markets with such relatively thin volume.

PORK BELLIES

The T-bond futures of yesteryear was the pork bellie market. Though price volatility in bellies remains high, trading volume has declined significantly from its high levels of the 1970's. At least two cycles were important from a short-term perspective in the 1970's and early 1980's—the approximate 40- to 50-day cycle and its one-half cycle of approximately 19 to 27 days, low to low. Figures 5.19 through 5.22 show some of the history of these cycles. Figure 5.23 shows the recent behavior of both cycles in February 1987 pork bellies.

COTTON

The cycles in cotton futures have been unreliable from a short-term perspective; however, they can be used for speculation if one is willing to accept the variability. Figures 5.24 and 5.25 show the approximate 33- to 43-day cycle as it stood in 1975 and 1981. Figure 5.26 updates this cycle to 1986. That the cycle has persisted is readily apparent, in bull and bear markets alike. The usual question of low trading volume applies, yet cotton has historically been a very good trending market, and this makes the relatively thin volume more acceptable. Though the short-term cycles in cotton are clearly still reliable, cotton trading should be approached from a more intermediate-term time-frame orientation due to the relatively longer

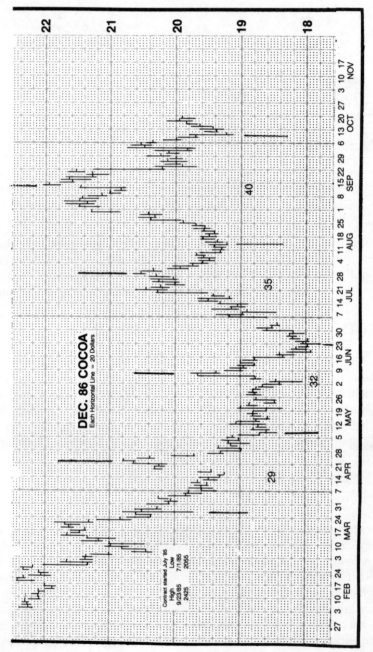

Figure 5.18 30—40-day cycles in cocoa futures.

Figure 5.19   Short-term cycle in August 1978 pork bellie futures.

lasting trends. The short-term cycle described here might more appropriately be used as an entry point for intermediate-term positions, either initial or secondary (i.e., initial or additional entries on the way up or down consistent with the intermediate-term cycles).

Figure 5.20   Short-term cycle in July 1977 pork bellie futures.

Figure 5.21   Short-term cycle in May 1975 pork bellie futures.

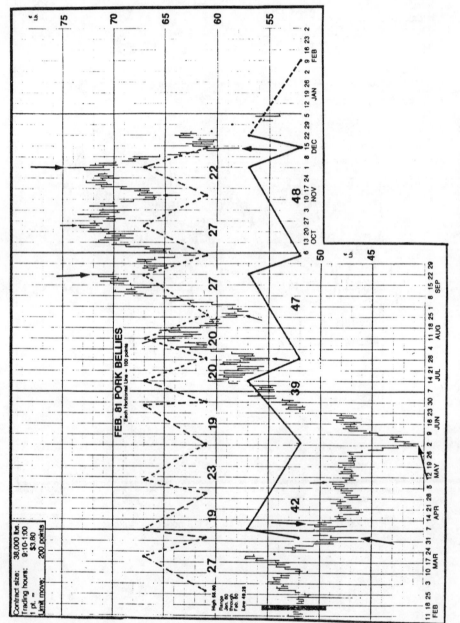

Figure 5.22   Cycles in February 1981 pork bellie futures. Arrows mark timing signals.

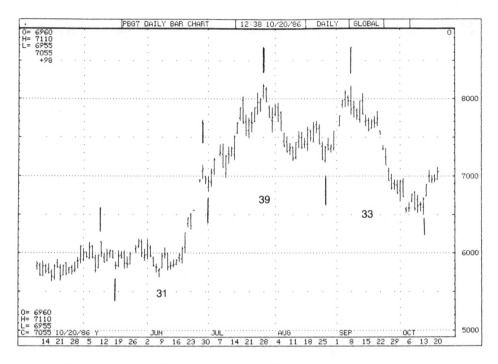

Figure 5.23　Cycle lows and highs daily pork bellies February 1987: approximate 7-week cycle.

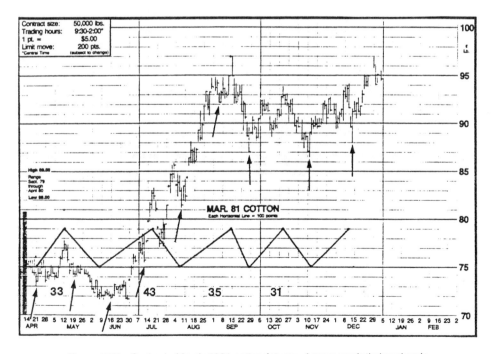

Figure 5.24　Cycles in March 1981 cotton futures. Arrows mark timing signals.

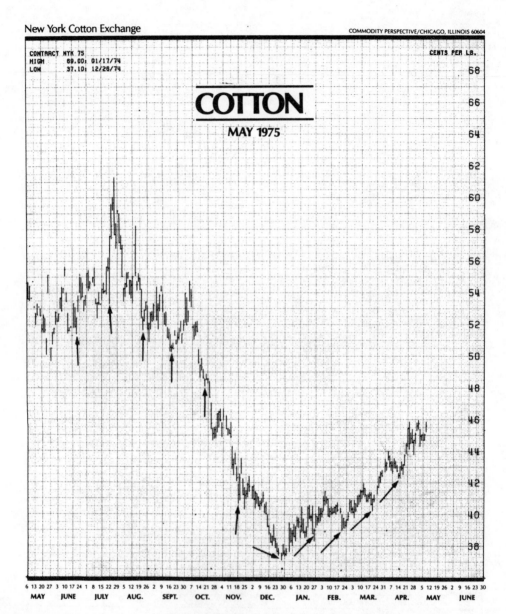

CONTRACT NYK 75
HIGH   69.00: 01/17/74
LOW   37.10: 12/26/74

CENTS PER LB.

COTTON

MAY 1975

Figure 5.25   Short-term May 1975 cotton.

Figure 5.26   Approximate 7-week cycle lows and highs December 1986 cotton.

SWISS FRANC

Swiss franc futures have become the leader in currency trading volume and, as a consequence, are expected to show the more reliable cycles of any of the currency futures. The 1979–1980 time frame showed this market with a short-term cycle of approximately 20 to 25 days, low to low, and a cycle of about double this length. In addition, a very-short-term cycle of approximately 14 to 23 days has also appeared valid.

The accompanying Figures 5.27 through 5.29 illustrate a number of these cycles. Though the short-term cycles are valid in Swiss francs, my inclination is to stay with the intermediate-term cycles, since trends here tend to be long lasting and quite large in terms of magnitude. The intermediate-term or long-term trader might be in a better position to profit from such large moves.

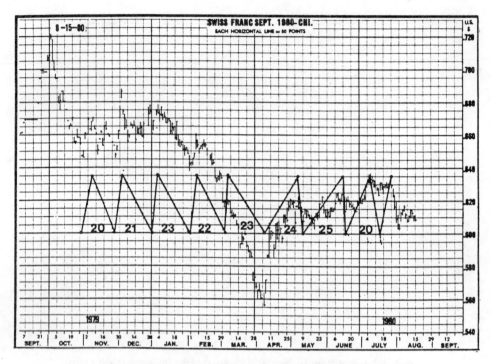

Figure 5.27   Cycles in September 1980 Swiss franc futures.

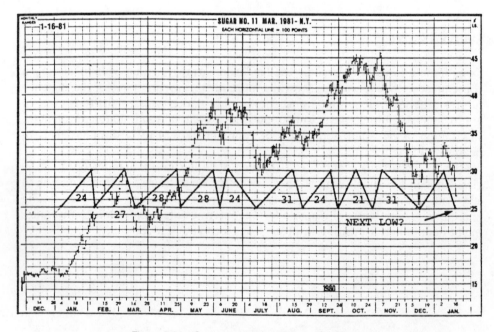

Figure 5.28   Cycles in March 1981 sugar futures.

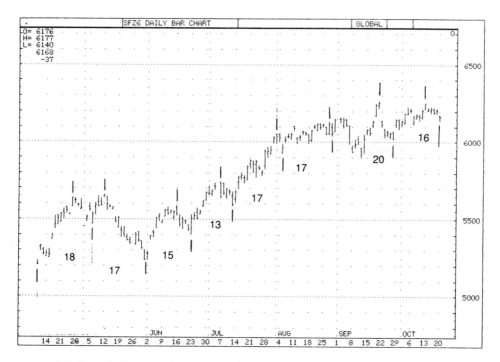

Figure 5.29   Approximate 13–17-day cycle in December 1986 Swiss franc.

6

The Basic Indicators and Their Use

The Handbook of Commodity Cycles[1] detailed four basic timing indicators as applicable during time frames of expected cyclic turns. These four indicators are *the price reversal, the low/high and high/low close, 3-H/3-L, and closing price chart penetrations*. These indicators are still valid and can be used as simple measures of cycle turns within the approximate time-window configurations. Figures 6.1 through 6.8 give graphic examples of the basic timing signals. Timing indicators that are considered buy signals are used only in time-window lows,[2] whereas timing indicators considered sell signals are used only in time-window tops. The appropriate risk or stop/loss point for each of these timing indicators, as well as examples of their application, are given in *The Handbook of Commodity Cycles*. I have had many questions in the last several years regarding the statistical reliability of the timing indicators referred to in this chapter. Though I have done some extensive studies on basic signals and their combinations, there are too many variables to consider in making any definitive statements about their "accuracy." Differences in size of move after a cycle turn, actual cycle low and high, and combinations of cycle length make a specific statement of accuracy impossible. However, an overwhelming majority of cycle turns will exhibit one or more of the basic or advanced signals. For general statistical guidelines on reversal signals see Figures 6.9 and 6.10.

VARIATIONS ON A THEME

Perhaps one issue to which *The Handbook of Commodity Cycles* did not devote sufficient attention was the method by which the timing signals can be used for entry subsequent to a cyclic high or low. In addition, another significant detail that deserves considerable attention is the issue of risk and stop losses. Let's take

---

[1]Bernstein, J. *The Handbook of Commodity Cycles: A Window on Time*, New York: John Wiley, 1982.

[2]"Time Window." That period of time during which a cycle is expected to turn. The mathematical computation of "Time Window" is: "Time Window" = average cycle length ±15% of average cycle length.

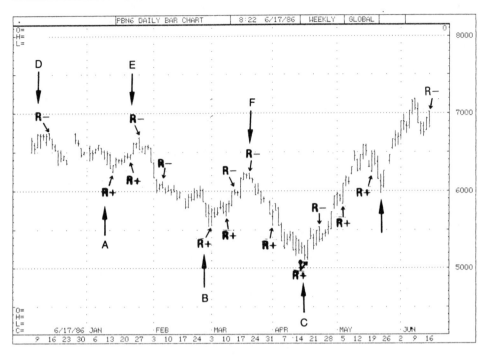

Figure 6.1. Some reversal signals: definition and examples. Arrows mark short-term cycle lows. Note buy signals at cycle lows (A−C) and sell signals at cycle-highs (D−F).

these points individually, beginning with market entry on timing signals. To do this, a brief review of typical market entry and exit is necessary, using the timing signal/time window approach. To refresh your memory or to introduce you to this topic, the following review is provided.

AVERAGE CYCLE LENGTH

Cycle length is determined over time, using as many actual cycle repetitions as can be acquired. A minimum sample size of eight repetitions is deemed reasonable as verification of long-term cycles; however, forty or fifty repetitions are preferable for short-term cycles. The average cycle length is computed simply by taking the arithmetic mean of the actual time span, low to low, and high to high.[3] Not all cycles are symmetrical, nor do they all run the same time length. Nevertheless, establishing the existence of cycles whose lows and highs fall within a reasonable range of ideal highs and lows is possible more often than not. Naturally, aberrations of the cycles caused by a number of factors may occur, yet the cycles typically return to their normal beat following dissipation of the distorting event(s.)

For the purpose of speculation or investing, cycles should be reliable to within plus or minus 10 to 15 percent of their mean cycle length. Anything in excess of

---

[3]Using trading days for short-term cycles.

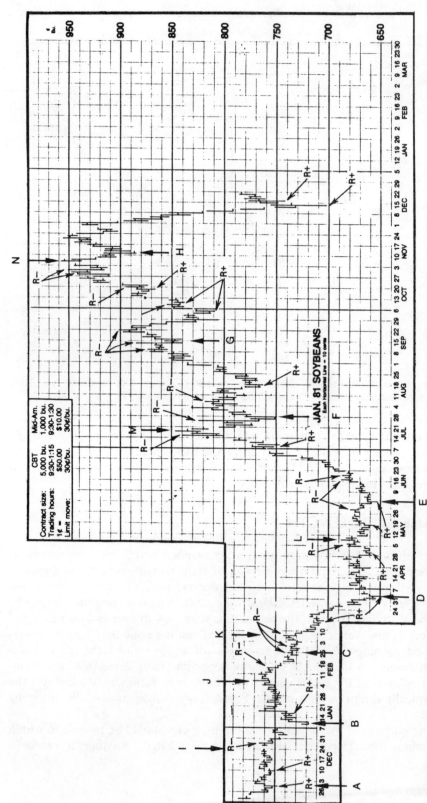

Figure 6.2 R+ and R– signals in January 1981 soybean futures. Note also my analysis of the approximate 28-day cycle. R+ (buy) signals were seen at or near cycle lows A, B, D, E, F and G. R– (sell) signals were seen at or near cycle highs I, J, K, L, M, and N.

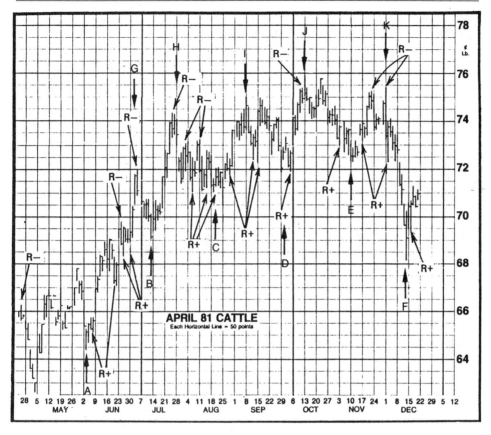

Figure 6.3 R+ and R− signals in April 1981 cattle futures. Note the R+ (buy) signals at or near cycle lows A, C, D, E, and F; note the R− (sell) signals at or near cycle highs G, H, J and K.

plus or minus 20 percent is considered too variable for accurate market analysis. By adding together all the cycle lengths that have been observed and dividing by the total number of cycles, the average cycle length will be determined (shown as X_c, for our purposes).

WHICH DAYS COUNT WHEN YOU COUNT?

Students and practitioners of cyclic trading differ in their methodology regarding market days and calendar days in cyclic measurement. While some analysts (such as myself) prefer to count only market days (i.e., trading days), others favor counting calendar days. That a cycle high or low might be projected to fall on a weekend or on a market holiday is therefore conceivable. Naturally, this might leave the trader or investor rather perplexed as to the proper action. In the past, I have felt that counting market holidays as part of the cycle length added an unnecessary element of complexity and confusion to the cycle picture. The investor would certainly be frustrated if a cycle low was projected to occur on a day during which he or she could not trade because the markets were closed. Since 1980, futures trading throughout the world has increased dramatically.

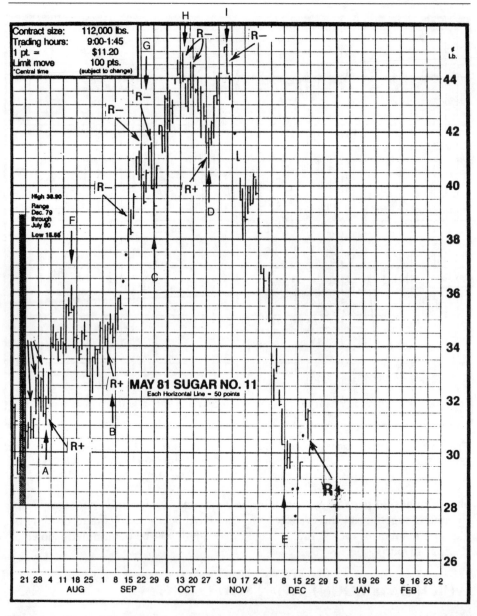

Figure 6.4 R+ and R− signals in sugar futures. Note R+ (buy) signals at or near cycle lows A, B, and D and R− (sell) signals at cycle highs F−I.

Trading in precious metal, currency, and interest rate futures virtually around the clock, up to six days a week is now possible. It is, therefore, likely for a market to top or bottom on a day that might be a market holiday in some parts of the world but not in others. For a low in the currencies to be made in European trading, overnight, while the U.S. markets are closed, or for a U.S. market to top or bottom when the European markets are closed would not be uncommon. Inasmuch as twenty-four-hour trading is now a reality, it is conceivable that calendar days would provide the most accurate cyclic count. Ultimately, however,

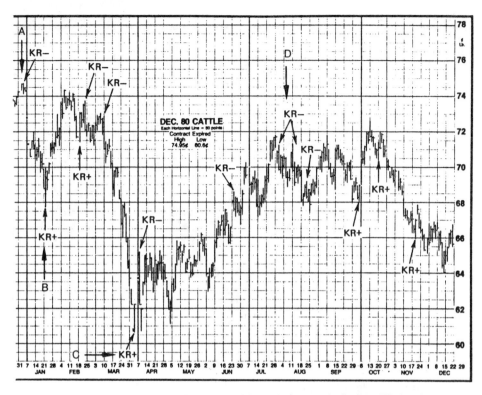

Figure 6.5   KR+ and KR− signals in December 1980 cattle futures. A−D show KR signals at or near major market turns.

I don't think that the differences would turn out to be particularly significant. I recommend, therefore, that you use whichever method you prefer, provided you remain consistent.

CYCLES AND TIMING

Figures 6.1 through 6.8 illustrate how the basic timing indicators can be used in conjunction with cycles. Timing indicators introduced in *The Handbook of Commodity Cycles* are still valid. In fact, as time passes I suspect that their validity will improve. More complex indicators (to be discussed later on in this text) are now available thanks to computer technology. For those interested in learning more about the basic indicators, their combinations, implementation, and performance, I suggest *The Handbook of Commodity Cycles*. The essential combination, however, is to employ timing indicators, either singly but preferably in combinations, only during the approximate time frame of an expected cycle top or bottom.

DEFINITIONS

Upside Reversal (R+)   If the current time unit (day, week, month) low price is lower than previous time unit low price and the current time unit closing price is

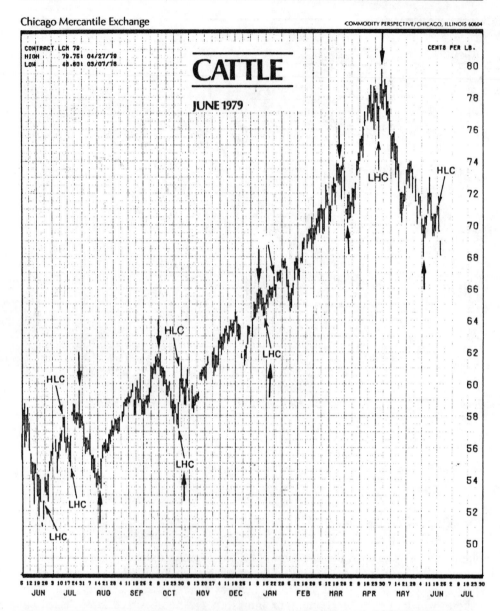

Figure 6.6 HLC and LHC timing signals in cattle futures. Although some of the signals were seen near cycle turns, they were not too common. This is why other signals should be used in addition to HLC and LHC.

higher than previous time unit closing price, then an upside reversal signal is established.

Downside Reversal (R−)   If the current time unit (day, week, month) high price is greater than previous time unit high price and current time unit closing price is lower than previous time unit closing price, then a downside reversal signal is established.

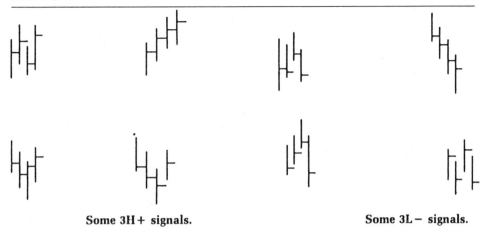

Some 3H+ signals.   **Some 3L− signals.**

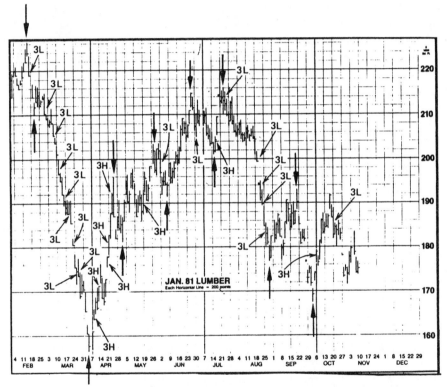

Figure 6.7   3H+, 3L− timing signals and short-term cycles in lumber futures. The 3H+ and 3L−
signals should ideally be used with other timing indicators, or for late market entry.

In determining reversals the only things taken into consideration are the time unit
highs, lows, and closing prices. We do *not* pay any attention to the opening price
in determining reversals. Nor do we look at open interest or volume in following
these signals. It is important that you understand precisely what is meant by a
reversal up and/or down. A way of stating the definition mathematically would be
as follows:

If H_1 = high of day 1   and H_2 = high of day 2
      L_1 = low of day 1 L_2 = low of day 2
and C_1 = closing price of day 1 C_2 = closing price of day 2
then upside reversal is

$$L_2 < L_1 \quad \text{and} \quad C_2 > C_1 = R+$$

downside reversal is

$$H_2 > H_1 \quad \text{and} \quad C_2 < C_1 = R-$$

Key Upside Reversal (KR+)   Any time unit (week, month, day, etc.) during which prices trade above their previous unit high, below their previous unit low, and close higher than the previous time unit.

Key Downside Reversal (KR−)   Any time unit (week, month, day, etc.) during which prices trade above their previous unit high, below their previous unit low, and close lower than the previous time unit.

   The key reversal is a special category of reversal signal and is considered much more important at major turning points of the market.

High to Low Close Signal (HLC)   If a market gives a COH one time unit and a COL on the very next time unit, then an HLC signal has occurred.

Low to High Close Signal (LHC)   If a market gives a COL signal one time unit and a COH signal the next time unit, then an LHC signal has occurred.

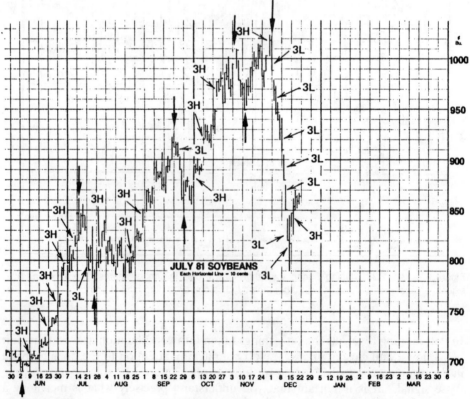

Figure 6.8   Some 3H+, 3L− signals and the short-term cycle in soybeans. Note 3H+ signals during cycle upswings and 3L− signals during cycle downswings.

For any given time unit (week, month, day, etc.):

Close on High (COH)   A closing price that is no more than 10 percent below the high of the given time unit.

Close on Low (COL)   A closing price that is no more than 10 percent above the low of the time unit.

A 3H + signal is used at or near cycle lows. The most recent 3 days' or 3 weeks' closing prices are compared to the current close. If the current close (fourth) is higher than the highest close of the last three days (or weeks), then a signal to buy has been given. Remember that the signal must occur within the proper time window! 3H+ can also be used with monthly data.

The 3L—signal is used to determine a cyclic downmove. Hence, it is used at a time window high. The most recent 3 days' or 3 weeks' closing prices are compared to the current close. If the current close is lower than the lowest of the last three closes, then a signal to sell has been given.

Graphically, these signals appear as in Figure 6.7. If no signal is present on the day (or week) after the 3 periods you have observed, drop the oldest day from the configuration and add the current day to your 3 unit period. Some examples of 3H+ and 3L— are shown in Figures 6.7 and 6.8.

CLOSING COMMENTS ON THE BASIC INDICATORS

Remember the following points in connection with the basic timing indicators:

1) The are used only in the time frame of expected cycle turns.
2) They are best used in conjunction with one another and with the other timing indicators in this book.
3) They must be used with stop losses or other risk limiting methods.
4) Their validity varies from market to market and from cycle to cycle. The Appendix provides specifics on the % accuracy of reversal signals in various markets.
5) If you have missed the opportunity to buy on or near a cycle turn, then you can use the basic timing indicators presented in this chapter for on market entry consistent with the existing trend so long as you realize that you may be taking on more risk due to later than optimum market entry. (See Appendix.)

7

The Stochastic Approach to Cycle Timing

Another useful cycle timing tool is the stochastic indicator. Its popularity in the 1980's is credited to George Lane of Investment Educators.[1] Although the interpretation and formulae used in my computation of the stochastic numbers are somewhat different from those employed by Lane, the concept of stochastics is similar. Regardless, its computation is not complex. It is interesting to observe that the dictionary definition of "stochastic" is "an educated guess."

WHAT STOCHASTICS DOES

The stochastic process mathematically "normalizes" price data. It then smooths the normalized data, using a moving average approach. The formulae for computing stochastics are shown in Figure 7.1. Computation of the stochastic numbers yields two values: % D and % K. % K is a derivation of % D. There are two types of output from this process, the "fast" and the "slow" stochastic data. The "slow" numbers are nothing more than a smoothed moving average of the "fast" numbers. Application of fast or slow stochastics is a matter of individual choice. Our concern will be with the "slow" or "smoothed" data.

There are numerous variations to the stochastic process. Methods of computation vary. Most computer quote services offer stochastics as one of the indicators their software provides. Since stochastic data are readily available, I will not take space to elaborate on the precise methods of calculation. They are relatively simple to compute. (See Figure 7.1).

CHARACTERISTICS OF STOCHASTICS

The stochastic data, as a function of its mathematical formulation, approach zero and one hundred as limits. High and low stochastic readings correspond with so-

---

[1]Lane, George. Investment Educators. 704 Graceland, Des Plaines, IL 60016.

1. Compute %K raw for time period.

$$\% \text{ K raw}_p = (\,(\text{Close}_p - \text{Low}_n) / (\text{High}_n - \text{Low}_n)\,) \times 100$$

where
    $\%\text{K raw}_p$ = the value for the initial **%K** or raw **%K** for the current time period,
    Close$_p$ = the closing price for the current period,
    Low$_n$ = the lowest low during the **n** periods,
    High$_n$ = the highest high during the **n** time periods and
    n = the time period you want to compute

2. Next compute the moving average of **%K.**

$$\%\text{K}_p = (\,(\%\text{K}_{p-1} \times 2) + \%\text{K raw}_p) / 3$$

where
    %K = the true **%K** for the current time period,
    %K$_{p-1}$ = the **%K** for the previous time period and
    %K raw$_p$ = the raw **%K** for the current time period.

3. Compute % D

$$\%\text{D}_p = (\,(\%\text{D}_{p-1} \times 2) + \%\text{K}_p) / 3$$

where
    %D$_p$ = the value for **%D** in the current period,
    %D$_{p-1}$ = the value for **%D** in the previous time period
    %K$_p$ = the value for **%K** in the current period.

Figure 7.1 How to compute stochastics.

called "overbought" and "oversold" conditions (to be defined). *High and low readings do not, however, correlate 100 percent with tops and bottoms, or with buy and sell signals.* Note that the stochastic formulae can be applied to any string of data, whether daily, weekly, monthly, yearly, or intraday. As long as high, low, and close data are used, stochastics can be computed.

The stochastic "period" (i.e. length or time span) can be adjusted to virtually any length of time desired by the user. In other words, a stochastic period of 3 days, 55 days, 14 days, 6 weeks—virtually any time length specified—can be used. The variation in time length or period selected either increases or decreases the number of timing signals generated by the stochastic indicator. The longer the time period, the less sensitive the indicator, and the shorter the time period, the more sensitive the indicator. Striking the proper balance of sensitivity and cycle length is very important, in order to keep the number of losing signals to a minimum. Typically, a stochastic period of one-half the cycle length tends to correspond best with cyclic turns. Before examining stochastics as a cyclic timing tool, however, let's take a closer look at the indicators.

WHAT STOCHASTICS LOOK LIKE

Figures 7.2, 7.3, and 7.4 each show the two stochastic numbers (% K, % D) plotted in chart form. The relationship between stochastics and underlying price won't be considered at this time. Let's simply look at the stochastic numbers in graphic form in order to illustrate some basic parameters and relationships.

Figures 7.5a, 7.5b, 7.5c, and 7.5d show stochastic readings for the same market, using periods of 5, 10, 15, and 25 units of time. Remember that these units of time could be minutes, hours, days, weeks, months, or even years. In this case, they happen to be days. Observe that stochastics turn slower or faster (i.e., sooner or later), depending on the time length of the stochastic period. One conclusion that can be reached about stochastics is that selection of the time length or period is very important in determining how sensitive (responsive) or insensitive (unresponsive) the indicator may be in relation to price. Essentially, the distinction here is between a highly responsive indicator for those who wish to trade more actively or a less responsive indicator, with fewer timing signals for those who wish to trade less actively.

Another important characteristic of stochastics is that its values fluctuate between a minimum and maximum of zero and one-hundred. I consider stochastic readings over 75% as indicative of "overbought" conditions. A reading of 25% or lower suggests an "oversold" condition. The terms *"overbought"* and *"oversold,"* though very popular among traders, are subjective and misleading. They are used herein for lack of more accurate or descriptive terms. Remember, "overbought" *is not synonymous with "sell signal,"* and "oversold" *is not synonymous with "buy*

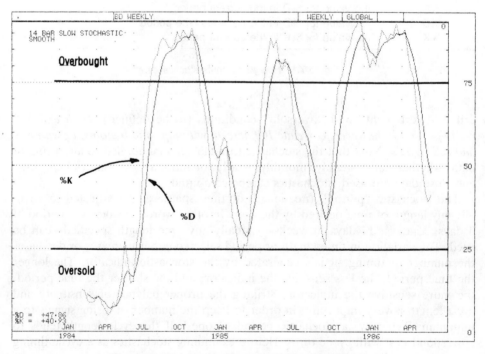

Figure 7.2 Two stochastic numbers plotted in chart form.

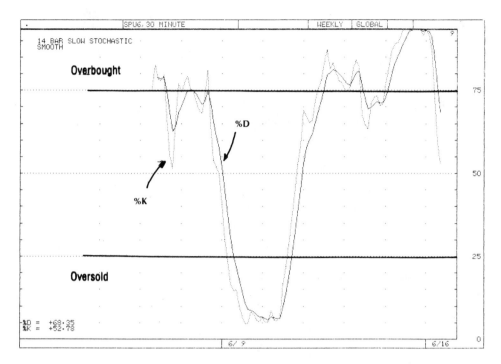

Figure 7.3   Two stochastic numbers plotted in chart form.

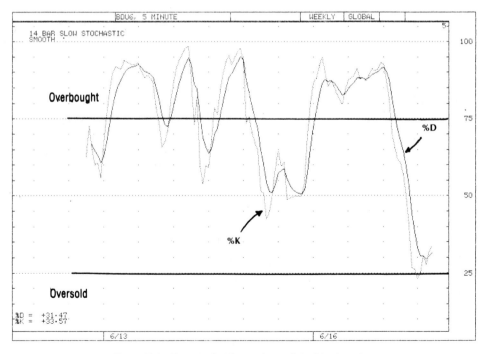

Figure 7.4   Two stochastic numbers plotted in chart form.

179

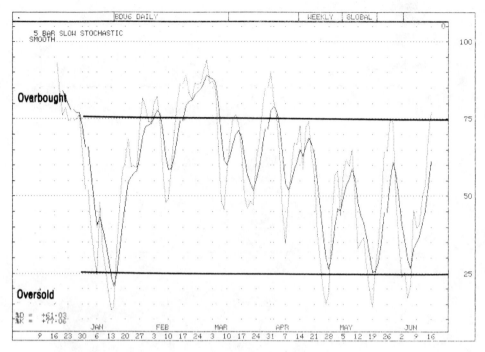

Figure 7.5a   Stochastic indicator—5 days for September 1986 T-bond futures.

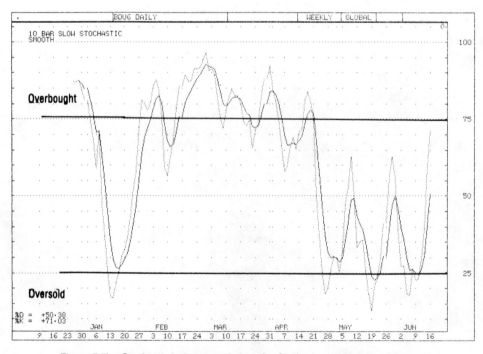

Figure 7.5b   Stochastic indicator—10 days for September 1986 T-bond futures.

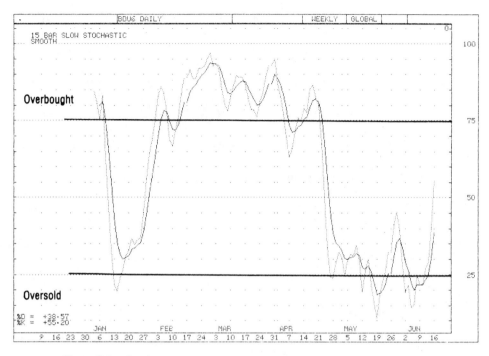

Figure 7.5c   Stochastic indicator—15 days for September 1986 T-bond futures.

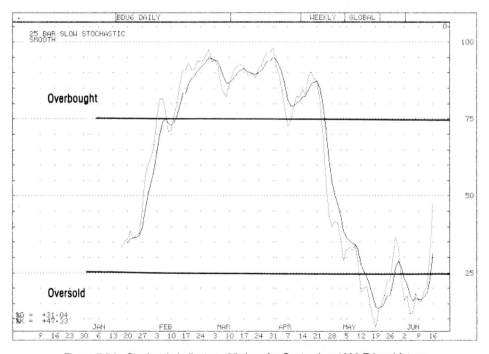

Figure 7.5d   Stochastic indicator—25 days for September 1986 T-bond futures.

signal.'' These terms are more appropriately replaced with *"cycle topping''* or *"cycle bottoming.''* We all know that the topping or bottoming process in any market is not a fixed-time event. In other words, no hard-and-fast rule exists about how long it takes a market to top or bottom. Some markets can top or bottom in a matter of minutes or hours, whereas others may take months or even years to top or bottom. Therefore, the terms overbought and oversold are not especially accurate. They can cause traders difficulty, particularly from a power-of-suggestion standpoint. The old saying "just because it's cheap don't mean it's good" expresses, in a way, the idea that an oversold condition does not automatically signal purchases. Conversely, the mere fact that a market is overbought does not necessarily indicate that selling is now appropriate. The issue of "overbought/oversold," "cycles topping/cycles bottoming," is a very important one, not only for the futures trader in general but particularly for those who make trading decisions based on cyclic and/or seasonal patterns.

Let's examine the stochastics on daily price charts. Figures 7.6 and 7.7 each show the stochastics plotted against price. Note how the stochastics tend to top or bottom near or at cycle turns. However, observe that stochastics cannot pick all turns! Here are a some of my guidelines for the use of stochastics as a general indicator (i.e. not necessarily in conjunction with cycles or seasonals). (1) While both stochastic indicators, i.e., % K and % D are in a downtrend (i.e., % K lower than % D) traders should not be long the market; rather they should be short, selling on rallies to resistance areas. (2) When % K is above % D and the trend is up, traders should be long, buying on breaks to support and taking profits

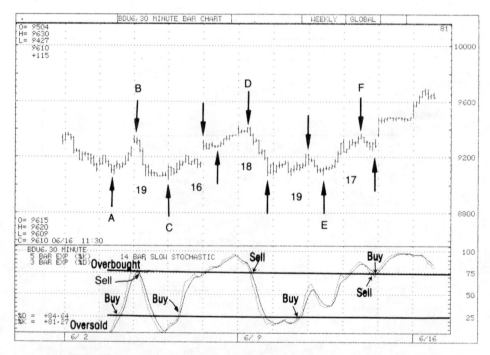

Figure 7.6 Stochastic indicator plotted on price chart of T-bond futures (intraday). Cycle tops and bottoms A–F were confirmed by stochastic signals.

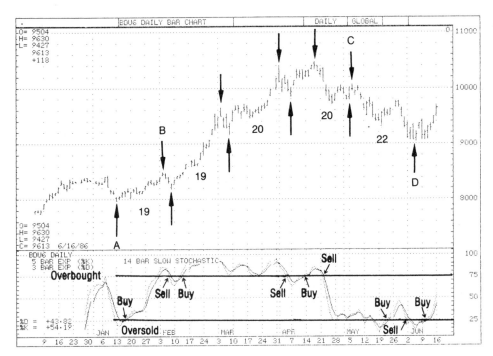

Figure 7.7 Stochastic indicator plotted on price chart showing buy and sell signals in conjunction with cycle turns A–D.

on rallies. (3) When % K and % D become oversold, falling to 25% or lower, traders should begin looking for a turn to the upside; however, no buying should yet be done. When both stochastic values equal or exceed 75%, traders should prepare to sell and/or sell short; however, they should do no selling yet. As shown in Figure 7.6, cycles and stochastic signals can be used in conjunction. (4) When stochastic has dropped to under 25% and when both indicators have turned back up over 25%, longs can be established. (5) When both stochastic indicators have exceeded or touched, 75% thereafter falling under 75%, selling can begin, either of long positions or to establish short positions.

Observe (from Figures 7.6, 7.7) that stochastics can enter oversold or over-bought, remaining oversold or overbought for an extended period of time. *There-fore, to anticipate turns in stochastics, or to act simply because the market is over-sold or overbought is not a wise decision,* possibly leading to repeated and sub-stantial losses.

STOCHASTICS AND CYCLES

The stochastic indicator can be used as a timing tool in conjunction with cycles. (Figures 7.6 and 7.7.) Two steps are used in the stochastic/cycles approach: First, isolate the probable time frame of a cycle low or high, and second, use the sto-chastic indicator to time market entry. Several examples (Figures 7.8 through 7.12) illustrate the application of this combined approach using various cycle

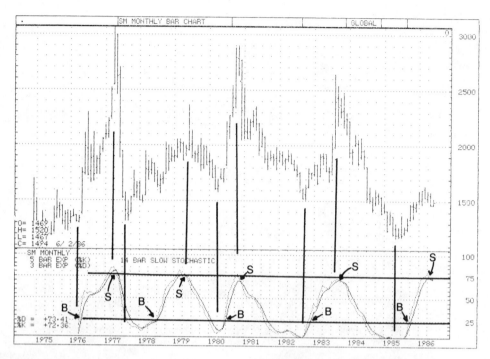

Figure 7.8 Stochastic and cycle turns (monthly soybean meal). Arrows mark buy and sell signals (B = buy) (S= sell). Vertical lines mark cycle lows and highs.

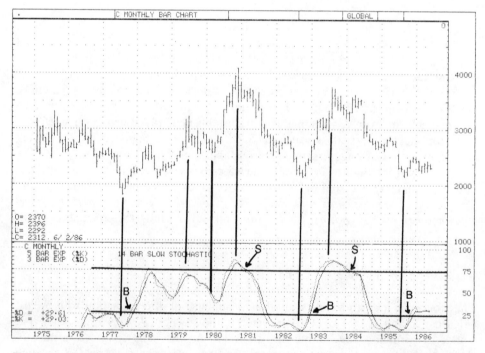

Figure 7.9 Stochastic and cycle turns (monthly corn). Arrows mark buy and sell signals. Vertical lines mark cycle lows and highs.

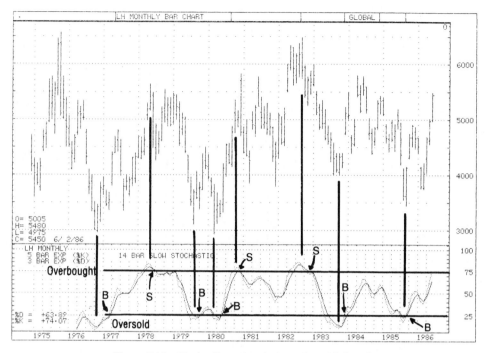

Figure 7.10   Stochastic and cycle turns (monthly hogs).

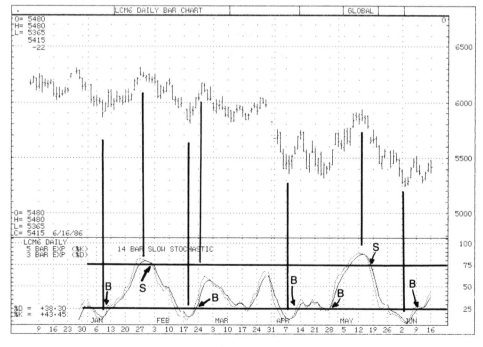

Figure 7.11   Stochastic and cycle turns (daily cattle).

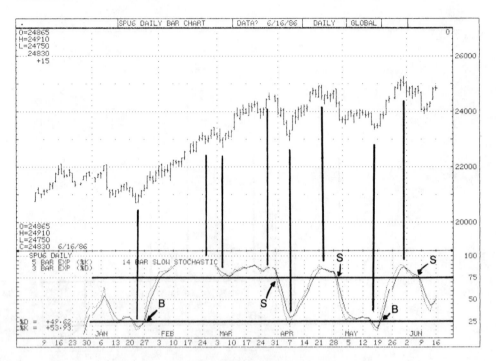

Figure 7.12   Stochastic and cycle turns (S&P daily).

lengths. Note from the examples given that stochastics can facilitate the timing of cycle turns. In selecting the length of stochastic (period of stochastic) used in timing cycle turns, a period of 7 to 15 time units is ideal. I find that periods shorter than 7 or longer than 15 are either too sensitive or too insensitive to cyclic turns. You may also consider using a stochastic period equal to about one-half the length of the cycle being studied.

STOCHASTICS: SUMMARY OF APPLICATIONS WITH CYLCLES

The use of stochastics with cycles is a most promising combination. There are some guidelines regarding practical implementation of stochastics as a timing tool.
1) Use the slow version of stochastics
2) A 14 period stochastic is best, however, a good general rule is to use one-half the cycle length.
3) Use stochastics to confirm a cycle turn.
4) When a cycle enters its time window high or low use stochastic signals to enter or exit the market.
5) Use several timing indicators to confirm a cycle low or high.
6) The most effective approach is to enter only when stochastics and cycle expectations are in agreement within a reasonable period of time (i.e., the time window or slightly before/after).

8
Support, Resistance, Price Projections, and Cycles

One of the criticisms of cyclic analysis is that it fails to provide price targets. But those who truly understand trading and cyclic analysis know that price projections are frequently unnecessary. However, for those who cling to the old belief that price is more important than time, I have developed a simple method for determining approximate price targets for a given cycle. I have also developed a secondary technique for determining support and resistance levels for cyclic up and down moves. Before explaining these techniques, I must reaffirm that price projection is not necessary, and it can, in fact, be damaging to trading results. The following explains why.

ARE PRICE TARGETS NECESSARY?

We all know that in the markets, "timing is everything." If the time for taking a particular action is right, then the price must necessarily also be right. Therefore, it makes little difference to those trading with cycles how high or low prices may be. If the time has come to take action, action must be taken without regard for price. In fact, if one allows price to affect judgment, the resulting decision can be inconsistent with one's original intentions. Assume, for example, the case of an individual who purchased gold at $300/oz. with a price target of $379/oz. Although the market may have risen to within $10 of the objective with the cycle peaking, the original price target has now become a benchmark. It prompts the investor to hold the position, awaiting the price target, even though market cycles may be saying that the trend has most likely turned lower. I conclude, that projecting price targets is not necessarily a practice that fosters sound investing or successful speculation. Price targets have a way of fostering dependency. The more you establish a specific price target for your trading or investing, the less attention you are prone to pay to the important aspects of timing. This is why I stated earlier that the use of price targets may actually prove detrimental to the investor or trader in the long run. I prefer to establish time targets as opposed to price targets. If the time is right, then the price must also be right, regardless of what the price may actually be. As mentioned earlier, determining support and resistance levels as well as price objectives is very important to many traders. Yet, to the true trend follower, these ideas are superfluous, and in actuality are not worthy of consideration. Precisely where prices will go, and what obstacles or resistance they may encounter on their journey is a fruitless exercise to the true follower of cycles and trends. The majority of technicians are convinced that if their methodology and analysis will help them determine when to buy and sell, then price target issues are not important. The trend follower who is truly committed to a technical system knows from experience that the system will permit market entry sufficiently early after inception of an important trend with reasonably good results over a period of time. Furthermore, the technical method should ideally permit market exit and position reversal when the trend has changed. Time spent calculating price objectives is not necessary, since the true trend-following system is primarily concerned with changes in trend and market entry/exit as soon as possible subsequent to such change. This ability (or lack of it) frequently separates profitable trend-following systems from marginal or unprofitable trading systems.

Some techniques of market analysis place great emphasis on price objectives, and their success is determined by the accuracy and ability of their methods to determine precise price points. Whereas this may be relatively simple to do over the short term, it becomes increasingly difficult to accomplish with accuracy over the long term.

In spite of the fact that many technical methods of futures trading do not, ideally, require the determination of price objectives, many traders and investors also have in fact, been trained to believe that price objectives are necessary. The principles of good investing, whatever they might actually be, have perpetuated the notion that in order to trade or invest successfully, one must have specific objectives both for the positive and negative alternatives. This idea has its roots in fundamental analysis and is anachronistic for the market technician.

Before I ruffle the feathers of those advocating technical methods whose ultimate goal is to forecast price, in all fairness, I must say that I have seen some of these techniques work quite well. In fact, they could be combined with cycles quite effectively. Yet, I am not certain whether this is necessary. You must decide for yourself. I won't name specific systems, but a number of popular techniques use exact price targets and derivations to establish buy, sell, or hold signals. At this point you may wish to reflect on your personal experiences with price projections, and draw your own conclusions accordingly. If you can use such techniques in combination with cycles, then, by all means do so!

Another dimension of the price-objective issue is the psychological one. Our education and training constitute one aspect of the need for price projection; however, human needs and human psychology constitute a more significant aspect of the propensity to establish price objectives. Throughout our lives we have been told that we need to know where we are going. Whether or not this is as true in trading, as it is in managing a business, we have been taught that specific goals are necessary if we are to acquire the things we want and need. This is why so many of us have difficulty following the dictates of a purely technical approach that does not provide specific price objectives but rather yields only buy and sell signals. Since it is not the purpose of this book to delve into trader psychology, I will move on to various techniques by which general ideas of support, resistance, and price targets may be determined (by those who cannot overcome the need to establish such objectives, or who, for other reasons, may wish to have some idea of where prices may go during a given cyclic phase). As a final point, I might add that specific price targets may be particularly important to hedgers, producers and intraday speculators. They are also useful in "key date" seasonal trading.[1]

MEAN PERCENTAGE MOVE METHOD (MPMM)

One technique for projecting price targets it the Mean Percentage Move Method (MPMM). MPMM is a simple technique that employs the average percentage move of a given cycle, up and down, over an extended period of time. By examining as many cycles as possible, and by determining the approximate magnitude of the price rise and fall for each of the cycles, the approximate average percentage price increase or decrease can be determined. In some markets there is a high degree of consistency for mean percentage price increase or decrease across many cycles, whereas in other markets consistency is not sufficient for trading purposes. Figure 8.1, which shows a hypothetical cycle with hypothetical price rises and declines for each repetition. Percentage price increase and decrease for each of the cycles is also shown. By taking as many observations of each cycle as possible, adding them together, and taking their average percentage move, we can project the approximate size of the next move as shown in Figure 8.1 and 8.2. Moving from theory to real time examples, Figures 8.3, 8.4, and 8.5 show three specific examples of how the projection technique applies to longer term cycles. A

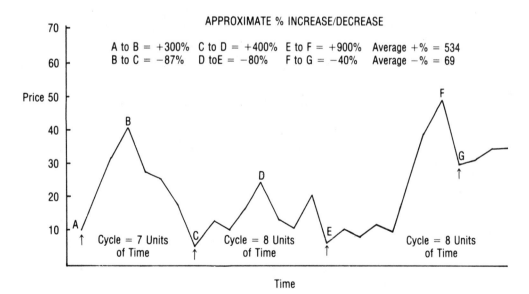

Figure 8.1   Hypothetical cycle showing price rises, declines, and % up/down moves.

[1]See Bernstein, J. *Seasonal Concepts in Futures Trading*. New York: John Wiley, 1987.

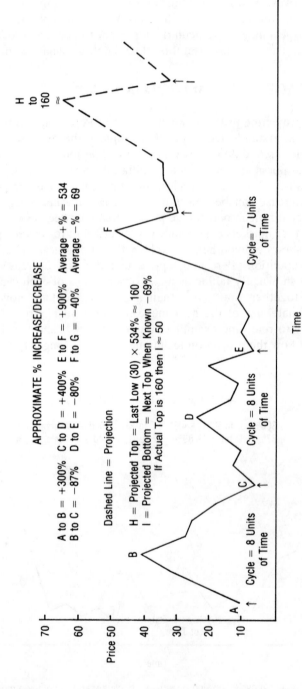

Figure 8.2 Hypothetical cycle showing price rises, declines and projection.

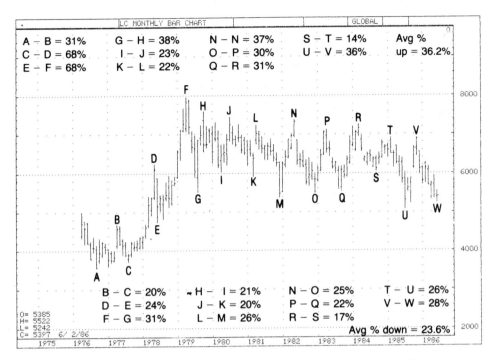

Figure 8.3 Monthly cattle futures cycle showing price rises, declines, and % up/down moves.

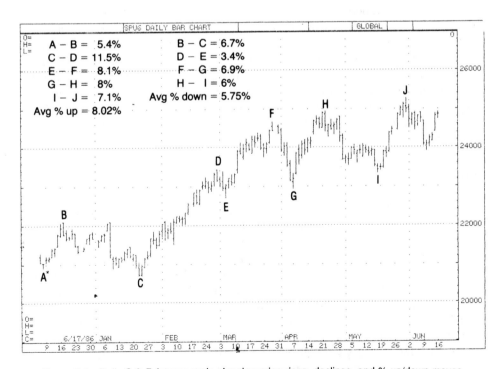

Figure 8.4 Daily S & P futures cycle showing price rises, declines, and % up/down moves.

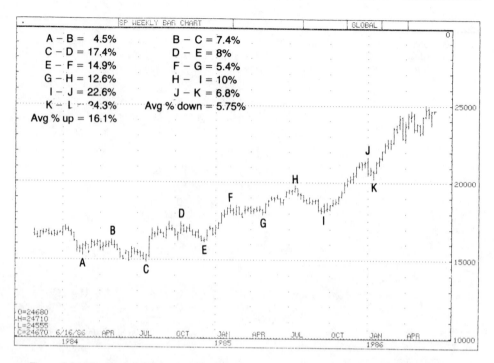

Figure 8.5 Weekly S & P futures cycle showing price rises, declines, and % up/down moves.

minimum of five repetitions is needed before a reasonable projection of bullish and/or bearish price targets can be obtained. The dashed lines show upside and downside price targets that were projected, using previous cycle up and down moves. Percentage price increase and percentage price decrease for each of the preceding cycles are averaged in order to make a price projection. Once the projected cycle has been completed and actual price highs and lows are known, the average up and down moves are recalculated and another projection is made. Theoretically, the passage of time allows for more accurate projection of possible high and low price targets.

PRICE BAND

The price projections derived from MPMM are given within a given price band of approximately 5%, plus or minus the magnitude of the move. In other words, if the average move for a given cycle is 100 price units (i.e., dollars, cents), then the projected price target band will fall into a range of 100, plus or minus 5%, or a band of 95 to 105 units. In addition to the raw calculations or price projection bands, the degree of forecasting confidence (i.e., confidence level) can also be calculated by determining how accurate previous projections were compared to actual results. Figure 8.6 illustrates this technique. Do your own projections on Figure 8.7.

The MPMM is a very general method for projecting approximate price targets using cyclic analysis, however, it seems to yield some fairly useful results. Ulti-

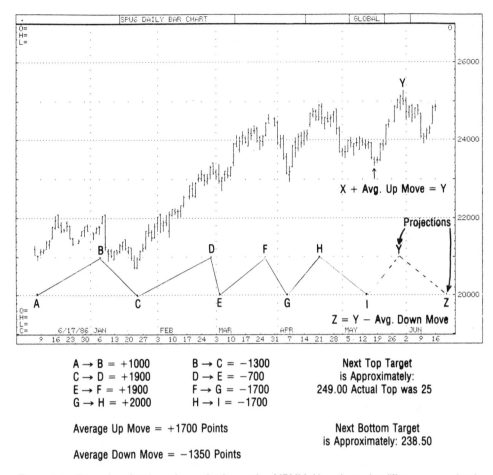

A → B = +1000	B → C = −1300	Next Top Target
C → D = +1900	D → E = −700	is Approximately:
E → F = +1900	F → G = −1700	249.00 Actual Top was 25
G → H = +2000	H → I = −1700	

Average Up Move = +1700 Points

Average Down Move = −1350 Points

Next Bottom Target
is Approximately: 238.50

Figure 8.6   Illustration showing price projections using MPMM. Note that point differences need only be approximate since MPMM is a method of projecting approximate price targets.

mately, price projections in combination with cycles and/or other technical methods may prove more of an art than a science. The technique I have just described appears to apply not only to long-term cycles but to short-term cycles and seasonals as well. Practice this technique on Figures 8.8, 8.9, and 8.10. Remember that MPMM does not provide exact price targets, but rather general levels of support and resistance.

THE PRICE PROBE AND SPIKE METHOD (PPSM)

It is said that the history of prices is very important in determining the future of prices. Every market exists as an individual entity as well as a collective entity in the economic world. What has occurred in previous cycles and throughout the course of history has a lasting effect on the future of prices. The most recent events have the most immediate effect, whereas the most distant events have more subtle significance. I have frequently observed that certain specific price

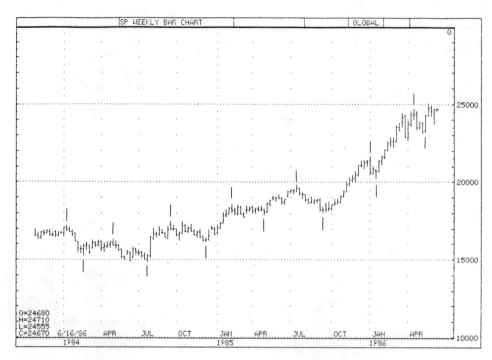

Figure 8.7 Use this chart and the indicated cycle tops/bottoms to make your own MPMM projections.

Figure 8.8 Short-term cycles and MPMM. Try your hand at projecting the next high/low.

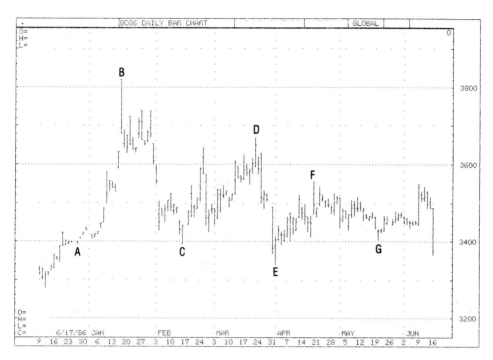

Figure 8.9   Short-term cycles and MPMM. Can you use the MPMM to project the next high/low.

Figure 8.10   Short-term cycles and MPMM. Can you project the next high/low.

levels established during a major market turning point appear to exert a continued effect on the market for a considerable period of time thereafter. Whether these effects are primarily economic or essentially psychological is really of no consequence. Determining the answer to this question might prove to be a totally fruitless exercise. Ultimately, it is speculators, investors, hedgers, and/or commercial interests who are concerned with price and timing. If previously significant price movements can be demonstrated to somehow exert a continuing effect in the future, and if some general rules for interpreting and understanding these effects can also be demonstrated, then results are clearly more important than reasons. Through the years I have observed that significant market turning points, usually those marked by important cycle highs and lows, tend to provide support and resistance to prices at some future point. This is perfectly logical, and certainly is no great secret or market discovery. The laws of supply and demand, which ultimately determine price, are reflected and affected by price. The circular relationship between the two is somewhat repetitive. Supply and demand affect price. Price affects producers and consumers by either encouraging production, discouraging production, stimulating demand, or stimulating consumer resistance. These, in turn, exert influence back on price, which, in turn, exerts influence back on the underlying variables. During periods of extreme fluctuation and/or price extremes, supply-and-demand factors are out of balance. This is true on a secular level as well as on a short-term basis. Hence, supply and demand influences can be observed on a monthly, weekly, daily, and intraday basis. To validate these assertions, we need only study price charts.

The technique about to be described is still somewhat general in its methodology, however, many applications are possible. You must remember that the price probe/spike method (PPSM) is not strictly operational, inasmuch as it does not yet define a specific set of procedures by which one can evaluate either price objectives or long-term support and resistance. The PPSM makes the following assumptions regarding any given market: (1) The month, week, day, hour, or minute a significant price high or low occurs is important in the future of each market. (2) The high and low price established during this important time frame is likely to have future significance as support or resistance. (3) Frequently, subsequent price highs and lows will fall within (or close to) the price range at previously significant highs or lows. (4) In a downtrend, the low of the spike top time frame is likely to become very important as the approximate high to which prices later rally (to be illustrated). (5) In an uptrend, the high of the spike-range time frame will become important later on after prices drop on a reaction during uptrend (this will also be illustrated). (6) Although conditions (4) and (5) frequently hold true, there are no totally mechanical rules regarding its application. Prices can top or bottom at any point in the range of the spike. The entire range of the spike time frame is important. Specific examples are shown in Figures 8.11, 8.12, 8.13, and 8.14. Figures 8.15, 8.16, 8.17, and 8.18 are given as further illustrations of this technique. Of all the methods discussed in this book, this is the one that requires the most practice and the best "sixth sense." The PPSM is not as objective a method as it should be, yet it can yield some especially good results, as is readily apparent from the charts that have been included as illustrations of this technique. By using a price band of approximately plus or minus 10 percent, you can further enhance the technique to allow for

Figure 8.11   Chart illustrating the PPSM on monthly D-mark.

Figure 8.12   Chart illustrating the PPSM on 60 minute T-bond chart.

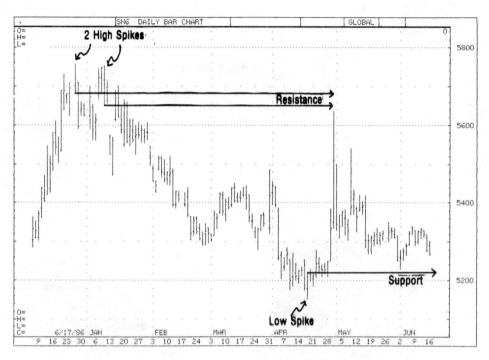

Figure 8.13   Chart illustrating the PPSM on daily July soybeans.

Figure 8.14   Illustration of the PPSM on weekly wheat chart.

Figure 8.15   Illustration of the PPSM with monthly soybean cycles. Cycle low E was in range of spike at low C. High F in range of spike B etc. Vertical arrows mark cycle tops and bottoms.

Figure 8.16   Illustration of the PPSM on monthly corn cycles. Vertical arrows mark cycle tops and bottoms. Note tendency for previous low spikes (i.e., A, F & E) to act as support for next cycle low. Note tendency for previous high spikes to act as resistance for next cycle (i.e., B and F).

199

Figure 8.17   Illustration of the PPSM on daily cycles. Note how lows G and I fell into previous spike support. Note also highs F, H and J at spike resistance.

Figure 8.18   Illustration of the PPSM on weekly T-bond cycles. Note spike support/resistance.

reasonable variations in support and resistance levels. Remember that the PPSM price levels must be used in conjunction with significant cycle tops and bottoms if they are to be used as part of the cycles approach.

CONCLUSIONS ABOUT PPSM AND CYCLES

The PPSM technique is highly versatile in its application and can be used as follows:

1. To project the approximate low of a cycle by examining previous spike highs, and projecting the range forward in time.
2. To project approximate cycle-price highs by examining previous spike lows and projecting the ranges forward in time and price.
3. To determine possible objective within the given range for a specific cycle.
4. To determine approximate price entry levels for the long and short side, once a cyclic turn has been established.

The PPSM technique does not constitute the trading system, but rather it is another tool that cycles traders may keep handy for use as needed. Personally, I find the spike-range technique to be very helpful in projecting price reactions during moves and determining entry levels in conjunction with cycle tops and bottoms. As mentioned at the beginning of this chapter, I have seen the spike-range technique do some amazing things. Logically, cycle lows and cycle highs as well as the price range established during these high periods are significant, since they reflect major changes in the underlying economics of each market.

USING THE 10/8 CHANNEL FOR SUPPORT AND RESISTANCE

The 10 high/8 low moving will be discussed thoroughly in Chapter Nine as a method of cyclic top and bottom timing. The channel method can also be used for determining support and resistance levels. These levels can, in turn, be used for the purpose of establishing approximate price targets for existing trades and/or for the purpose of entering trades consistent with the cyclic trend. Figures 8.19 through 8.22 illustrate some of these applications. Note commentary accompanying each figure.

The major benefit of this approach is that it is very specific. At any point in time, you will know the precise moving average channel values. when trading with the cycle, specific price orders to buy or sell can be entered at or near these values. Take some time to study this approach. You will be impressed with its ability to help you spot specific reaction levels for taking positions consistent with the cyclic trend. For more information see Chapter Nine.

I must stress that the channel support and resistance technique has its greatest success when used in conjunction with the cyclic trend. Remember also that for cycles of less than about 14 to 18 days duration, the 10/8 channel should be used on intraday data as opposed to daily data. Specific examples on hourly and half-hourly charts are shown in Figures 8.23 through 8.26. As you can see, the 10/8 channel is highly versatile in conjunction with cycles and, by itself, can be used as a measure of trend, support, and resistance.

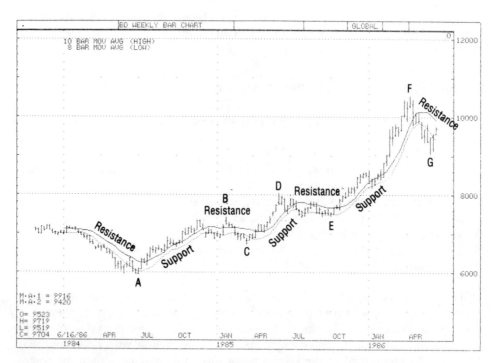

Figure 8.19 Support and resistance on weekly T-bond cycle using 10H/8L channel. The channel consists of two moving averages; one consisting of 10 units of the highs; the other being 8 units of the lows.

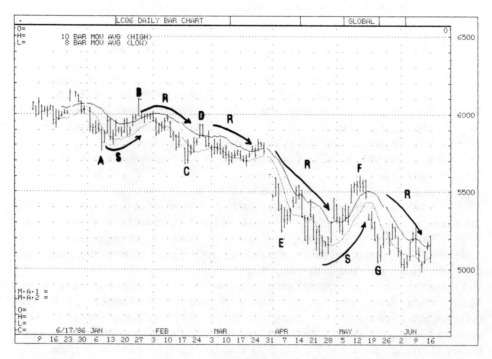

Figure 8.20 Support and resistance using 10H/8L on daily price chart. A–G are cycle lows and highs. R = resistance during down cycle. S = support during up cycle.

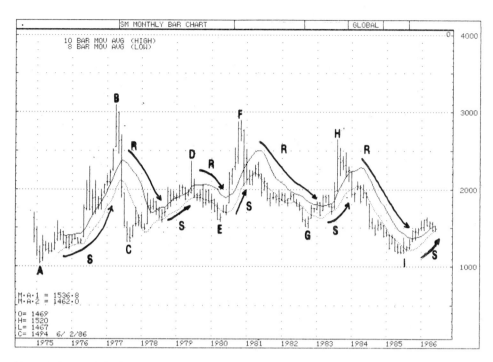

Figure 8.21   10H/8L channel resistance and monthly soybean meal cycles. Cycle lows and highs
A−I and support/resistance based on 10/8 channel.

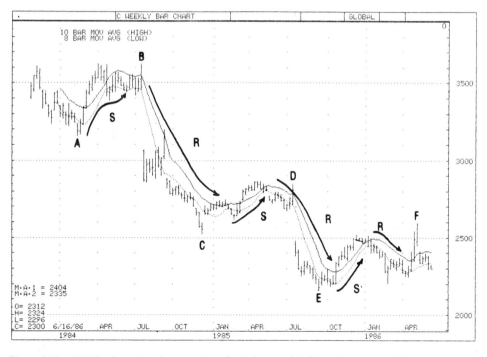

Figure 8.22   10H/8L channel and corn cycles. Cycle lows and highs and support/resistance based on
10/8 channel.

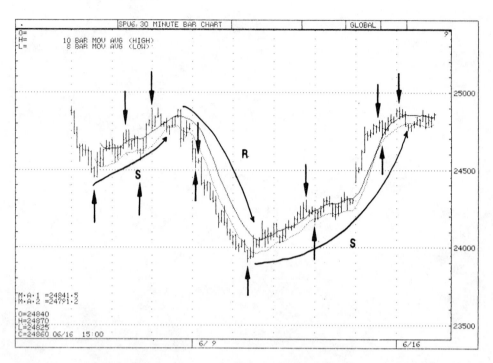

Figure 8.23   10H/8L channel and 30 minute S&P chart. Note cycle lows and highs marked by vertical arrows.

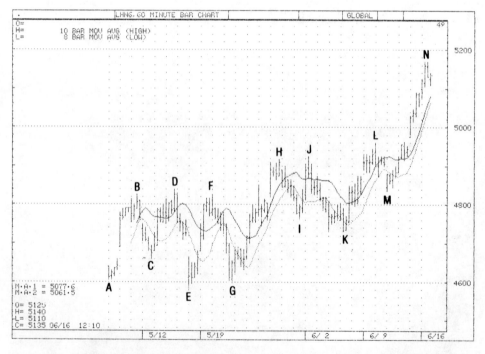

Figure 8.24   10H/8L channel and 60 minute live hog chart (note that 10/8 is too slow for such a short-term cycle). Cycle lows and highs A–N.

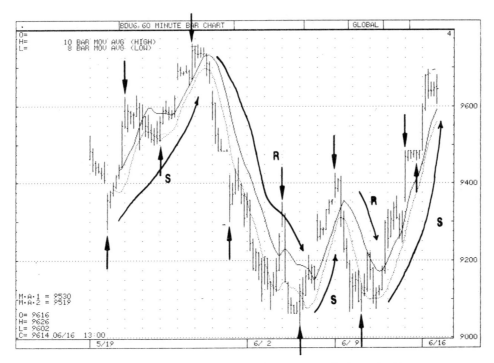

Figure 8.25   10H/8L channel on 60 minute T-bonds. Cycle lows and highs marked by vertical arrows.

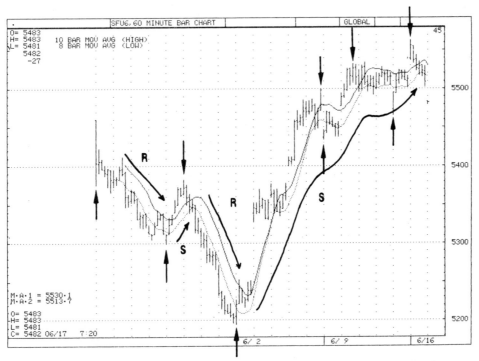

Figure 8.26   10H/8L channel and 60 minute Swiss franc, support/resistance, and cycles.

SUMMARY OF SUPPORT, RESISTANCE AND PROJECTION

Support and resistance methods are important to the cycles trader inasmuch as they can permit market entry and exit consistent with the cycle trend *after* the cycle has turned. Projection of price highs and lows is not considered to be very important. However, there are various techniques for doing so.

9

Moving-Average Channel and Cycle Timing

Moving-average* systems have enjoyed a perennial following among stock and futures traders. Other systems have come and gone, but moving averages have endured. The simple fact that moving averages and their many variations are still with us today is a strong testimonial to their efficacy. Indeed, many stock and commodity fund money managers employ moving averages in their various forms as a primary method of trade selection. Computer technology has made possible many variations on the moving average theme. It is now possible to compute, within seconds, a host of different moving averages, differences of moving averages, weighted moving averages, smoothed moving averages, and exponential moving averages. Moving averages are "naturals" for today's computerized trading environment.

We have certainly come a long way since the days of Richard Donchian, the man who is affectionately called the "father of moving averages." Donchian popularized the notion of using moving averages as a trading method in the 1950's. For a review of the many different types of moving averages, see Kaufman (1980).[1] The formula for computing simple moving averages is shown in Figure 9.1.

$$\text{Data Point \#1 for Moving Average:} = \frac{P_1 + P_2 + P_3 + P_4 \ldots + P_N}{N}$$

$$\text{Data Point \#2 for Moving Average:} = \frac{P_2 + P_3 + P_4 + P_5 \ldots + P_N}{N}$$

where P = price
N = number of time units

Figure 9.1 Calculating a simple moving average.

*MA = moving average
[1]Kaufman, Perry J. *Commodity Trading Systems and Methods*. New York: John Wiley, 1980.

The process of computing a simple moving average is most elementary. One variation on the moving average theme is to compute a moving average of other price parameters, such as highs, lows, opening prices, average price, etc. In other words, rather than computing the moving average of closing prices (which is the common application), one could compute the moving average of other price parameters. Figure 9.2 shows a daily futures price chart with a ten-day moving average of the closing price plotted on the chart. Figure 9.3 shows the same chart with a ten-day moving average of the median price (high plus low divided by two). Although some differences between the two are apparent, they are not outstanding.

Now let's examine the same price chart with a new moving average: specifically, a ten-day moving average of only the high prices (Figure 9.4). This chart is especially noteworthy. You can readily see that the ten-day moving average of highs seems to act somewhat as a resistance level. In other words, on the downswing, prices tend to touch or briefly exceed the ten-day[2] High MA (moving average) line, and once an uptrend begins, the ten-day High MA line no longer serves as a resistance level. Instead, the ten-day High MA line seems to become a support level, which prices touch on downside reactions within the uptrend. The ten day MA of highs can be of potential value as follows:

Figure 9.2   A daily futures chart with a ten-day moving average of closing prices.

[2]Note that although I refer to the MA's in terms of "days" they are applicable to virtually any unit of time, whether days, weeks, months, hours, or minutes.

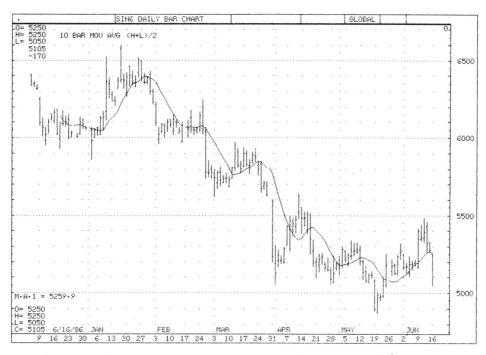

Figure 9.3   Chart showing the ten-day MA of the median price.

1. The ten-day MA of highs serves to identify specific price levels at which resistance should appear on corrective rallies during downtrends.
2. This line can serve as a point against which traders can sell on bear-market rallies.
3. Once the ten-day MA of highs has been exceeded by price, an uptrend has probably started. Now the ten-day MA of highs takes on different significance: namely, that of support (as opposed to resistance).

Let's take our illustration a step further. Figure 9.5 shows the same market as Figure 9-4, but with a ten-day MA of lows, instead of highs. What has happened? A situation exactly the opposite of what was earlier discussed for the day MA of highs is now apparent. In other words, the ten-day MA of lows tends to serve as support under the market during rising trends. Corrective reactions during the trend usually dip down to very close to the ten-day MA of low line (or level). By examining Figure 9.5, you can see why I reach the following conclusions about the 10 day MA of lows:

1. The ten-day MA of lows serves as support on corrective declines during rising trends.
2. Traders who wish to buy on downside reactions during bull trends can do so at or near to the ten-day MA of low line.
3. Once price has successfully penetrated the ten-day MA of lows, a bear trend is said to have started, and the ten-day MA of lows now serves as a resistance level on price rallies.

Figure 9.4   Chart showing a ten-day MA of only high prices.

Figure 9.5   Chart using a ten-day MA of lows.

Used individually, moving averages of highs or lows can be very helpful to futures traders; however, used in combination with cycles, they can be more valuable to those interested in catching that portion of the downtrend or uptrend that has the greatest acceleration and normally carries the least amount of risk. To do this, the moving average of highs and lows in combination could be employed to form a channel. Figure 9.6 shows such a channel without price, and Figure 9.7 shows the same channel with price. Some observations about the moving-average channel are worth noting prior to a discussion of its use.

Sideways, or "trendless," markets that repeatedly hit their upper and lower parameters are not uncommon, finding resistance at, or close to, the top of the channel and support at, or close to, the bottom of the channel. The condition of price bar within the channel may be defined as "equilibrium." In other words, when a price bar (defined as the high and low range for a given unit of time) is either partially or entirely within that price channel or envelope, the market is said to be "at equilibrium" (in economic terms, "fairly priced").

However, my work has shown that markets are not often fairly priced. I disagree with the old economic theory that price at any given point represents a fair balance of buyers and sellers, and that such a balance is maintained most of the time. Although this definition may have been true in the economics of yesteryear, I do not believe that it is true today for more than brief periods. As long as price bars remain partially or totally within the moving-average envelope or channel, the market is fairly priced. However, more often than not, bars remain primarily outside the channel. In cases in which markets fall below the channel or envelope, the market has a condition of oversupply, and prices must be continually adjusted

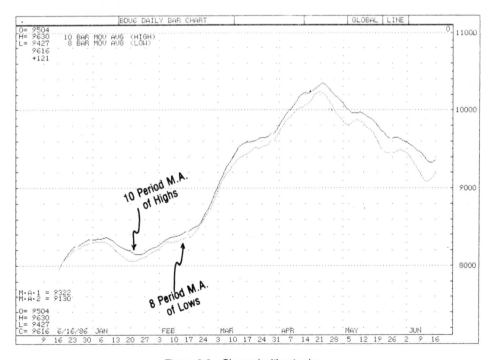

Figure 9.6   Channel without price.

Figure 9.7   Channel with price.

downward until equilibrium is again reached. On the other hand, once price bars move above the channel or envelope, the market has entered a condition of undersupply, or increasing demand, and prices must continue to adjust upward until equilibrium has again been attained.

The application of this "economic" theory is really quite simple: As long as price bars remain within the channel (as defined), the market is in a state of equilibrium with the channel highs and lows representing support or resistance areas. A trader could have resting orders to buy in the lower area of the channel with resting orders to liquidate longs and go short in the upper area of the channel. Once the market has entered a condition of oversupply or undersupply as defined, the system will so indicate by showing two consecutive price closings outside the channel (i.e., not touching either extreme of the channel, and not within the channel at all). On the downside, two successive closings below the lower end of the channel often indicate that prices have reached a condition of oversupply, and that a bearish trend has begun. Conversely, if the market shows two successive price closes outside the top of the channel, it indicates that a condition of undersupply has started and prices are likely to climb until an equilibrium level has been reached. (See Figures 9.8 through 9.12 for different time lengths and notes.)

To assume that all markets will, at all times, move in regular patterns of equilibrium to undersupply, equilibrium to oversupply, etc. is idealistic. Markets will often have brief spurts of oversupply or undersupply with alternating periods of equilibrium. In fact, within one's defined time frame (i.e., hourly, daily, weekly, monthly, or yearly), brief interruptions of trends, periods of equilibrium, and

Figure 9.8   Channel on monthly T-bond chart showing buy (B) and sell (S) signals. Buy signals are given when two successive closing prices are above the top of the channel; sell signals occur when two successive closings fall under the bottom of the channel.

Figure 9.9   Channel and weekly buy (B), sell (S) signals. (See Figure 9.8 for explanation of signals.)

Figure 9.10 Channel and daily buy (B), sell (S) signals. (See Figure 9.8 for explanation of signals.)

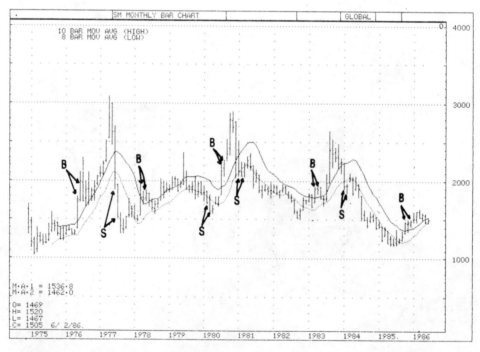

Figure 9.11 Monthly soybean meal chart with buy (B) and sell (S) signals. (See Figure 9.8 for explanation of signals.)

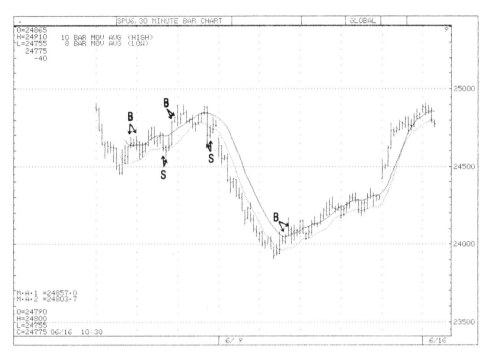

Figure 9.12   Channel and intraday (30 minute) buy (B), sell (S) signals.

returns to the major trend are not uncommon. this is a roundabout way of saying that the channel equilibrium theory is not a 100 percent occurrence. What can we do to make the theory more workable? One important ingredient is adding cyclic expectations to the channel technique to arrive at a more accurate indication.

THE CHANNEL AND CYCLIC TURNS

Now that I have examined the manner in which daily averages of the highs and lows act as support and resistance (among other things), let's study how these indicators can be used in the timing of cycle turns, both to the upside and the downside. If you understand how these averages work, you will understand how they can serve as timing indicators for cyclic turns. In an uptrend, the normal pattern for prices is to maintain upward momentum, with the general rule of thumb being "higher highs and lower lows." Figure 9.13 shows how the typical bull market unfolds, there is a strong tendency toward higher highs and higher lows. This does not mean that each successive daily price must have a higher high or higher low, but rather, in a majority of days, a bull market will have a higher high than the previous day and a higher low than the previous day. Conversely, the typical bear market pattern is for lower lows and lower highs. Figure 9.14 shows this tendency in a typical bear market. Naturally, then, when a moving average of highs is calculated, the average will have a strong tendency to move in a fairly consistent and minimally erratic uptrend as long as the bull market remains in a healthy state. Due to the nature of the moving average, a certain amount of movement contrary to the trend is acceptable and can occur without

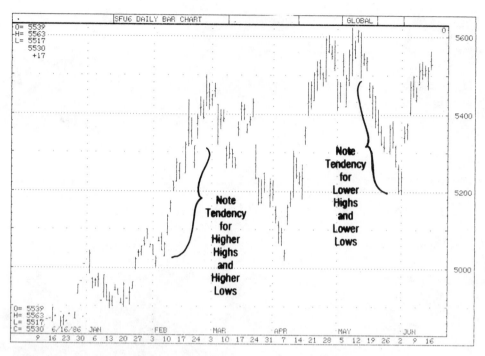

Figure 9.13   Tendency toward higher highs and lower lows in bull market, and vice versa in bear market.

Figure 9.14   Lower highs and lower lows tendency in bear market.

turning the moving average of the high lower. If, however, the market enters a sideways pattern or begins to trend sideways to lower for a period of X number of days (X being the moving-average length), the moving average of the highs will indeed turn lower, and, before too long, the moving average of the highs will be above or greater than the actual price highs established by the market. This, according to my definition, would turn the trend lower. To a certain extent, markets tend to exhibit characteristics that are in many ways similar to physical or chemical properties. Consider the following comparison between price and a physical object in motion:

If a ball is thrown in the air with a given amount of energy, it will continue to rise until the forces of gravity and friction overtake its energy and it begins to fall. Unless an intervening push of additional energy is exerted on the ball, it will reach a point at which its upward speed begins to slow, and, for a brief moment, the ball will actually move neither up nor down. The ball will then reverse course and begin to move lower. The course will continue lower until the ball hits the ground or obtains more energy input to the upside. In such a perfect situation, many measures of velocity and acceleration, friction, gravitational pull, intermediate energy input, wind velocity and direction, mass of the ball, etc. could be taken into consideration. Even a relatively new student of physics could make a fairly accurate forecast about such things as how high the ball will go, how long it will remain in an uptrend, when it will turn lower, and how quickly it will return to its original position.

The 10/8 channel technique can serve to assist such calculations for the market in the same way that various formulae from physics can be applied to the analogy of the ball. The predictability of the market cannot be as accurate as the predictability of the ball in motion, since not all inputs (i.e., variables) can possibly be known. However, the 10/8 channel is a relatively good way of assessing when the market has run out of energy. Sometimes a market will turn lower, but it will receive an additional energy input that will propel it higher, thereby turning the moving average of highs to the upside once more.

To compensate for the degree of error normally associated with the cycles indicator, the MA channel is used as a filter that determines whether the cycle is likely to turn higher or lower. The channel and the cycle compliment each other.

As an example, Figure 9.15 illustrates how the combination of cycle and MAH (Moving Average of Highs) can work together in spotting market turns. Specifically, this figure shows a number of things: First, it shows an approximate 28-day cycle in stock index figures. In addition, it shows a moving average of the highs of daily prices.

A number of things tend to occur when the approximate 28-day cycle bottoms: First, a low is expected anywhere from 25 to 31 days after the preceding low. Second, as the low point approaches, prices are usually below their MAH plot. Third, the price high for most days, is equal to, slightly higher, but most often lower than that of the MAH. Finally, as the cycle begins to bottom out and turn higher, price tends to penetrate the MAH values, and eventually close above the MAH. The reverse holds true for expected cycle tops using the MAL valves. Figures 9.16, 9.17, and 9.18 illustrate this tendency. Note, that the MAH and MAL values would need to be changed for especially long-term or short-term cycles.

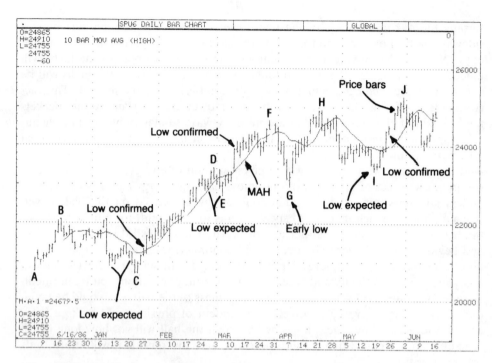

Figure 9.15 Combination of cycle and MAH, showing MAH penetrations confirming cycle lows.

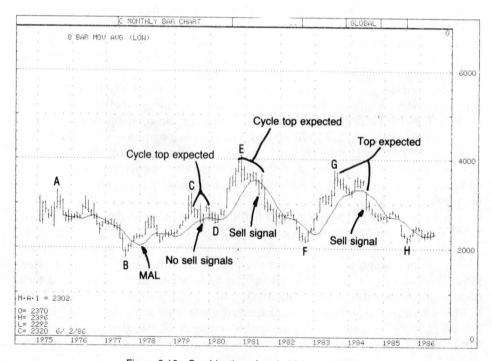

Figure 9.16 Combination of cycle highs and MAL.

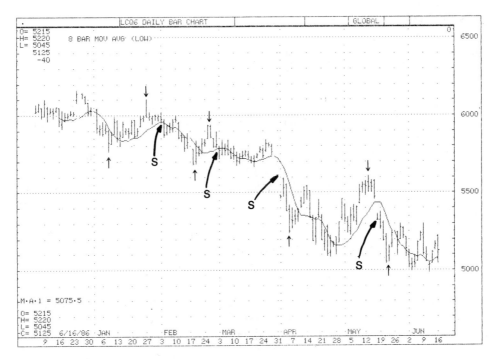

Figure 9.17   Cycle highs and MAL. (S = sell signal.)

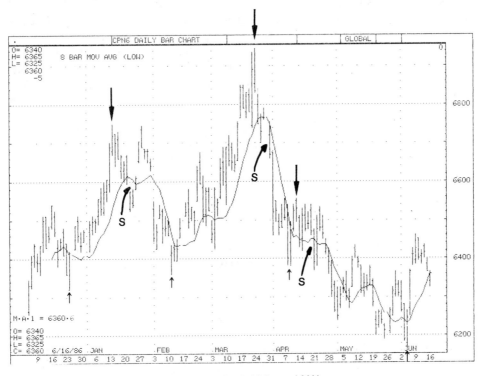

Figure 9.18   Cycle highs and MAL.

USING THE MAH AND MAL

In general, the following conclusions can be reached about the relationship between cycles, the MAH and the MAL.

1. Cycle lows are usually established as prices begin to make consecutive closes above the MAH value. Generally, two or three consecutive closes tend to indicate that a cycle low has been established.
2. During the rising portion of the cycle, price lows tend to remain slightly above, equal to, or slightly below the MAH value.
3. During the rising portion of the cycle, the MAL values tend to serve as major support levels to which prices tend to fall during normal bull market corrections.
4. As price cycles begin to peak, the MAH values slowly but surely become greater than the actual price lows, and the moving average of the lows (MAL) now becomes an important technical indicator in determining when the trend has changed to the downside (i.e., cycle has peaked).

   Now let's examine the MAL in relation to cyclic downtrends. Downtrends normally begin after an upmove and a period of consolidation, or distribution, during the time frame of a cyclic top. The situation described for the start of bullish cycles is now repeated, only in reverse. As prices approach their top, the MAL generally continues to move higher with price lows slightly above or below the MAL, but more often than not above it. During the rising phase of a bull market, the MAL would usually serve as a major area of support into which prices can fall during corrective phases. As the top begins to develop, prices begin to fall below the MAL as well as the MAH, and at some point, prices begin to close consistently below the MAL as well as the MAH. In terms of timing, both the MAL and the MAH can be used to arrive at indications of a change in the cyclic pattern. As the bearish phase of the cycle continues, prices begin to drop well below the MAL, and at some point, price highs for any given day, week, or month approach the MAL on a corrective rally as a level of strong resistance.
   A number of conclusions can be reached regarding the relationship between the MAL and the declining phase of a cycle. They are as follows:

1. As prices begin to peak, lows usually begin to approach or fall below the MAL.
2. In a bullish cycle, the MAH and the MAL serve as areas of support; however, the MAL usually provides major support on corrections during a bullish cycle.
3. As the bear cycle begins to take full force, price highs begin to approach or touch—possibly slightly—exceed the MAL, which now serves as a resistance level during the declining portion of the cycle.

   The MAH is a good indicator to employ when a cyclic low is anticipated. The MAL, on the other hand, is a good indicator to employ when a cyclic top is expected. Figures 9.19, 9.20, 9.21, and 9.22 show a number of different markets and time frames for various cyclic tops, using the MAL and MAH indicators for timing.

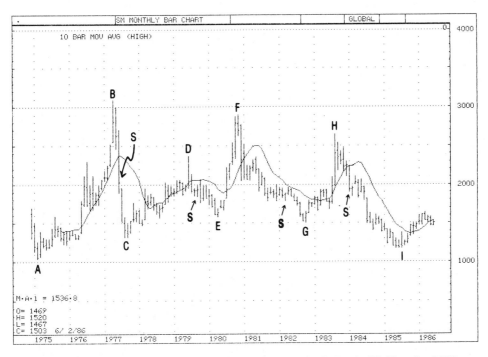

Figure 9.19 Monthly soybean meal cycles and MAH timing of sell signals (S). Note that MAH can be used for selling as can the MAL.

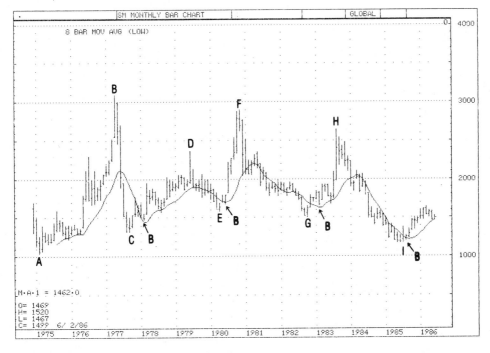

Figure 9.20 Monthly soybean meal cycles and MAL timing of buy signals (B). In this case the MAL is being used to time buy signals at cycle lows, rather than the MAL.

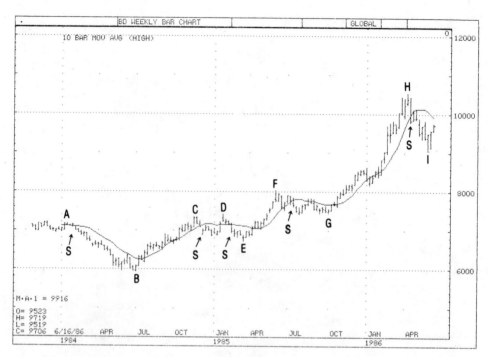

Figure 9.21   Weekly T-bond cycle tops and MAH sell signals (S). (Cycle tops A, C, D, F, H. Cycle bottoms B, E, G, I.)

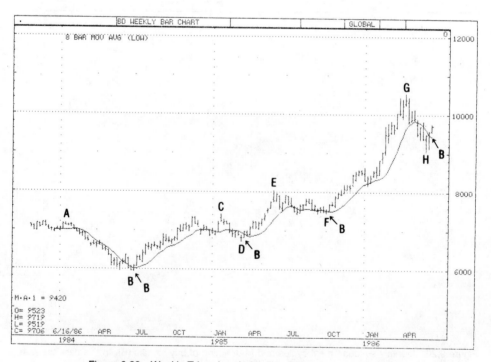

Figure 9.22   Weekly T-bond cycle lows and MAL buy signals (B).

Observe that the moving averages employed for MAH and MAL are slightly different. Whereas the MAH appears to work ideally using a ten-unit moving average of the highs (i.e., hours, months, days, weeks, etc.), the MAL seems to have its greatest efficacy when calculated on the basis of eight units of time. I have determined these ideal lengths empirically, through the course of my studies and trading. An eight-unit MAL is apparently preferable, since a more sensitive indicator of lows is desired in order to trigger more prompt entry on the short side after the start of the cyclic downmove. The reason for this is simply that bear markets tend to fall much more quickly than bull markets tend to rise.

10
Moving Average Oscillators (MAO) and Cycles

Another interesting variation of moving averages is the price oscillator. With so many different possible combinations of length for moving averages, a technique that incorporates several moving averages and their differences can certainly prove confusing to the speculator. There are many possible combinations of moving average oscillators but, essentially they share the same basic features. A moving average oscillator is defined as the difference of two moving averages. Figure 10.1 shows a price chart with a moving average oscillator consisting of the difference in the MA values shown.

The theory behind the implementation of a moving average oscillator is that it combines the best features of two moving averages and allows for a mechnical interpretation of market strength or weakness. The 1980's have witnessed increased use of oscillators by market technicians. For a more thorough study of oscillators, their theory, construction, and use, consult John Murphy's book *Technical Analysis of the Futures Markets.*[1]

More recently, another variation on the theme of oscillators has been popularized by Gerald Appel.[2] The use of the moving average oscillator and the moving average of the oscillator itself (when exponentially smoothed), comprises what Mr. Appel has termed "the MACD (Moving Average Convergence/Divergence)." For purposes of simplicity, the exponential aspect of the MACD will not be discussed.

[1]Murphy, John J. *Technical Analysis of the Futures Market.* New York: Prentice Hall, 1986.
[2]Appel, Gerald. 150 Great Neck Road, Great Neck, NY 11021.

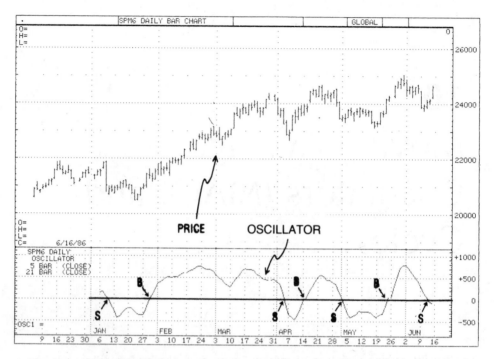

Figure 10.1   Price chart with a moving average oscillator and basic oscillator buy/sell signals.

APPLICATIONS

By employing different values for the component MA's of the oscillator, you can obtain distinctly different results. Figures 10.2, 10.3, and 10.4 show the same market with three different oscillators. Varying degrees of sensitivity to market turns can be achieved by employing oscillators of different lengths. In addition, MACD oscillators, can be manipulated by applying smoothing or exponential techniques. Figures 10.5 through 10.7 show the same market as Figures 10.2 through 10.4, using smoothed and/or exponential oscillators. Use of such variations is a matter of individual preference and experience. No strong conclusion in favor of or opposed to the use of any of the three approaches (simple, smoothed, exponential) if offered herein.

The use of oscillators for timing approximate cycle tops and bottoms can be effective, however, the problem with using of only one oscillator is that it still leaves one without a good trigger mechanism for timing a possible cyclic turn. By using two indicators (namely, the oscillator and the moving average of the oscillator), one can get a very good indication of when the rising object (remember the ball analogy) has lost momentum and is about to turn significantly lower (or higher). The construction of such an oscillator is fairly simple but involves a number of calculations. When exponential averages are used, such an oscillator is termed an *MACD*. Computer technology will, of course, deliver virtually instantaneous results without the laborious process of manual calculation. Even in the case of computing an MACD oscillator, which involves the use of exponential

Figure 10.2   Oscillator with different values of moving average (5/21).

Figure 10.3   Oscillator with different values of moving average (3/11).

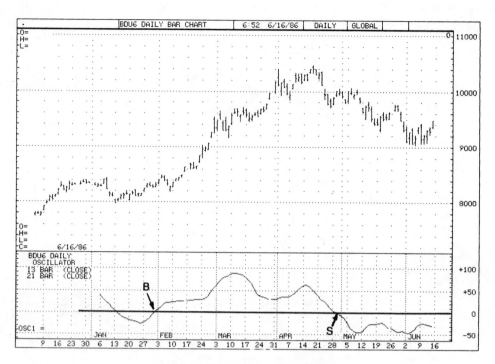

Figure 10.4   Unsmoothed 13/21 oscillator.

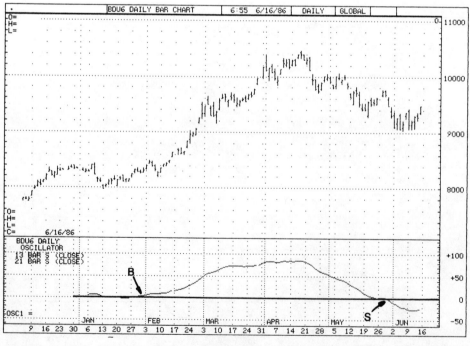

Figure 10.5   "Smoothed" 13/21 oscillator. Note different timing of buy/sell signals than unsmoothed oscillator in Figure 10.4.

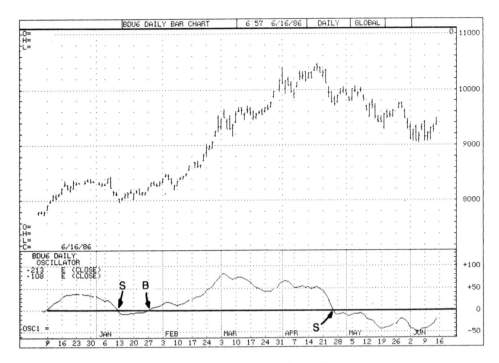

Figure 10.6   Exponential 13/21 oscillator.

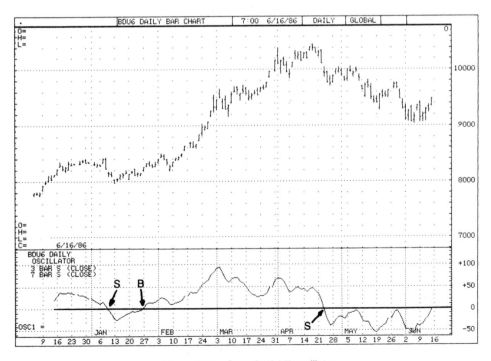

Figure 10.7   Smoothed 3/7 oscillator.

229

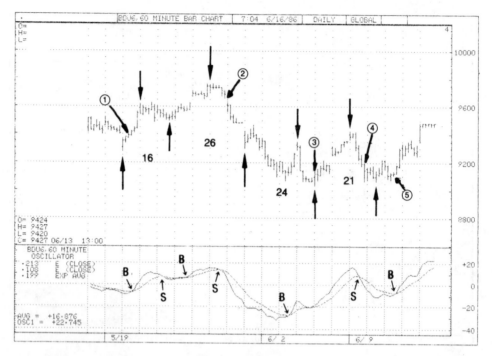

Figure 10.8 Dual oscillator timing signals on intraday data showing oscillator signals in agreement with cycle highs and lows (① through ⑤).

moving averages, computer results can be generated within seconds. Manual computation of exponential moving averages, however, is not a simple matter.

The application of oscillator moving average combinations, or what has been called convergence/divergence, is illustrated in chart form in figures 10.8, 10.9, 10.10, and 10.11 for various time lengths. The rule of application is, of course, very simple: Specifically, buy and sell signals are generated on crossovers of oscillator and moving average or moving average and oscillator. The combination of cycles and convergence/divergence indicator will frequently filter out the false signals generated by the oscillator or cycles alone. Ideally, then, the best application of the oscillator in conjunction with a cycle would be during the cyclic time window, which has been discussed previously in this book. Additional examples of how this combination functions, examine Figures 10.12, 10.13, 10.14, and 10.15, and study my notes, which describe the combined technique just illustrated.

In summary, the rules of application for moving average, convergence/divergence indicators in conjunction with cycles are these:

1. Buy and sell signals of the oscillator/moving average combination are generated on crossovers.
2. The oscillator/moving average combination when incorporated with cycles should ideally be employed during the time window top or bottom for the given cycle.
3. Positions should be entered at the market for a short-term cycle, or at resistance and support levels for intermediate and long-term cycles.

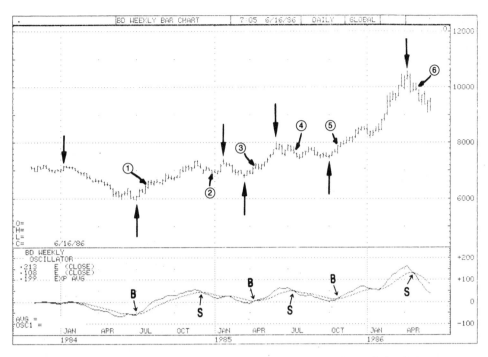

Figure 10.9 Crossover signals, dual oscillator weekly data, and cycle buy/sell signals in agreement with oscillator signals (① through ⑥).

Figure 10.10 Crossover signals, dual oscillator weekly signals, and cycle buy/sell signals in agreement with oscillator signals (① through ⑧).

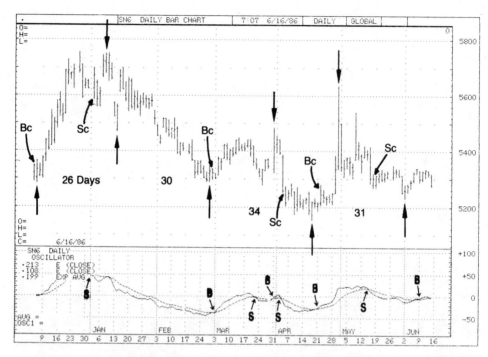

Figure 10.11   Crossover signals on dual oscillator daily signals, and cycle turns. B (Buy) and S (Sell) show buy and sell signals for which cycle and oscillator are in agreement.

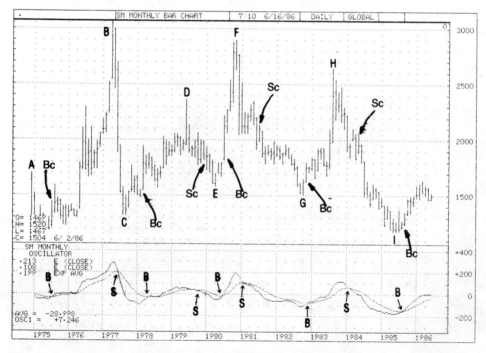

Figure 10.12   Cycles and dual oscillator buy/sell signals. Bc = Buy signals in agreement with cycle. Sc = Sell signals in agreement with cycle.

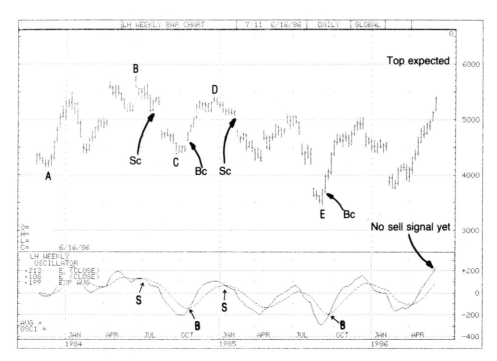

Figure 10.13 Cycles and dual oscillator signals. Bc = Buy signals in agreement with cycle. Sc = Sell signals in agreement with cycle.

Figure 10.14 Crossover signals and daily cycles. Bc = Buy signals in agreement with cycle. Sc = Sell signals in agreement with cycle.

233

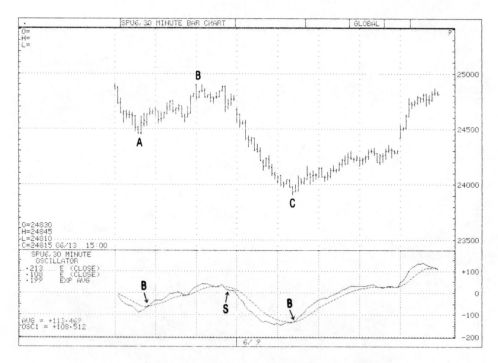

Figure 10.15   Oscillator signals on intraday cycles.

4. The oscillator/moving average combination could be combined with the MAH, MAL, or Channel Indicator discussed in Chapter Nine. As an illustration of this latter technique, examine Figures 10.16 through 10.18, which show the combination of cycle, oscillator/moving average, and channel method. The combination of three indicators does, of course, tend to limit the number of trades, but it also increases the validity of those trades. Finally, my work has shown that the oscillator/moving average combination tends to be very effective in tracking short-term cycles as well as intraday cyclic patterns based on true cycles or time-of-day tendencies.

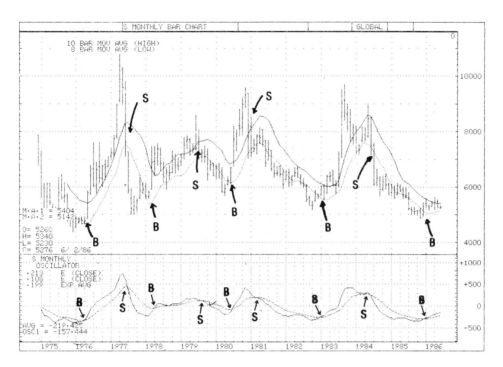

Figure 10.16　Oscillator signals, 10/8 channel and monthly soybean cycles.

Figure 10.17　Weekly copper cycles with oscillator and channel timing signals.

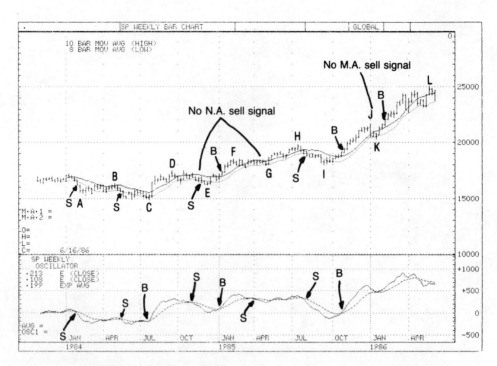

Figure 10.18 Weekly S&P cycles with channel and oscillator timing. Note that by taking only signals on which all three indicators agree, many losing trades are avoided.

11
Cycles, Trendlines, and Timing

In *The Handbook of Commodity Cycles: A Window on Time*,[1] I discussed the use of traditional trendlines as an adjunct to the technique of cyclic timing. My discussion at that time focused on the use of closing price charts (i.e., weekly, daily, monthly, intraday), and penetration of trendlines during cyclic time windows as buy or sell indicators. This technique is certainly as "old as the hills." Its longevity speaks well of its efficacy and simplicity. In spite of today's trend toward greater complexity, the use of trendlines and close only charts (as a combined technique for isolating the start of cyclic up and down moves) continues to have great validity. This chapter is devoted to an update and synopsis of the trendline timing technique with cyclic turns. For individuals who are limited in time and resources, this technique is ideal. Recent advances in computer programming permit trend-line analysis on the computer screen.

REVIEWING THE BASICS

Because markets move in trends, the analysis of trends in terms of support and resistance is a valuable approach. The simplest way of determining support and resistance for any trend is to draw support and resistance lines above down moves and below up moves. This elementary task is known to even the most inexperienced stock and commodity trader. In spite of the seeming ease of application, the trend line technique is a natural "rubber pencil" method. By this I simply mean that most individuals fail to follow specific rules when determining trend lines. They are frequently tempted to use too much "technical license" as to where their trend lines are drawn, and in how they are interpreted. All too often, trend lines are said to be valid after the fact. Technicians are tempted to use 20/20 hindsight in their placement of appropriate support and resistance lines.

---

[1]Bernstein, J. *The Handbook of Commodity Cycles: A Window on Time*. New York: John Wiley, 1982.

Since I have spent many years working with trend lines, I am intimately familiar with their use. Consider my attempt to operationalize this technique as an effort to minimize its misuse or abuse. The result will ultimately be beneficial to all who are interested in technical market analysis and the proper application of cyclic trading techniques.

DEFINITIONS

I define a trend line "a line consisting of a minimum of three points above or below a price plot, provided that these points are: (a) nonconsecutive, and (b) that they occur over a period of 10 units of time (i.e., ten hours, days, weeks, months, years), or more."

A *support trend line* is one that can be drawn below a rising or sideways price trend. Support lines must always be drawn on a sideways or rising slope. *Resistance lines* are drawn on a sideways or declining slope above a falling or sideways price trend. Penetration of a resistance line occurs when price has made at least two consecutive closings above a resistance line. Penetration of support occurs when price has made at least two consecutive closings below a support line.

APPLICATIONS

In a rising cycle, support trendlines are drawn under price trend. In most cases, placing or drawing a support line under a bull market price plot is fairly easy. The application of trend line timing in such a case is rather simple: When a market enters the time frame for a cyclic low, penetration of resistance line (according to the definition provided) is a primary indication that the cycle has probably bottomed. Conversely, in a rising cycle, support will run under the market. Penetration of support, according to the definition, is considered an indication of a probable cyclic top. By definition, the rules of application are quite simple indeed. In practice, however, these definitions are, unfortunately, subject to interpretation. Interpretation enters the situation as a confounding variable since, as in most cases, the human element is the weak link. Strict adherence to the trading rules provided should, ultimately, avoid the detrimental effects of poor discipline.

Before giving any attention to some of the pitfalls of interpretation, I suggest you study the ideal application of these rules. In order to assist you, I have provided eight different figures (i.e., Figures 11.1 through 11.8 illustrating some clear as well as some not-so-clear situations.

LIMITATIONS

One of the problems with trendline analysis has been interpretation. Perhaps the operational definitions provided here will help resolve this problem. The examples chosen for illustration vary from the ultrasimple and obvious to the complicated and more subjective, precisely for this reason. My point is that experience is part of the art of trendline analysis. Even though art may account for only 20 percent of the entire technique, it is, nevertheless, a crucial 20 percent.

Figure 11.1 Support and resistance trendlines.

Figure 11.2 Support and resistance trendlines.

Figure 11.3   Support (S) and resistance (R) trendlines.

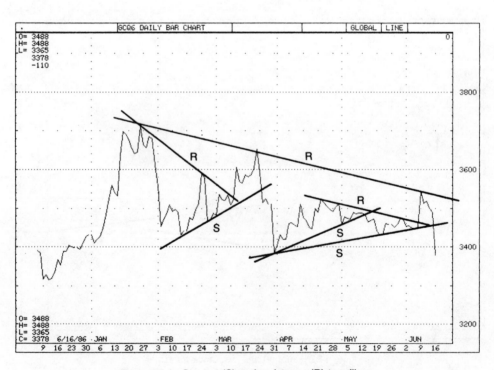

Figure 11.4   Support (S) and resistance (R) trendlines.

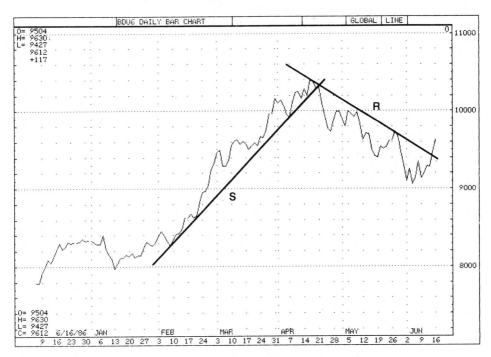

Figure 11.5   Support (S) and resistance (R) trendlines.

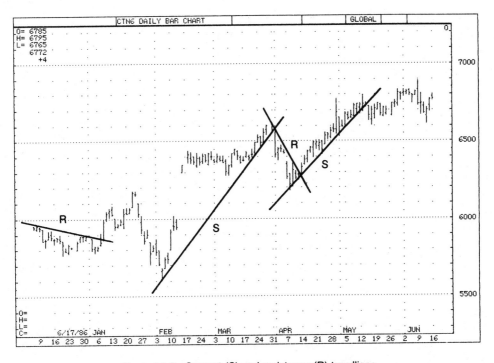

Figure 11.6   Support (S) and resistance (R) trendlines.

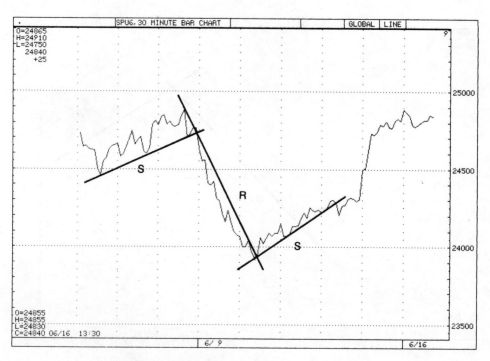

Figure 11.7   Support (S) and resistance (R) trendlines.

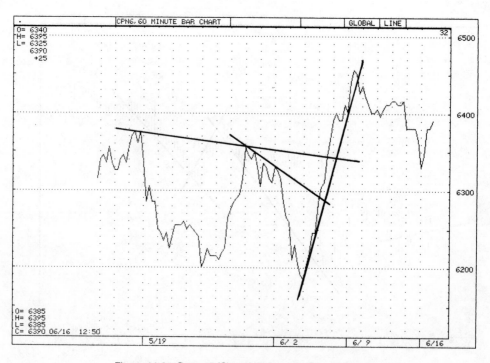

Figure 11.8   Support (S) and resistance (R) trendlines.

To make the procedure more operational and pragmatic, I provide the following procedural listing:

1. Determine the cycle you wish to evaluate.
2. Determine the ideal time window, top and bottom, as discussed previously in this book.
3. To time entry after a cyclic top, draw a support line under the market according to the instructions provided previously. Make certain that: (a) the support line is sloping sideways or up, (b) at least three nonconsecutive points touch the trendline, and (c) the trendline is continuous and interrupted by no more than five nonconsecutive closings slightly below the trendline (see Figures 11.9, 11.10, and 11.11). The term *"slightly"* as used here is not operationally defined; however, the trendline "violations" should be considered part of the line only if they are fairly minor. The extreme intra time unit price highs and the extreme intra unit price lows, however, may penetrate the trendlines by a significant amount. *We are only concerned about the closing penetrations.* (d) The trendline should be drawn connecting as many extreme price lows as possible. (e) You may use either closing charts or (open) high, low, close charts. . . . Either approach is acceptable; however, closing penetrations can more readily be seen on close only charts. Some illustrations of the support and resistance technique using both types of charts are provided in this chapter. Remember that trendline penetrations alone will not signal every cycle turn. Other timing indicators must be used in conjunction with these signals and the cyclic turns. Also remember that closing price charts won't readily

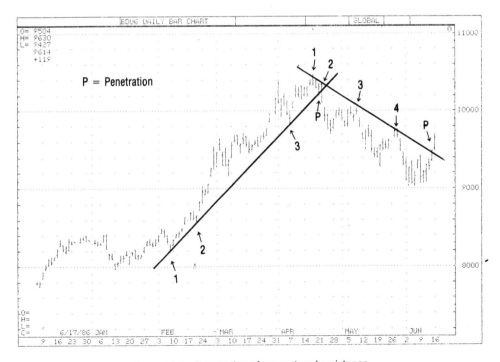

Figure 11.9   Penetration of support and resistance.

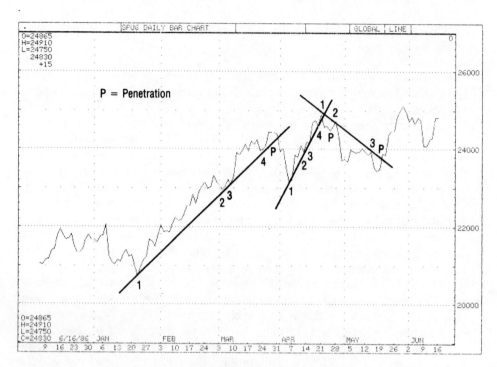

Figure 11.10   Penetration of support and resistance.

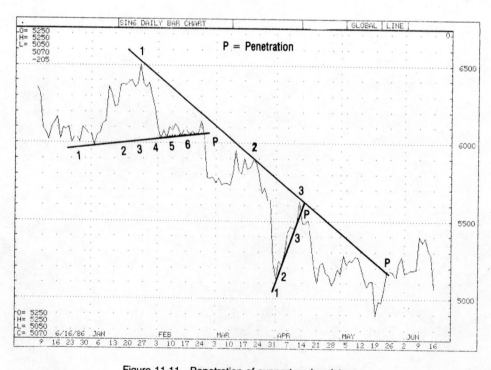

Figure 11.11   Penetration of support and resistance.

show you your stop losses (see #5 and 6 below). (f) Use a reasonably thin line to draw support and resistance. The most operational procedure you can perform here is to use a sharp number 2 pencil as opposed to a thick marking pen line.

4. Once price has made two consecutive closings below support within the time window of a top, a peak is likely to have occurred.
5. If a short sale is initiated, risk is determined to be a new closing high (namely, a close above the highest previous intra time unit high). My illustrations have marked the suggested stop/loss levels.
6. The procedure for buying is essentially the same, only in reverse. The trendline is drawn above the market. Decisions are made within the time window of the low. Risk or stop loss is determined as a close below the previous low that occurred on an intra time unit basis.

Illustrations provided earlier in this chapter serve to provide examples of these rules. Perhaps one of the best ways I can assist you in developing your understanding of this technique is to provide several more visual examples. This has been done in Figures 11.12 through 11.20. Note how the cycle lows and highs are considered as the prerequisite for buy and/or sell signals.

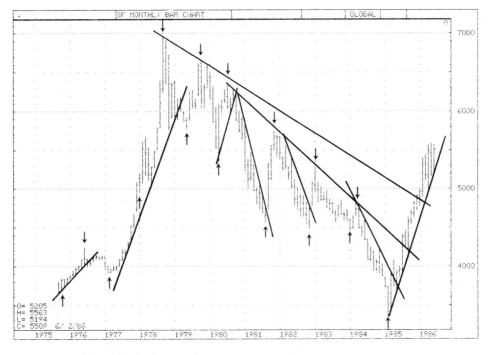

Figure 11.12 Monthly Swiss franc cycle tops and bottoms (arrows) and trendline penetrations. Note that not all tops or bottoms were accompanied by or followed by penetrations.

Figure 11.13 30-minute Swiss franc cycles and trendline penetrations. Note that cycle tops and bottoms (arrows) do not always yield trendline penetrations.

Figure 11.14 Monthly live cattle showing approximate 20-month cycles (arrows) and trendlines. Note that the lack of trendline signals suggests that a weekly chart should be used.

Figure 11.15   Monthly Canadian dollar showing cycles (arrows) and trendlines. Note lack of signals. This suggests that a weekly chart should be used for analyses.

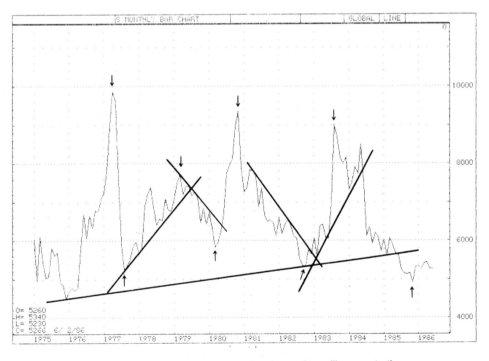

Figure 11.16   Monthly soybean meal cycles and trendline penetrations.

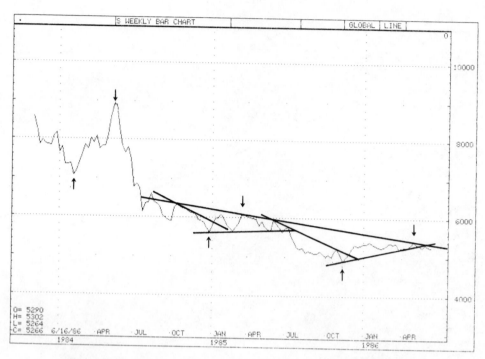

Figure 11.17　Weekly soybean cycles (arrows) and trendline penetrations.

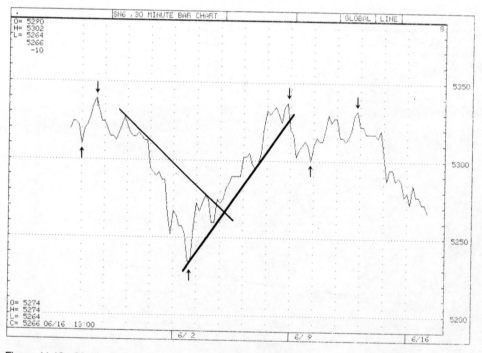

Figure 11.18　30-minute soybeans showing cycles (arrows) and trendline penetrations. Note that only two signals transpired.

Figure 11.19   30-minute crude oil showing cycles (arrows) and trendline penetrations.

Figure 11.20   Monthly corn showing cycles (arrows) and trendline penetrations.

12

Openings and Closings

In the early days of futures trading, opening prices were considered very important. Perhaps for the sake of simplicity, many traders began to ignore opening prices. My work, however, suggests that opening prices, particularly in relation to closing prices on daily charts, can help confirm cyclic turns. Computer research has shown that important high and low prices for any given day are often established at or near the opening of the day's trading.[1] The closing price theoretically represents the balance of buyers and sellers at the end of the day. Therefore, they are important in any analysis of market trends. The comparison between opening and closing prices yields even more meaningful information. Why is this so? To understand the importance of opening versus closing price relationships, we must take a brief excursion into the daily characteristics of bull and bear markets. My closing price pattern studies suggest that closing price and opening price are valuable indicators of market trends and trend changes.

DAILY CHARACTERISTICS OF BULL AND BEAR MARKETS

In a bull market, the trend of prices is, by definition, higher. Naturally, the intensity of one bull market differs from the market of another. Intensity is defined as the upward acceleration of the market as measured by the angle of ascent. If, for example, the base of a bull market or the apex of a bear market was used to measure its angle, it would be found that they approach a 90-degree angle of upward movement or downward movement as their limit. A market cannot exceed 90 degrees as its upward or downward angle. The longer a bull market lasts, the less will be its upward angle, and, conversely, the longer a bear market lasts the less will be its downward angle. Figures 12.1 and 12.2 illustrate a bull and a bear market respectively, showing the angle of each as measured by a standard protractor. Note that we attempt to use the start of a trend as our point of origin for measuring.

Since the price tendency of the daily trend in a bull market is higher, this tendency is often reflected on an intraday basis as well. Short-term speculators

---

[1]Hadaday, Earl. Hadaday Corporation, 61 South Lake Avenue, Suite 309, Pasadena, CA 91101.

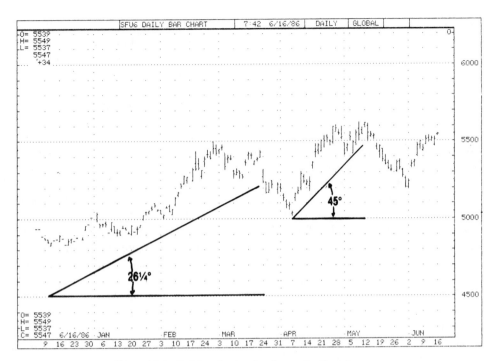

Figure 12.1   Bull trends showing the angle of each wave.

Figure 12.2   Bear trend angle.

and day traders have known about this tendency for many years; hence, the old adage "buy lower openings in bull markets." In a strong bull market, prices often tend to open at or near their low of the day, moving higher during the day, and closing near their high. Conversely, the saying "sell higher openings in the bear markets" characterizes the tendency of bear markets to open near their high of the day and close near their low of the day. Figures 12.3 through 12.6 illustrate the open/close tendencies in a number of bull and bear markets.

As a point of information, one can also observe this tendency on weekly and monthly price data. This phenomenon might be observed more readily by plotting the price difference between opening and closing for bull and bear markets in order to observe how these two values function in various types of markets. Examine Figures 12.7, 12.8, and 12.9. They show the price difference between open and close for different types of markets (i.e., bull and bear) and different time frames. The general trend difference between opening and closing prices is readily apparent and reflects the general trend of the market. Note the persistence of closings higher than openings in the uptrend portions of each chart and vice versa in the downward portion of each chart (Figures 12.3 to 12.6).

At some point, however, the difference between opening and closing price begins to change with the market trend. In other words, when a bullish market changes to bearish, an eventual change in the relationship between the opening and closing price differences would theoretically be expected. Such a change should occur sooner rather than later, and it should reflect a situation in which opening prices slowly begin to increase or become greater than closing prices. As

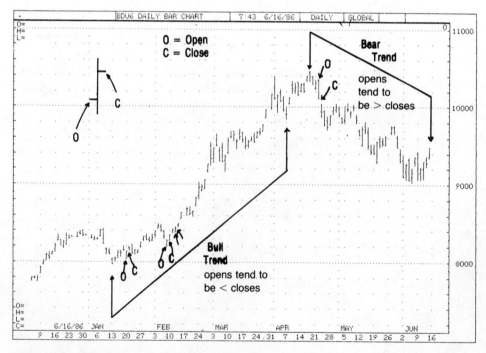

Figure 12.3   Daily open/close tendencies in bull and bear trends. Only several days are singled out as examples. There are, however, many more. Can you find them?

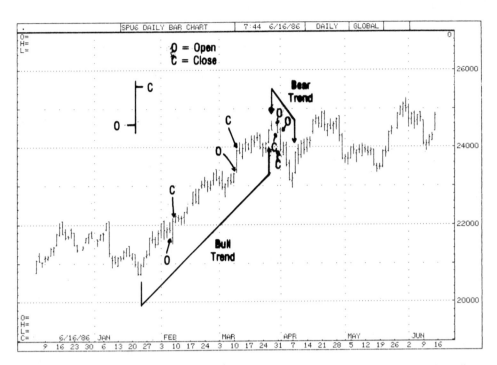

Figure 12.4 Daily open/close tendencies in bull and bear trends. Can you find the rest of the days illustrating this concept?

Figure 12.5 Daily open/close tendencies in bull and bear trends. Can you mark the days accordingly?

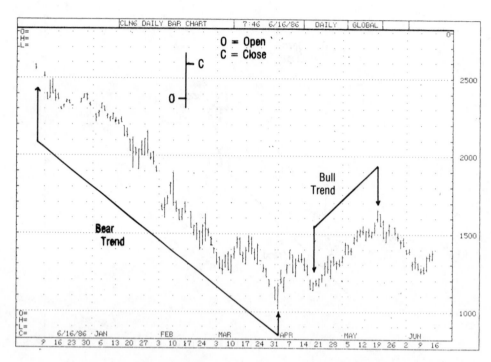

Figure 12.6   Daily open/close tendencies in bull and bear trends. Can you find the days illustrating this concept?

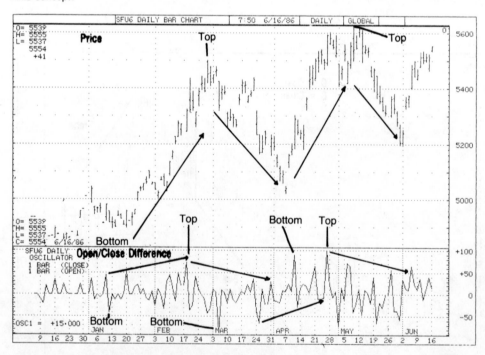

Figure 12.7   Price vs. difference of open and close. Chart shows price trends (arrows) and opening/closing price difference as an oscillator (bottom). Note similarity of trends. Note also tendency of open/close difference line to top and bottom ahead of price!

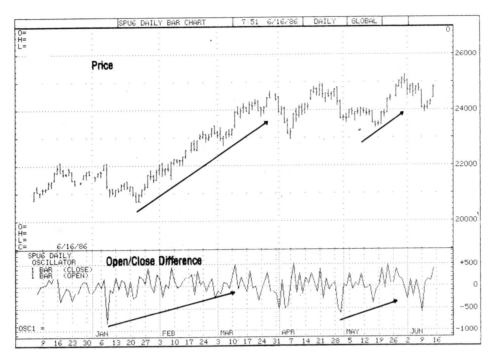

Figure 12.8   Price vs. difference of open and close.

Figure 12.9   Price vs. difference of open and close.

255

the downtrend continues, opening prices should continue to be relatively greater than closing prices on most days. As the trend of the market begins to change back to the up side, closing prices should begin to turn higher relative to opening prices. This is the ideal fashion in which the opening/closing relationship should function.

The open/close difference line (see Figures 12.7 to 12.9) can be smoothed by applying a moving average calculation to opening and closing prices. Empirically, the ideal combination has been determined to be five units of time.[2] Because opening/closing price relationships are so sensitive, a period of five units is ordinarily sufficient to smooth the data while minimizing the number of false turns.

Figures 12.10 through 12.13 show four price charts for which the 5 open/5 close moving averages have been calculated. Observe my notes. Notice that as price begins to turn higher, the moving average of closing prices crosses above the moving average of opening prices. Also observe that as the trend begins to turn lower, the moving average of closing prices falls below the moving average of opening prices. This condition reflects the situation just described. These relationships are consistent through many different time lengths.

Such a combination can of itself prove very helpful with timing. But the potential for false signals is cause for concern. One way to avoid this is to use a cycle as the determining factor for market direction, and 5 open/5 close crossovers for

Figure 12.10   Price vs. 5 open/5 close moving average.

[2]Bruce Babcock of Commodity Traders Consumer Report, 1731 Howe Avenue, Suite 149, Sacramento, CA 95825, deserves full credit for introducing me to this concept.

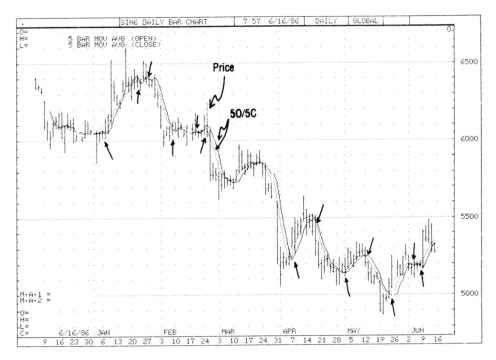

Figure 12.11   Daily price chart with 5 open/5 close moving averages and crossovers (arrows). Note tendency of crossovers to signal start of up and down trends in Figures 12.11 to 12.13.

Figure 12.12   Daily chart showing 5 open/5 close crossovers (arrows).

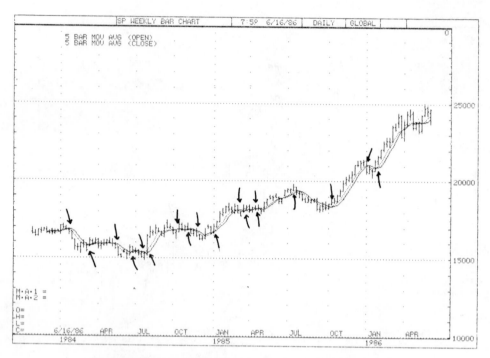

Figure 12.13   Price chart with 5 open/5 close crossovers (arrows).

timing. Assume, for example, that the approximate 30-month cycle in soybean meal prices was expected to bottom. The 5 open/5 close moving average technique could be used as a method for timing the approximate market turn. See Figures 12.14 through 12.16 for illustrations of how this works in practice. Naturally, cycles that have very short time spans such as the approximate 14-day cycle in stock index futures might require the use of a shorter moving average period, perhaps three of the open and three of the close, or less.

In summary, the following rules apply to the use of 5 open/5 close moving average timing methods in conjunction with cycles:

1. A five-unit moving average of open and closing prices for the specified time length is used as the timing indicator.
2. When the closing MA plot is greater than the opening MA plot, the trend has probably turned higher and the cycle has bottomed.
3. When the closing MA plot is less than the opening MA plot, the trend has probably turned lower for the given cycle specified.
4. Use of the 5 open/5 close moving average timing appears to be most effective in conjunction with cycles, during the anticipated time frame of a cycle top or cycle bottom (i.e., time window).
5. If a cycle is due to top or bottom but if no 5 open/5 close signal appears within the time window, no action is taken, and vice versa.

The 5 open/5 close timing method should be carefully studied by all those interested in timing market entry with cycle turns. Very few cyclic trend changes

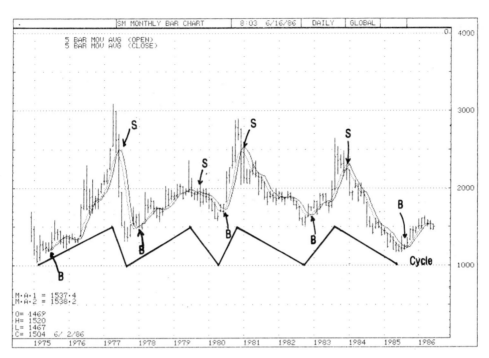

Figure 12.14   Monthly soybean meal cycle and 5 open/5 close timing signals (B = buy   S = sell). Observe the ability of 5 open/5 close to confirm a cycle turn very close to its actual low or high.

Figure 12.15   Cycle lows and highs in daily live cattle futures and 5 open/5 close timing (L = cycle low, H = cycle high, B = buy, S = sell).

259

Figure 12.16   Daily S&P showing cycle lows (L), cycle highs (H), buy signals (B) and sell signals (S) using 5 open/5 close timing signals.

fail to be signalled by a turn in this indicator. When combined with the many other timing tools presented in this book, the resulting arsenal of timing tools will prove highly valuable to cyclic traders. My statistical analyses of 5 open/5 close timing and cyclic turns suggest that well over 80% of cycle turns are confirmed by 5 open/5 close very early in their inception, and without an excessive degree of "false" starts or "whipsaws".

13

Making Cycles Work for You

Most of this book has been dedicated to a discussion of the philosophical and technical aspects of cyclic analysis. In spite of my efforts to quantify and operationalize systems, methods, and procedures involved in the process of cyclic analysis, the use of cycles in futures and/or stock trading remains an art as well as a science. Today, six years after publication of *The Handbook of Commodity Cycles: A Window on Time*[1] considerably more is known about technical and timing indicators that facilitate the overall method. Yet the cyclic method is still somewhat subject to interpretation as are the various cycle theories.

Few professionals in the field can be consulted for verification and/or corroboration. Perhaps in one sense this is good, since it shows that the majority are not looking at cycles. Since the majority is usually wrong, some degree of comfort can be taken in being part of the minority. On the other hand, the relative lack of professional practitioners leaves the cycles trader in a lonely place. Granted, The Foundation for the Study of Cycles is an excellent organization providing quality research . . . but they are not futures traders. Some advisory publications claim to analyze cycles, but there are very few. Yes, some brokers claim to use cycles in their trading and research, but they are often too difficult to talk to without concern about their potential conflict of interest. They are frequently too busy to give nonclients advice, consultation and/or time.

There is no definitive direction in which the cycles trader may foray without the persistent and nagging insecurity that he or she is out there alone. Though an element of excitement accompanies this lonely voyage, it is not the kind of excitement that serious futures traders seek. As traders we want answers and direction.

In addition, the problem also arises of how to obtain, implement, analyze, and execute the kind of information and systematization that is likely to produce profitable results. I certainly don't have all the answers, and many of the answers I do have are still subject to additional verification, validation, and alteration. My work in the field of cycles, which has evolved since 1972, is still regarded as

---

[1]Bernstein, J. *The Handbook of Commodity Cycles: A Window on Time*. New York: John Wiley & Sons, 1982.

relatively minor when compared to the work that still awaits. We have only scratched the surface of cyclic analysis as a trading vehicle. However, I know for a fact that the individual trader and/or investor can put cycles to work in a trading program of either short-term, intermediate-term, or long-term duration. However, as with any venture, there are many potential pitfalls that can lead you astray or confound your approach. This chapter seeks to provide some concrete guidelines and hands-on suggestions designed to keep you on track and mindful of your goals. I suggest that you use this chapter as a roadmap in developing an approach that fits your temperament, time orientation, and trading objectives.

FIRST, DECIDE ON YOUR TIME FRAME

Time frame is, perhaps, the single most important decision the trader must make. Although the desire to trade in all time frames (i.e., short-term, intermediate-term, long-term) is only natural, this is an objective that only very few individuals can achieve consistently. Trading in all three time frames is limited not only by the amount of time available but also by the psychological effect of time-frame interaction. Specifically, traders frequently have difficulty establishing a trade based on one time frame and then establishing an opposite position in another contract month using a different time frame. The tendency will be to confuse time frames, causing use of signals from one time frame in another.

For the novice trader or for the trader who is becoming reacquainted with the marketplace, I suggest finding one time frame that makes you comfortable and staying with it as your major time orientation. Only after you have gained considerable experience with your chosen time frame should you consider adding or switching. Based on my observations, I suggest that the shorter term time frame (three- to five-day positions) is initially best suited to the orientation and ability of most traders. I say this for several reasons: First, when learning or relearning a particular approach, seek an immediate, or as close to immediate, feedback of results as possible. With the shorter term time frame, a trader will get prompt feedback, win, lose, or draw, thereby enhancing the learning experience. Second, the shorter term time frame tends to provide more opportunities. This allows more learning opportunities. Third, commissions, which in the past have been a detriment to active trading, are no longer the major issue (at least as of this writing), and the trader need not be concerned about paying away too much of his or her capital in the form of commission. Finally, as of this writing, there are many high-volume large-move markets (i.e., currencies, Stock Index Futures, and Interest Rate Futures) that are readily tradeable on a three- to five-day basis. (This does not, however, rule out trading other markets.)

Consider all of the above when making your decision about time frame. But whatever you decide, make sure that you *do* decide. While you may wish to study or analyze all three time frames, I urge you to trade in only one of these initially.

THEN DETERMINE YOUR RISK CAPITAL

Note that this topic has been placed ahead of many others because of its importance. Knowing your risk is an important aspect of your trading approach. If you accept the fact that futures trading using any form of analysis is a game of probability, you must also accept the fact that losers clearly outnumber winners. Nothing is definite when it comes to profit. Individuals can lose their entire starting amount very quickly.

In spite of this, one thing is definite: the individual who starts with a larger amount of risk capital is more likely to succeed than is the individual who has little to risk. This is true because, first and foremost, the individual who can risk more is probably a more sophisticated, more knowledgeable, and wealthier individual who has probably been engaged in speculative investments frequently in the past. Second, the individual who can afford to take greater risks will not be as prone to run scared before his or her system indicates that taking a loss is appropriate. Finally, most systems take time to test.

Consequently, I urge you to consider these facts when making your decision about how much risk you are willing to accept. The less you can afford, the less likely are your chances of success, regardless of the trading system you plan to employ. Furthermore, you must have the discipline to stay with your original intentions. If you have decided you can risk $10,000 and you lose it all, don't add more unless you have more risk capital available.

DON'T FORGET TO ORGANIZE YOUR APPROACH

Organization is third on my list of prerequisites. Traders frequently lose money for reasons other than the inherent inaccuracies or randomness of their trading system. Such errors are clearly avoidable through the use of consistent, organized, and disciplined trading rules. Since the odds of profitable trading for many trading systems are between 60 and 75 percent, decreasing these already low odds by committing unnecessary blunders that are not related to the system itself is ludicrous. If you do so, then you are only defeating your own goals. Perhaps the best way to keep the odds in your favor is to eliminate most, if not all, nonsystem errors. This can be accomplished by a logical and, most important of all, an organized approach.

WHY THE TRADING APPROACH IS NOT FIRST ON THE LIST

As is apparent, the trading approach or methodology is not first on my list, because I don't regard it as the single most important aspect of trading. More important are the items previously listed. Cyclic and seasonal analysis are certainly both valid and worthwhile techniques, but they are very broad methods. They need to be narrowed down to make them specific and pragmatic. One can't be in all places at all times, and, unless you make trading your full time occupation, you won't be able to study all of the revelant indicators. For example, you may decide that seasonal analysis and seasonal trends are the most logical in terms of your personal situation. If this is the case, I recommend that you either obtain a copy of *Seasonal Concepts in Futures Trading* (1986),[2] and/or do your own seasonal research, developing a trading plan from it. If short-term cyclic analysis is best

[2]Bernstein, J. *Seasonal Concepts in Futures Trading.* New York: John Wiley & Sons, 1986.

suited for you, then determine precisely how you will implement the short-term techniques, which markets you will trade, and what you hope to achieve. These are all important considerations relating to technique.

Evaluate and work with some of the indicators presented, so you will feel at home with them. Retain the ones that work best for you. Once you have formulated all these concepts, considered all the facts that require deliberation and development, and made the necessary decisions, you're ready to trade.

STAYING ON TRACK

My experience has taught me that one of the most difficult things for a trader to do is to stay on track. This is true not just of the market but also of virtually any of life's disciplines. Temptations, side trips prompted by success and failure, distractions, new ideas, and psychological excuses may alter your program. If you succumb to these, you will not be giving your program a fair opportunity to show what it can or can't do. You won't have an adequate test of your own ability to implement the cycle trading program, and you will never know the truth.

I recommend that you do whatever you need to do to stay on track for any given period of time. This permits your system, method, and trading abilities to be tested fairly and thoroughly. This will eventually become even more difficult, because computer technology and software development will tempt you with promises of better results. You must resist temptation. Give your system a fair test. There will always be faster cars, bigger houses, "better" systems, methods, computers, or those you perceive to be better than what you have. Every time you go for one of these, you're giving in to inconsistency and distraction, unless you have given your system a fair evaluation period.

BE OBSERVANT

Many traders are considerably more perceptive than I am. When they begin to work with cycles, markets, and indicators, they may observe relationships and parameters that I have not found. I hope that this book will stimulate you to do additional research, resulting in the development of new indicators that will serve you better. If you are observant and keep records of your trades, signals, etc., you will learn from these and you will know the many nuances that take years of experience to acquire. Each exposure to the market, each trade, each analytical session, and each of your studies should be a learning experience. They will provide either verification that something works, that something is going on, that something doesn't work, or that nothing is going on. These are vital and significant pieces of information for the futures trader. Observe them and learn!

MONEY MANAGEMENT

The point has repeatedly been made that effective money management is critical to the success of any futures trading program. I needn't go into this issue in great detail again, but will remind you that the way your account is managed may be the determining factor in success or failure. Regardless of whether your trading system is one of the better ones, it will be of secondary importance if it is not instituted within the guidelines of sensible and effective money management. Essentially, there are three specific elements of good money management:

1. Do not overextend your margin. A good rule of thumb is to have no more than 50 percent of available capital committed to the market at any point in time.

2. Don't ride losses. In other words, don't let a small loss turn into a large one. Take those losses when your system says to do so—no sooner, no later.

3. Avoid markets that would require you to take too much risk relevant to your account size.

IN CONCLUSION

Before you begin trading with the cycles approach—or, for that matter, any system or method—be prepared: Know your methods and procedures and study your alternatives and game plan. Develop sufficient confidence to avoid unnecessary errors. It may sound rather strange or paradoxical, but not too many individuals can stick with the guidelines of a totally mechanical system. In the long run, those individuals who can develop and maintain a trading system that is, perhaps, 75 percent automatic will probably fare very well. Note that I do not advise a 100 percent mechanical or automatic approach to cycles. Since cycles and the cyclic approach are not 100 percent reliable, one *must* employ some degree of judgment.

The importance of research cannot be over emphasized. To thoroughly test and evaluate all of the indicators presented in this book would take considerable effort and funds. The complexity of testing all indicators in conjunction with one another at cyclic turns adds yet another dimension of cost and effort. My work, though tested thoroughly for a limited time sample in some cases, and for a more lengthy time sample in other cases, is, by no means complete. In fact, by the time this book is in print the characteristics of many markets may have changed sufficiently to alter the efficacy of certain indicators. This is why I urge you to do your own research; even if it is limited to manual methods as opposed to computerized study.

14

Core Issues in Cyclic Analysis

Due to the changeable nature of markets, I seriously doubt whether a totally mechanical system will ever prove to be a consistent performer over time. Trend-following methods such as moving-average systems have their periods of better and worse performance. Performance is a function of trend. When trends are relatively free of "whipsaw" behavior, systems based on cyclic trend following concepts work best.

My approach to cyclic analysis is not mechanical, nor is it without its subjective aspects. If cycles were presented as anything other than partially objective, the picture would not be portrayed honestly. Ultimately, each individual must think and act at his or her discretion with what is, I hope, a good understanding of the marketplace.

Can the trading process be facilitated by forms of artificial intelligence? This technology is certainly growing in popularity and contains important features of construction that allows users to learn from their experiences. Yet I maintain that the human mind is capable of much deeper understanding if it considers important issues revelant to any given situation. Of course the human mind has its limitations and negative aspects. Somewhere a meaningful and functional balance must be found between the rationality, speed, objectivity of the computer, and the creativity of the human mind. My experience teaches that the single most important aspect of cyclic analysis—or, for that matter, of any trading approach—is an understanding of how the approach functions within the context of the marketplace. This chapter is designed to convey that concept. Therefore, I regard it as the single most important chapter in this book. The concepts and issues presented in this chapter are both theoretical and pragmatic. Yet they are all central to an orientation and proper implementation of cyclic techniques.

THE IMPORTANCE OF UNDERSTANDING PRICE, TIME, AND CYCLE RELATIONSHIPS

Price cycles are relatively independent from reactions to events and factors prompted by human actions. We have certainly seen the distorting effects of war on certain cyclic patterns. Yet various researchers have clearly demonstrated that cyclic tendencies occur in international conflict. To a certain extent, such conflict can be predicted using cycles.[1] Seasonal patterns are only partially determined by humankind, they are a function of various economic forces as well as weather patterns. Cycles, therefore, are naturally imposed time spans that maintain validity through their repetitions. To understand cycles can add immeasurably to the ongoing analysis of supply and demand.

Price cycles are a backdrop against which price relationships are measured by the supply-and-demand equation. Ultimately, price cycles probably have their basis in patterns of human consumption. Such patterns may be prompted or regulated by astronomical or geophysical events such as magnetic fields, polar ice-cap shifts, planetary alignment, sunspots, or all of the above (as well as many other unknown forces). Nevertheless, achieving an effective understanding of virtually any market situation is possible by a concise analysis of price, time, cycles, and the relationship between buyers and sellers. Price and time interact to create opportunity.

THE BASIC UNIT OF ANALYSIS

If you permit cycles to be your basic unit of market analysis, virtually all other decisions will be facilitated. Two significant factors exist in determining when price cycles have reached their top or bottom. First, and of utmost importance, is the "time window", or ideal time frame for a turn. Yet the response of buyers and sellers is equally important, and, this second variable is termed "timing".

Price is a method by which buyers and sellers are attracted to a market. Ultimately, price must go high enough to attract all significant sellers or low enough to draw in all significant buyers. Therefore, the function of price is, as Peter Steidlmayer suggests, "to advertise" for market participants.[2] Two key elements must be learned if you are to acquire a complete understanding of cyclic methods: They are, the *status of the cycle* and *the activity of buyers and sellers* as measured by timing indicators. Cycles can be progressing, topping, or bottoming. Buyers and sellers can either respond or wait. Price, time (i.e., cycles), and market response must always be evaluated when issues of timing are concerned.

WHAT MAKES CYCLES LATE/WHAT MAKES CYCLES EARLY?

The interaction of these three key elements accounts for early cycle tops or bottoms or late cycle tops or bottoms. In a cycle down, an early bottom is indicated by a willingness of buyers to step into a market and/or an absence of sellers prior to the ideal low. A late cycle bottom is probable when buyers are unwilling to

[1]Dewey, E. R. Selected Writings, Foundation for the Study of Cycles: Pittsburgh, 1972.
[2]Steidlmayer, J. Peter and Koy Kevin. *Markets and Market Logic*. Chicago: Porcupine Press, 1986.

act at current prices, or when sellers are still willing to pursue their course of action.

The task of the cyclic analyst is to determine when sellers are in control, when buyers are in control, and, moreover, when the balance is shifting or has indeed shifted. When this balance shifts during the proper time frame of a probable cycle turn, your risk will be at its minimum and your potential reward will be at its maximum. The timing indicators discussed in this book, as well as timing indicators and methods found elsewhere, are designed to detect such balance shifts.

Yet you don't need to be one of those brave souls who seeks to participate only in areas of major turn. Since price cycles tend to progress in a stepwise fashion, sufficient time usually exists to evaluate a change in trend (i.e., buyer/seller balance), and to act consistent with the new cyclic trend, or to take advantage of price reactions within the new trend. In other words, you need not buy at the extreme low or sell at the extreme high in order to be successful.

FUNDAMENTAL CONSIDERATIONS AND CYCLIC ANALYSIS

The technical trader is often said to have little or no use for fundamentals. In fact, many traders claim that fundamentals are too often known after the fact, and that technical considerations tend to forecast fundamental changes in the supply/demand situation of markets. Other technical traders maintain that a knowledge of fundamentals is counterproductive to their goals and objectives, since it frequently prompts them to take actions not consistent with their technical indicators. Yet others claim that only "insiders" are aware of important fundamentals at the right time. I have been guilty at times of underplaying the role of fundamentals as well as the importance of fundamental changes and developments. For the purely technical trader, following a totally mechanical or artificial-intelligence approach to the marketplace, fundamentals may indeed be a minor consideration. However, I have learned that fundamentals are useful to all traders in various ways. Fundamentals are, perhaps, much more useful than many of us would care to admit. What follows is a review of some of the aspects of fundamentals as they relate to cycle trading, and illustrations of a number of situations and applications of fundamentals that could prove profitable for those who incorporate cyclic analysis in their trading approach.

In the traditional sense, fundamentals consist of the basic factors that are purported to play an important role in the supply/demand and price structure of the marketplace. These factors may have either a short-term or long-term effect on prices, or they may play a secondary role. Such things as supply-and-demand statistics, foreign orders, exchange rates, foreign competitive products, and a host of other statistics are often considered part of the fundamental structure of a given market. Some fundamentals are relatively intangible; others appear to have a direct effect upon prices. As a rule, any one or several fundamentals may have a relatively brief impact on price-trend developments. In certain instances, however, some fundamentals, such as an abrupt change in weather patterns or other natural catastrophes can have a severe and lasting impact on prices. Yet, it is not ordinarily possible for fundamental forces to make a major shift without markedly affecting prices. It has been said that well capitalized commercial interests who

have good contact with fundamentals throughout the world take action in anticipation of changes based on these factors, and if their activity is monitored, the
development of the next major move can be determined. Yet, commercial interests are aware that their activities may be closely monitored by many traders, and
hence, can take measures to mask their entry into and exit from the marketplace.
It appears, then, that fundamentals, once known, may not have the impact typically expected.

THE CONTRARY NATURE OF MARKETS

Traders are well aware of the fact that fundamentals are frequently known in
advance by professional traders, and that prices often fail to respond to the current fundamentals. Instead, they tend to show their greatest response when the
fundamentals are about to change in another direction. Fundamentals and market
direction often seem out of phase. For example, consider situations in which fundamental factors are at their most bullish very close to the top of the market, and
most bearish towards the bottom of the market. Those dedicated to the fundamental approach will argue that this is illusory. They will assert that the important
fundamentals are not known, or that traders are not cognizant of their developing
importance. Those who are strictly dedicated to technical analysis will correctly
argue that fundamentals are reflected in prices. Since prices are an effect of fundamentals, one merely need study price trends and relationships to ascertain the
existing and anticipated trend of the marketplace. As in virtually all cases of po-
larized thought, the truth is likely to be found somewhere in the middle. I suspect
that technical considerations and fundamental considerations are both important.
I have found through years of trading and research that both factors at certain
times provide valuable data; that the fundamental trader can take advantage of
the technical situation and vice versa. In other words, both types of information
create opportunities for traders, and these opportunities can facilitate profitable
trading, particularly at major market turning points. The main consideration is
that fundamentals and technicals must always be taken within the context of the
cyclic patterns. Market response to fundamentals and technicals is more important than the timing signals generated by fundamental or technical factors.

EVALUATING RESPONSE

Numerous facts and factors influence the action of buyers and sellers in the marketplace. These events, whether directly related to the individual market and/or
the overall economic picture, shape investor or trader attitudes and expectations.
Traders respond to price opportunities according to their expectations and per-
ceptions. Two individuals examining the same set of statistics can frequently arrive at two totally opposite conclusions due to expectation, anticipation, attitude,
and perception. This is where the marketplace fulfills its function. It provides
buyers and sellers with an avenue of expression called "buying and selling."

Remember, that the quintessential aspect of market information *is buyer and
seller response!* A trader or investor who holds an opinion or who is impacted by a
news item but who does not translate the impact into action is not a significant

force in the marketplace. Three basic conditions of potential market response to fundamental or technical considerations are apparent:

1. *No Response.*
2. *Consistent Response* (i.e., consistent with the news; buying response to bullish news, selling response to bearish news.)
3. *Opposite Response* (i.e., selling on bullish news, buying on bearish news.)

In the marketplace, a frequent—indeed, a generally accepted maxim—is that traders should buy on anticipation and sell on realization. In other words, the epigram "buy the rumor, sell the news" is practiced by many. This is not unreasonable when you remember that the marketplace is an anticipatory game. Traders often buy stocks or futures in anticipation of an uptrend, or sell in an anticipation of a downtrend. Knowledgeable traders take advantage of news-created opportunities to establish their positions on the opposite side. For example, bearish news is frequently used to mask entry into long positions by large commercials and knowledgeable speculators. Conversely, bullish news is used as a vehicle for entering large short positions or for liquidating large long positions with relative ease.

Legendary speculator Jesse Livermore quipped, "It's amazing how much stock there is for sale in a rising market." The crux of my commentary here is that fundamental and technical factors cannot be considered bullish or bearish without reference to their impact on the marketplace. A bear market that is barraged almost daily with negative fundamentals and technical considerations but which fails to move lower in response to these factors, clearly indicates that bearish news is being used by long-term traders and commercial interests to accumulate significant long positions for a probable upmove. Conversely, fundamental and technical developments that should have a bullish impact on prices but consistently fail to do so cannot be considered positive developments. To take a piece of fundamental information out of context is as absurd as making an evaluation of any measurement without reference to anything. It is as absurd as the weather forecaster who jokingly says, "And here are some temperatures from around the country: 63, 72, and a whopping 88 degrees!" This type of information tells you nothing because there is no reference point. If the weather forecaster had noted a whopping 88 degrees in Anchorage, Alaska, for example, the information would have had significance and impact. It would indicate an important development. Yet, if the weather forecaster had reported 88 degrees in Key West, Florida, the news would mean nothing out of the ordinary.

The situation regarding fundamental and technical developments in the marketplace is exactly the same, but, of course, in a different sense. The student of fundamentals must constantly evaluate all fundamentals with respect to market impact. The impact may be immediate or delayed. It may be consistent with past experience or inconsistent with it. *In any event, information, whether fundamental or technical, is important only in relation to its effect on the marketplace.* Did the information result in an upturn, or a downturn? Did the information initially result in a downturn followed by an upturn, or vice versa? Did the information fail to have an impact on the marketplace? How long did the news take to affect the marketplace? These questions must be asked and studied; the answers must also be analyzed.

HOW A CYCLES TRADER CAN USE THIS INFORMATION

Knowing that a market is due to make a major top or bottom—or, for that matter, a minor top or bottom—based upon the cycles, the trader can begin to evaluate the impact of news on the marketplace. For example, assume that you are awaiting a bottom in the nine-year wheat cycle. You know that the bottom is due to occur within a given time frame. You also know that certain characteristic technical conditions will frequently accompany such a bottom. These conditions consist of some of the technical signals illustrated in this book. Of course, many other technical indicators could be evaluated in determining the approximate timing of the nine-year cycle low (or any other cycle low or high). Typically at such a bottom, the fundamental considerations will be bearish: the price of wheat will be low; consumption will be low; crop conditions will be good to excellent; world competition and lower prices in foreign countries will be significantly negative factors; projections of supply/demand statistics will generally be negative; and a succession of reports and/or developments interpreted as primarily bearish will frequently occur. Yet the observant trader or investor will know that at some point the bearish news will cease to have a bearish impact on the marketplace. The astute trader will note that bearish news will increasingly have less and less negative impact on the marketplace and may, in fact, have a slowly but surely developing positive impact on prices.

Important fundamental reports will initially affect daily trading in a negative fashion, only to be followed later in the day by a reversal of the downturn and/or a strongly positive response. The bearish fundamentals will begin to result in sideways to higher prices, while fundamentals continue to barrage the marketplace with purportedly negative news. In such a situation, the cycles trader can have great confidence in his or her work, since the market's response to news clearly demonstrates that the cycle is about to turn higher. Frequently, such responses will develop prior to the occurrence of any timing signals. These developments, although difficult to quantify and often subtle, are of great importance.

On occasion, there will be a clear-cut demonstration of the market's unwillingness to accept the supposedly negative news in a negative fashion. Such situations are easily detected by traders who know what to watch for. Typically there will be an initial negative market response to bearish news, such as a lower daily price opening. The day may, however, end with a higher closing price. The reverse would hold true as a cyle is peaking. When presented with a succession of such responses over an extended period of time during the appropriate cyclic time frame, little doubt exists (or ought to exist) in the mind of the cycles trader that an important turn is developing. What has taken place, is that the market has rejected the news, and with it, lower prices have not been accepted. Consequently, the market has only two choices: namely, to turn sideways, or to go higher. The process of rejecting bearish news with bullish market response is a classic situation in a developing cyclic low.

The opposite will occur as a cycle tops. Markets will be bullish; bullish news will occur almost day after day; traders will be bullish; the public will be bullish; the press will be bullish; and yet, the market will consistently fail to respond higher on bullish news, indicating to knowledgeable traders that something is definitely wrong. Should this develop in the time frame of a cyclic top, the informed trader will have good reason to believe that the top has either developed or is about to occur.

For the reasons just cited, cycles traders should be aware of, and remain in touch with fundamentals. By knowing market response, lack of response, or opposite response to fundamentals, you will have more evidence upon which to evaluate the cyclic patterns. In addition to the information provided by fundamentals in relation to prices and cycles, fundamental developments, reports, etc. can provide you with an opportunity to enter a given market on a trend reaction. To the cycles trader, bearish news in a bullish market constitutes a buying opportunity and vice versa for bullish news in a bear market. News may be your greatest ally. You can take advantage of opportunities created by news to establish positions on reactions within the major trend. Furthermore, the news can be used to liquidate positions within existing trends. For example, assume that you are holding a short position in a bearish cycle that is approaching the projected end of its move. Assume also that a major bit of fundamental news pushes prices sharply lower on a given day. The well rounded cycles trader will use such a market reaction as an opportunity to leave the short side, since the end of the move is likely to be close at hand. The cycles trader, in this way, can take advantage of fundamental developments in the marketplace that create trading opportunities.

As is apparent, the important factors in evaluating fundamentals are different for the cycles trader than they are for the traditional fundamentalist. Yet these same factors should be important to the fundamentalist, since he or she is also concerned with market response to news and fundamentals. To review my suggestions:

1. Fundamentals are important only to the extent that they affect prices in either the expected or the unexpected direction.
2. Fundamentals are important only to the degree that they prompt speculators or investors to act.
3. Persistent market response to fundamentals in the direction opposite of expectations strongly suggests that the market trend is changing. Should this occur during the time frame of an expected cyclic trend, it would be even more significant and would constitute evidence that a trend change either has occurred or is about to occur.
4. Fundamental developments create opportunities for cycles traders to evaluate, enter, and/or exit positions.
5. Cycles traders should study market response to fundamental and technical developments to determine the efficacy of suggestions discussed herein.

A LITTLE MORE ABOUT RISK AND REWARD

To a great extent, the issue of market response is closely related to the risk/reward aspect of futures trading. Aspects of risk/reward have been previously discussed in this book, but a brief commentary at this point is indicated. Traditional understanding measures risk in terms of dollars or prices. A different avenue of assessing risk is recommended for the cycles trader. I suggest that risk be evaluated as a function of market behavior. Since cycles and cyclic analysis are not perfect or mechanical, your understanding of the existant conditions in a given market at any point in time will be different from that at another point in time. In some cases, your understanding will be very clear, and you will feel that the situation is explicit, giving you very little doubt as to expected price trends. Your analysis of the cycles will be complete, and you will have virtually no uncertainty as to what position you should establish or the direction in which prices are likely to move. In such cases, your risk in trading is relatively small compared to the risk you would take in cases where your understanding of the factors and market interrelationships is unclear. Therefore, I suggest that you constantly evaluate risk in terms of knowledge as well as in terms of technical factors in the marketplace. Situations in which your understanding is lowest are those in which your risk is likely to be the highest. Your lack of understanding will leave you in doubt as to where and/or when you should buy or sell, as well as when or where you should leave your position, either with a profit or a loss. Lack of understanding creates greater risk. At times, even a thorough understanding will prove to be incorrect. Yet your understanding will still prove beneficial since it will let you know when you are wrong, and you will leave and/or reverse your position. The lower your understanding, the greater your risk in trading. More specifics regarding risk in Chapter 14.

HOW MUCH TO TRADE/HOW OFTEN TO TRADE

An important issue for all futures traders regardless of the system they are using relates to the size of the positions they will trade (i.e., number of contracts), and the time frames in which they will trade. Clearly, shorter term cycles will yield more trading opportunities; however, these opportunities may be at smaller profits. Longer term cycles will yield fewer opportunities, but, as a rule, the opportunities will be more profitable on a per trade basis. A number of factors should be taken into consideration when making these decisions. They are as follows:

1. *What Type of Trader Are You?*
   If you are a trader who wishes to maintain a more active approach to the markets, then shorter term cycles are clearly preferable to your temperament.
2. *Time Commitment*
   Short-term trading requires more time input and greater attention to the marketplace. Trading longer term cycles may be more suitable for individuals who have other jobs and less time to devote to the marketplace.
3. *Multiple Positions*
   A good strategy to incorporate is the use of multiple positions established on initial entry. This technique is described below.

USING MULTIPLE POSITIONS

A very sensible approach to futures trading using virtually any system is to take on more than one contract on your first market entry. When a cycle low or high has been made and your timing signals confirm entry, instead of establishing one unit of the trade, establish two, or perhaps three or four. Then, if the market moves quickly in your direction and you find an opportunity to take a quick profit, you could sell out one or two of your positions while maintaining the rest for the longer trend. The logic of this approach is very clear: Since other cycles interact with the major cycles at any given point in time, you could take advantage of this opportunity by trading some of your contracts while maintaining others. This approach is not a traditional pyramiding approach but rather a multiple-contract approach designed to take advantage of short-term, intermediate-term, and long-term swings. This approach allows accumulation of positions at various points, starting with the largest position at the lowest price and successively adding fewer contracts as the cycle moves in one's favor. (I do not recommend this approach for most traders until more understanding and considerable experience with cycles has occurred).

SHOULD YOU DO YOUR OWN WORK OR SHOULD YOU USE AN ADVISORY SERVICE?

I'm a strong proponent of doing your own work in the marketplace, even if it means that you must follow fewer markets. Yes, many services could be purchased that would provide you with some of the charts and information needed to evaluate the cyclic patterns. In spite of the time you would save by buying someone else's work, the information you will acquire by doing the work on your own will be much more valuable, since you will learn from it. Until you have learned the proper approach and implementation of the trading plan, I suggest you do your own work. After you have learned it, you will have a basis upon which to evaluate the work of others, thereby making informed decisions regarding the service of your choice.

Another point to consider is that few services today provide cycles research consistent with my approach. In fact, I believe I publish the only such service. As you know, many chart services provide the basic information you need; yet, among the available services that cover cyclic analysis, there are significant points of difference in their analytical approach. This may not be to your greatest advantage. It could prove to be quite confusing. When all is said and done, I believe you will be most pleased and much better off doing your own analysis as well as your own charting.

15

Frequently Asked
Questions

Virtually every day I receive numerous questions from individuals who are familiar with my work. Through the years I have found that many of the same questions are asked, and that people generally have difficulty with the same issues or topics. This chapter presents some of the frequently asked questions along with their answers. I hope that some of your queries will be addressed and resolved. If not, I invite you to write me.

Q. WHAT IS A GOOD CHARTING SERVICE?

A. There are many excellent charting services that the cyclic trader can use. Before choosing, obtain a sample of each service and make sure that the one you ultimately select contains the following features:

1. Large charts (preferable 8 1/2 /x 11 or larger).
2. Easily updated. The charts should be designed to permit easy user updating regularly.
3. Space. Each chart should have considerable space to the right to permit the projection of the next one or two cycles.
4. Your chart service should provide weekly and monthly charts on a regular basis. Preferably, the service should not analyze the markets for you, nor should it make recommendations or otherwise complicate the issue by cluttering your mind with excess information.

Remember also that many computer quote systems will allow you to view daily, weekly, monthly, and intraday charts as well. Some of these computer quote systems also permit the overlay of many of the studies described in this book. In view of the many alternatives, I suggest you take the time to sample. various services, selecting what suits you best.

Q. WHY NOT INCLUDE ALL CALENDAR DAYS WHEN COUNTING CYCLES?

A. As mentioned before, when counting daily cycle lengths I include only those days for which a market is open. However, I don't feel that this approach is the only valid way to count cycles. Whether you use market days or calendar days, I believe that the end result will be essentially similar: an approximate time frame during which prices are likely to change direction. I would suggest, however, that whatever approach you employ, do so consistently. I have seen studies relating market days to calendar days that show some interesting relationships between the two. Regardless of which approach you use, be consistent.

Q. SHOULD MY STOP LOSS ORDERS BE "IN THE MARKET"?

A. Some traders claim that stop losses or other resting orders have a tendency to be "picked off" by the floor. They also feel that this occurs only to their disadvantage. In other words, if they are long a market, with a stop loss below the market, they fear that the market will come down to hit their stop. This is one of the most popular suspicions about resting orders. Consequently, many traders prefer not to enter their orders, but rather to act at a given price or at the market when necessary. I don't see any particular problem with this procedure, yet I don't subscribe entirely to the school of thought that promotes the "stop-picking" argument.

You have three choices regarding the implementation of stop losses and/or buy/sell stops: First, you can enter a stop with your broker. Second, you can have a stop. A third choice, which is usually not given much consideration in most trading systems, is to use no stops during the trading day, but rather to use closing prices or opening prices to generate signals. Such an approach has not been given sufficient consideration, since it fails to conform to many of the principles of sound money management. Given sufficient thought and consideration, this ultimately appears to be the most sensible approach, and could be developed into operational procedures.

If a position in the market is the "right" position, then the use of buy or sell stops consistent with, or as required by the system should not be a cause for concern. While some markets are notorious for "picking off" resting stops, the serious cycles trader should not be overly concerned since the cyclic methods employed should keep him or her on the right track.

In conclusion, the issue of stops, their use, and precise manner of execution is also an individual matter, specifically related to the trader's needs and modus operandi. There may be some validity to the fear that resting orders will be triggered, but this is only true in thinly traded markets and/or for very large positions.

Q. HOW DO NEWS, GOVERNMENT REPORTS, WEATHER, AND "INSIDE" INFORMATION AFFECT THE CYCLES?

A. This is one of the most commonly asked questions, and probably the simplest to answer. My experience with cycles strongly suggests that cycles anticipate most of these events, and that these occurrences rarely develop out of phase with the cycles. Though cycles are not perfect, they do seem to have an uncanny ability to forecast major market events.

News will often provide an entry opportunity within a given cyclic time frame. A bearish report released during a strong cyclic bull market will probably result in a price reaction or decline into a support area, followed by a move to higher price levels. Though I would certainly say that the news should be ignored most of the time, acting contrary to the news is often a very sensible policy, particularly when there are good cyclic reasons for trading from a given market orientation.

Q. WHY AREN'T CYCLES MORE ACCURATE?

A. I suppose that if we were to know all of the different cyclic periods operating in conjunction at any given point in time, we could probably formulate a very accurate synthesis of all the cycles. We could then project tops and bottoms (as well as prices) more accurately. However, since not all of the inputs are known, turns cannot be predicted as accurately as we might like. If cycles were perfect, markets, theories of cycles, and timing indicators would not be needed. Nature, itself, which is probably the root cause of cycles, is not perfect. Cycles themselves are much more accurate than we know. However, our inability to completely understand the machinery of cyclic cause and effect limits our ability to make more accurate determinations of tops and bottoms. The implementation of advanced computer methods and hardware technology will undoubtedly help us find many answers. Greater accuracy will be achieved in the years to come. But for now, we must be satisfied with the limits of our current understanding.

Q. HOW MUCH PROFIT CAN I EXPECT TO MAKE TRADING WITH THE CYCLIC APPROACH?

A. That depends on you. There are so many variables in the study and implementation of cycles, that I would certainly be out of line if I gave you a specific answer. Two traders can use the same basic tools; one can win and the other lose. I have no specific guidelines, nor can I claim that a clear understanding of cyclic trading will make you money. The fact remains that the application of cycles—or, for that matter, any trading system—is an individual matter. You alone will ultimately be the determining factor in your success, magnitude of success; failure, or magnitude of failure.

Q. WHICH MARKETS HAVE THE MOST RELIABLE CYCLES?

A. I have found that some markets behave better than other markets when it comes to cycles. In addition, some markets appear to have more reliable characteristics with regard to timing indicators. In the 1960's and 1970's, shell egg futures had some of the most reliable cycles as well as a highly predictable seasonal price tendency and large price moves. Unfortunately, shell eggs were so volatile the traditional timing indicators did not work as well as they did in other markets.

The reliability of cycles should be evaluated according to several parameters.

They are as follows:

1. Trading volume and open interest. As a rule of thumb, markets with the highest volume and open interest tend to exhibit the best characteristics cyclically, as well as from a timing-indicator standpoint. Therefore, one should avoid exceptionally thin markets, or markets that characteristically have very wide intraday price swings without high volume.
2. Cycle length. Attempt to stay with the more common cycle lengths such as the 14- to 17-day, 28- to 34-day, 9- to 11-month, and 30- to 34-month cycles. These (and several others) are reliable in most markets.
3. Seasonality. As you know, seasonals have shown highly repetitive patterns. The probability is that most markets will continue to behave in a very predictable fashion seasonally. All markets should be evaluated from a seasonal perspective.

Summing up, then: These three criteria are ones that should be considered in determining which markets are "best" to trade from a cyclic perspective. Since the most reliable markets, by name, will vary from year to year, no blanket statement can be made. As an example, however, in 1986 the most markets to trade with cycles are S & P futures, T-Bond futures, copper, silver, gold, live cattle, live hogs, pork bellies, corn, soybeans, wheat, lumber, foreign currencies, sugar, and a few others. Inactive markets such as palladium or orange juice are not ones I favor for cyclic trading. Although their cycles may be reliable, trading volume is too thin. Seasonally, the markets that have exhibited the most reliable tendencies for many years are copper, the meats, lumber, wheat, soybeans, gold, and silver.

As indicated earlier, leadership and specific characteristics favoring certain markets will change over time. The knowledgeable cycles trader will keep an eye on most markets at least on a monthly basis to determine whether conditions are changing and if new opportunities are developing.

Q. IS IT POSSIBLE TO PREDICT PRICES USING CYCLES?

A. As you know, I have already stated in this book that the use of cycles to predict or project prices is not a scientific procedure. Although I illustrated some techniques that might be employed to this end, I generally do not favor the use of cycles for price prediction. This is because cycles are time-based indicators. Price itself is relatively unimportant and can actually be at any level when cycles turn. I suggest that you pay less attention to price and more attention to cycles and timing indicators. Looking merely at price will probably dissuade you from making trades as a function of price level, since the human mind has been conditioned to think in terms of price, price level, historical price level, and value. The concepts of value, relative value, historical highs and lows, and recent price history are certainly valid tools as an adjunct to cyclic trading, however, price alone should not be used for trade selection. Some trading systems and methods employ price derivations extensively in their analyses. They certainly have merit in the proper context. However, as part of my cyclic approach, they play only a secondary role in terms of timing.

Q. WHAT IS THE BEST WAY TO GET STARTED TRADING WITH CYCLES?

A. My response is both simple, and complicated at the same time. The answer is "get started." There is no better teacher than hands-on experience. Therefore, I recommend only a minimal period of paper trading prior to hands-on or real-time experience in the markets. An understanding of the basics of futures trading is certainly an absolute prerequisite. I strongly recommend that you have a thorough understanding of the principles, philosophy, and indicators discussed in this book and/or *The Handbook of Commodity Cycles; A Window on Time*.[1] These are the prerequisites. Once you have mastered these, once you know your direction, the best way to get started is simply *to begin*. Take the plunge, make some trades, keep your positions small, your risk relatively low, and your objectives reasonable. Experience is the best teacher.

Q. CAN YOU REFER ME TO A GOOD BROKER?

A. It has been my experience that what constitutes a good broker to one trader is not necessarily a good broker to another. It all depends on what you are looking for in a broker. Personally, I prefer minimal broker input and maximum broker service. Therefore, I have no need for brokerage house research, reports, recommendations, etc. Why pay for it? I find that all too often traders can be swayed from their own valid opinions by input from brokers and other sources. If you cannot filter the input of brokers, knowing what to accept and what to reject, then I suggest you secure the services of a discount brokerage firm, one that provides prompt and efficient order execution, reasonably low commissions, and courteous service. I have my personal preferences about brokers, but the decision must ultimately be yours, so do your homework and find the firm or firms that you can work with best. Remember that price alone must not be the final factor on which your decision is made.

[1]Bernstein J. *The Handbook of Commodity Cycles: A Window on Time,* New York: John Wiley and Sons, 1982.

16

Computer Technology and
Its Role in Cyclic Analysis
and Trading

The early 1980's witnessed almost exponential growth in the field of computer technology. What was once the size of several large refrigerators now fits into a small typewriter-size container. The information that was once stored on large disks can now be stored on small diskettes. While technology has moved up, price has moved down. And more changes are in the offing! By the time you have read this chapter, further progress will have been made, all designed to bring computer technology into the hands of more people. Having such powerful technology at one's disposal for a reasonable price has been a great boon to technical traders and investors. The chart studies and analyses that once took many tedious hours to complete can now be performed by computers in a matter of minutes or seconds, and with greater accuracy.

Every day, there is new software to further decrease our work load. This also permits highly complex mathematical manipulation of raw data previously either impossible or too costly to perform. In addition to the hardware and software revolution, the availability of futures data for traders has also improved dramatically. Obtaining many years of historical data at a reasonable price is also possible. Furthermore, tick by tick data. can be obtained for the purpose of studying intraday and short-term patterns. No tool lends itself more readily to use by cyclic analysts and technical traders than does the computer. I would, therefore, recommend that all serious futures traders, whether short term, long term, or even intermediate term, consider the acquisition of a computer system and access to either on-line or stored historical data. I could, at this point, enter into a discussion on which computer systems are best suited for futures studies, however, I can assure you that by the time this information reaches you it would be obsolete. In fact, it will probably be obsolete by the time I finish writing it. Excellent product reviews are available in the literature. They cover hardware and software for futures traders and investors. I will, however, provide you with some general guide-lines for evaluating any computer system, present or future.

PREPACKAGED OR ORIGINAL?

For those who are not familiar with computer technology and terminology, I will attempt to keep this discussion as simple as possible. Any of the items I discuss can certainly be explained to you more fully by your local computer salesperson or by a friend who is familiar with the field. In selecting a computer system that will help analyze futures prices, one could go in either of two directions. The first is to purchase a prepackaged system, one that is specifically designed for the analysis of futures price data. This approach has its pros and cons. One advantage is that everything you need to do has already been done for you. Specifically, the pre-packaged systems will already have self-contained data-analysis software to provide you with the studies you may wish to perform. They may also be set up as quotations systems that will provide prices you will need for ongoing market anal-yses. Furthermore, many of the systems have graphics to display charts on a screen or transfer them to paper (hard copy) by a printer or plotter. Therefore, such systems seem to be ideally suited for the futures trader. They can provide you with the information you think you need. In another sense, however, they may limit what you can do because they do not allow you to move beyond the limits of what is provided in the software package. In the future, advanced com-puter systems will permit the user to identify specific variables and systems that he or she will want to test in conjunction with the data. This type of system will certainly be ideal. It will provide the futures trader and the investor with the flexibility required for effective research and development.

One of the drawbacks of buying a prepackaged system is that many other indi-viduals who have acquired the same system will be analyzing the data in virtually the same way as you will. Hence, they may act on many of the same signals and indicators. This could prove to be detrimental to your performance, since the market may be affected by many traders entering and exiting markets at the same time. Though most prepackaged systems have features you will need, they may not provide you with some features you will want to have in order to do original research on futures prices and cycles.

Another type of prepackaged computer system that lends itself readily to com-modity analysis is one that works upon the user's-group principle. The user buys a computer system that is compatible with the particular data and services offered by a given organization. The individual then subscribes to the service, paying a monthly fee (or membership fee). The user's group frequently has many different technical approaches and trading programs. A large number of these approaches deal with the statistical analyses relating to cyclic studies. Frequent access to these programs is available at a standard charge. The user can realize substantial sav-ings by subscribing to one of these services.

Assuming that you have your own prepackaged system or one served by a user's group, you have no need to read any further, since most of the decisions have already been made for you. However, some individuals want to strike out on their own, searching for original techniques, employing their own programs, and doing their own research. I encourage this type of approach, since it often produces unique results. Those individuals who wish to embark upon this course should note the general guidelines given below and on page 283 regarding the purchase of computer systems. I realize that within several years, if not sooner, some of my observations will be outdated. I suspect, however, that most of the points I am now raising are of a sufficiently general nature that they will not be outdated too quickly.

MEMORY

In the old days of computer technology, memory was an important feature and a significant consideration. In fact, most research in the early days of computer technology was centered on the development of systems that provided more memory. The 1980's have, however, seen the development of advanced technology that makes available extremely large amounts of memory at exceptionally low prices. In the old days, the availability of 32 kilobytes of memory was standard, with 256 kilobytes considered large. Today, one megabyte of memory is not uncommon. In most analytical work, memory larger than 1 megabyte would really not be necessary. I'm certain, however, that before too many years pass, 5 to 10 megabytes of memory will be standard. The availability of more memory is certainly desirable, since it lets the user employ more complex programming, which allows faster information processing and less user interaction. Complex mathematical procedures that require great amounts of memory and intermediate storage in memory can now be achieved with more efficiency and greater speed. However, overkill is certainly not necessary, and every dollar spent does not necessarily produce another dollar in terms of results. Therefore, I advise not to go overboard with too much memory, but rather to purchase a system with expandable memory capability, which will be able to handle efficiently and with reasonable speed the work you need to accomplish. Spend more money on good graphics, fast printing, and large storage.

STORAGE

One of the weakest links in a computer system is storage capability—the amount of information that can be stored in the computer without being placed in active memory. The storage capability of the computer is, in many ways, like a telephone book that the computer will access when it needs certain programs or data. The more storage you have at your disposal, the more data you can keep in the machine at any time without having to change disks too frequently. As time passes, the amount of data available for analysis will increase, making the need for high-capacity storage more important. One of your key considerations in purchasing a computer system should be the amount of storage the system has or the amount of storage that can be added. Based on current data availability, I believe that 20 megabytes of storage is reasonable, and certainly 10 megabytes is acceptable. Storage is just as important as if not more important than memory size.

GRAPHICS

Another feature to consider when buying a computer system is its ability to display high-resolution graphics. You will want to see, in chart form on your screen, the results of the particular system or cyclic method you are testing. By putting the data in chart form on the screen, you will not need to waste time and expense plotting or printing the data to hard copy (i.e., paper). Therefore, buy a machine that has the ability to give you high-resolution graphics. (Contemporary trends are toward color-graphics monitors. Although certainly an interesting feature, color graphics are not a necessity.)

PRINTER

An equally important consideration is the printer, since it can be the weakest or slowest link in the chain. A printer that is slow can often hamper your entire operation while the computer is waiting for the printer to finish its work. A fast printer is, therefore, desirable. Alternatively a printer buffer or spooler can be helpful.

SERVICE

I need not say much about service. You know that it's important to get your computer repaired promptly when it malfunctions. Most service problems should be resolved within 24 hours. Active futures traders with considerable funds in the market should consider a standby system as a backup for those rare times when their hardware fails. Remember also that off-brand hardware may not be as readily serviced as are the major brands. This is an important consideration to those who need service promptly. Down time costs money and could result in losses and/or smaller profits if the delay is too lengthy.

SOFTWARE

The availability of software compatible with your system and methods of analysis is a key issue to consider in purchasing a computer system. Though you may want to develop your own software, data suppliers are generally keyed into data transmission in the formats for more popular hardware systems. Though fewer and fewer choices are available as the hardware giants win out over the competitors, many hardware clone systems sell at lower prices than the popular brands. They will run the major software just as well as the well-known brands, so shop around and save money.

17
Where You Fit In

A serious shortcoming of most futures market texts is that they fail to provide the reader with a set of guidelines to help determine his or her ability to employ the given techniques. This is unfortunate, since most systems and methods are ultimately used (and abused) by people. We must, then, consider carefully by juxtaposition, our assets, liabilities, abilities, and/or capabilities, with regard to any system or technique.

As you can well appreciate, the subject of cyclic analysis is malfaceted. With so many different cycles, seasonals, patterns, and methods, determining where you fit into the cyclic picture is a difficult task. There are many choices available to you as a trader or investor. You can elect to trade for the short term or for the long term; you can choose to be a day trader, or you can choose to be an investor. Each of these choices requires to further decisions. If, for example, you decide to be an investor, you will want to use techniques, methods, and systems consistent with your selection. If, however, you decide that you are best at day trading or short-term trading, you will want to examine data, charts, patterns, methods, and techniques consistent with this strategy. Your work will need to be more focused, and you will need to make a more thorough commitment to money management and sound trading principles than you would need had you selected long-term trading. You may decide that you want to use cycles for the purpose of hedging crops or livestock. If this is the case, you will need to study the types of cycles and data that will allow you to make the specialized decisions required of you as a producer or end user. In addition, the psychologies of short-term versus long-term trading are distinctly different and must be internalized.

The purpose of this chapter is to help you determine where you belong in the vast world of cyclic trading. Since the cyclic approach is comprised of various different aspects, a brief assessment of your goals, objectives, abilities, techniques, and motivation will determine more precisely your best fit. Once you have found your niche, you can trade with confidence and direction. Here are some things to consider in making your decision—I recommend that you study each of the following points carefully, being as honest with yourself as possible. The decision you make will ultimately have its greatest effect on you, so complete honesty is truly the best policy.

FINANCIAL ABILITY

Perhaps the single most important factor in determining the type of cyclic trading that best suits you is your financial ability. Since market conditions change from month to month and year to year, it is difficult to state with finality the amount of capital required for a particular orientation to the market. Generally, however, some comparisons are reasonable considerations when making such a decision. For example, the individual who is willing to trade higher risk positions for shorter term moves would need to be more highly capitalized than the individual who tends to trade for longer term moves with reasonably low risk. On the other hand, some individuals who wish to trade for major long-term moves may want to take larger risk using wider stops. In such instances, more capital would be required than in the case of individuals wishing to trade for shorter term moves with very small stops. I recommend the following broad pragmatic considerations:

A. Short-Term Trading for Limited Risk or With Small Stop Losses

A relatively small amount of capital would be required to trade cycles, according to this approach. Remember, however, that such techniques can often result in a fairly long string of losses, quickly depleting one's capital. Although it might seem that less risk is taken using such an approach, in the long run, more capital may actually be lost since the total number of losses may be large. The smaller your starting capital, the more stringent you'll need to be in your money-management program. Consider, too, that the individual who cannot take a small loss when it should be taken may actually be taking a much larger loss than he or she should. You can see that what may seem to involve less risk may actually involve more risk and more losses. Therefore, before you decide that you will become a short-term trader using short-term cycles and short-term techniques, make certain you have a very firm approach to money management. You must not let your losses run larger than they should. The most certain way to deplete a small amount of starting capital is to allow your losses to run away from you.

B. Intermediate-Term Cycles With "Reasonable" Stops

Another approach to cycles trading is based on the use of intermediate-term cycles, such as those discussed in this book and in *The Handbook of Commodity Cycles: A Window on Time*.[1] Intermediate-term cycles are defined as cycles running from 8 months to 14 months or approximately 40 weeks to 64 weeks. Such trading should require an approximately 3- to 7-percent stop loss or risk from the entry point. Therefore, a purchase of gold futures in the $400/oz. area using a 3-percent stop would entail approximately twelve dollars per ounce of risk, or $1,200 of risk based on current contract specifications. The same amount of risk with gold at $800/oz. would require $2,400 risk, since the price is higher. Conversely, at $200/oz., only $600 risk would be taken. Some individuals may feel that a 7-percent risk is too large. They may scale back to 3 percent. However,

[1]Bernstein, J. *The Handbook of Commodity Cycles: A Window on Time* New York: John Wiley & Sons, 1982.

they may not be giving themselves sufficient leeway in the event that their cyclic timing is not exact. As you know, cyclic timing can never be as exact as we would wish. Therefore, wider stops are preferable. Assuming that you will commit 5-percent risk on any one position you can readily see that a fairly large account size would be necessary. Based on conditions in 1986, an account of $30,000 to $50,000 would be sufficiently large to trade a reasonable portfolio of futures contracts, committing one contract per market. My concern is not that sufficient capital will be available to meet the requirements, but that sufficient capital is present to permit several successive losses while still keeping the account size large enough to maintain positions. Based on my experience, the intermediate-term time frame is adequate for most traders, however, it requires a great deal of patience and discipline, two qualities just as important as finances.

C. *The Long-Term Approach*

If you have discipline of steel and the patience of a saint, the long-term approach is probably the single best application of cycles. Unfortunately, those who can employ this approach with discipline and organization are rare individuals indeed. I can honestly say that in my many years of trading I have not met more than a handful of individuals who can achieve success in trading for the long term. There are many reasons for this inability; however, they are not the subject matter of this book. They have been covered quite adequately in my previous books, *The Investor's Quotient*[2] and *Beyond the Investor's Quotient.*[3]

The long-term trader, of course, seeks to capture major moves, and in so doing is willing to risk taking larger losses in order to make larger profits. A risk of 10 percent in gold, for example, may eventually yield a 200-percent profit. The difficulty in implementing such an approach is not that one is unwilling to take the necessary risk; it is the inability of most individuals to be patient while awaiting the opportunity to enter or exit at the optimum time. In this respect, no matter what your trading system may be, it will prove totally useless unless you can administer it in a proper and functional way. Long-term trading with cycles is a most rewarding undertaking, but it requires large stops, considerable patience, and complete discipline.

COMMITMENT

The availability of sufficient capital for trading is merely one aspect of the success equation. Another significant variable involves the willingness and ability to remain dedicated to a trading system. I mentioned previously that I have met only a few individuals in my many years of trading who were capable of maintaining a consistent, patient, and disciplined approach to cycles trading. Discipline and commitment are the core elements of success for any trading method. How often have you been in the situation of knowing that the technique you used was valid, yet you failed to correctly administer the rules? You abandon your system, know-

[2]Bernstein, J. *The Investor's Quotient.* New York: John Wiley & Sons, 1980.
[3]Bernstein, J. *Beyond the Investor's Quotient.* New York: John Wiley & Sons, 1986.

ing in your heart that if you had been persistent and disciplined, the technique would have been profitable. It does not take much experience to conclude that commitment and discipline form the cornerstone of success in the marketplace. Whether one is using long-term or short-term cycles is really of no consequence. Many mistakes can be made, and many potential profits can be thrown away, regardless of whether long-term, short-term, or intermediate-term trading is your fare. Therefore, the vital question is "Can you make the commitment to trade?" Are you ready, willing, and able to implement a specific method or trading approach with discipline, consistency, and commitment? If you are not, then I strongly suggest you avoid cyclic trading, or, for that matter, all trading systems, since they will probably not work for you regardless, of the principles on which they are based.

For the short-term trader who is interested in making a commitment and in keeping it, I contend that a cyclic approach is certainly a good idea. Short-term cycles provide sufficient repetition and signals to give the trader a very good opportunity to test his or her ability to interpret signals and to maintain self-discipline. The long-term trader will also require discipline and commitment, since his or her trading system will require thorough and consistent application of principles and techniques. Trading signals must be acted on and not second-guessed. Objectives must be followed clearly and specifically without frequent deviation.

Long-term cycles, as you know, may take many months to develop, and the urge to buy or sell too early will always prey on the mind of the trader. During this period, the undisciplined trader may give in to these feelings, clearly violating the basic principles of the system. The short-term trader who is guilty of such weakness will certainly realize his or her shortcomings much more quickly than will the long-term trader. This is why I advise every individual to spend some time and money educating himself or herself in short-term trading. The learning process of acquiring discipline will be quickened, and experiences may be more promptly engrained in the trader's mind. To make a mistake several times a week as opposed to several times a year (i.e., the short-term versus the long-term investor) certainly results in faster learning of important skills.

Therefore, in order to determine if you can make the commitment to trade using cyclic methods, I suggest you do some soul-searching as well as hands-on practice. In other words, make certain that you have the discipline and commitment to trade. Furthermore, make a commitment to either short-term or long-term trading. I can't overstate the fact that without discipline and commitment, no trading system will be effective either in the short run or the long run.

AVAILABLE TIME

Another important variable in determining where you fit in is your time availability. This is important, because in making a commitment to a type of trading that requires intensive time and study when, in fact, you cannot make this commitment is a losing proposition from the start. Therefore, determine specifically the amount of time you can invest before you make any commitments whatsoever to the market. The individual who wishes to trade for the very short term (i.e., scalping or day trading) should not even consider this form of trading unless he or she is willing to make this a full-time occupation. Naturally, the time commitment required of a short-term trader is much greater than the time commitment required of a long-term trader.

In the futures market, keeping up-to-date on your technical studies is critically important. Consequently, if you do not have the ability or intention of staying with a short-term trading approach by doing your work, then don't make the commitment, because you are sure to fail. Even a long-term approach is doomed to failure if you cannot invest the time, regularly and without exception, to keep your analyses current.

Although other small areas of importance may be present determining where you fit into the overall picture of cycles, I believe that I have covered the most significant ones. If you can't evaluate yourself based on the areas just discussed, and if you can't provide meaningful, realistic answers, you may wish to take some time to think about the different areas I have mentioned. You may find that other significant considerations are unique to your life-style and life situation. Perhaps, for example, your health may be such that the intense pressure of short-term trading is not advisable. Other considerations may be professional commitments, family commitments, and/or educational commitments. Each of these has a direct bearing on your individual situation. Therefore, I urge you to take them all into consideration when making your final decision. Important decisions such as these are necessary before you can begin trading with cycles.

Afterword

The book you have just read has taken more than two years to complete. The considerable time and effort expended reflect the actual research process as well as ongoing manuscript revisions. During the last several years, my understanding of and insights into futures trading via cyclic analysis have prompted changes in approach, organization, and philosophical orientation. While these changes may not appear either obvious or substantive to some readers, they were, nevertheless, especially important to me. Some of these changes are reflected in the final product.

As hard as I have tried to produce a complete work on a complex and poorly understood subject, it is a sad-but-true fact that by the time this book appears in print, it will, to a certain extent, be out of date. This is good and bad at the same time. It is good since it suggests that research in cyclic analysis continues at a rapid and growing pace. It is bad in the sense that it may outdate some of the concepts and indicators I have illustrated herein. Yet, this is the price of progress. Technological and scientific research are so rapid today that a work is often out of date before it leaves the author's desk. But to bemoan this fact or to permit it to limit our further studies and investigations would merely be an excuse for complacency. Instead of focusing on our time lag, let's concentrate instead on our progress.

The changes and the improvements in this work compared to *The Handbook of Commodity Cycles: A Window on Time*[1] represent a quantum jump toward more precise cyclic timing. I find that now, more than ever before, cycles are proving not only more reliable but also more easily discerned and more readily implemented. Markets that have, in the past, failed to show any obvious repetitive tendencies have been found to contain some truly significant and especially reliable cyclic phenomena. These patterns have both impressed and encouraged me.

With the new understandings presented in this book, with the increased reliability of cyclic patterns, with the additional timing methodologies discovered via the assistance of computer technology, and with what appears to be a growing acceptance of repetitive price patterns, I know that this book will serve you better than have any of my previous writings. But do not allow this book to be an ending point. Rather, allow it to be your beginning point. Let this exposition of cyclic methods be your stimulus to more concise research and greater profits. Certainly, if I can be of assistance in clarifying concepts, ideas or methods presented here, do not hesitate to contact me. In the interim, I wish all of my readers the very best of success and the very best of good fortune in researching and finding improved methods of cyclic analysis and timing.

Winnetka, Illinois   JACOB BERNSTEIN
January 1988

[1]Bernstein, J. *The Handbook of Commodity Cycles: A Window on Time* New York: John Wiley & Sons, 1982.

Appendix

Accuracy of weekly & monthly R+ and R− signals.

MARKET*	START	CORRECT % R+	CORRECT % R−
T-bonds	1977	50%	78%
T-bills	1976	50%	43%
Orange Juice	1968	62%	54%
GNMA	1975	74%	71%
Palladium	1968	83%	75%
Comex Gold	1975	57%	73%
Feeder Cattle	1972	54%	76%
Japanese Yen	1972	75%	67%
Live Cattle	1965	59%	64%
Swiss Franc	1972	59%	81%
Lumber	1970	74%	72%
Sugar	1960	67%	75%
Coffee "C"	1973	76%	75%
Chicago Wheat	1960	53%	72%
British Pound	1972	56%	55%
Corn	1962	69%	63%
Canadian Dollar	1972	67%	83%
Oats	1960	57%	59%
Soybeans	1960	66%	67%
Deutsche Mark	1972	53%	79%
Platinum	1962	69%	77%
Hogs	1966	72%	50%
Pork Bellies	1962	76%	67%
Cotton	1960	72%	71%
Soyoil	1960	73%	63%
Cocoa	1963	56%	70%
Copper	1960	63%	58%
Comex Silver	1967	71%	78%
Soymeal	1960	63%	66%

MONTHLY

*Markets listed in order of decreasing activity.

MARKET*	START	CORRECT % R+	CORRECT % R−
British Pound	1977	71%	63%
Canadian Dollar	1977	60%	78%
Chicago Wheat	1978	70%	64%
Cocoa	1978	67%	66%
Coffee "C"	1978	72%	71%
Copper	1977	57%	63%
Corn	1978	60%	73%
Cotton	1978	60%	73%
Deutsche Mark	1977	67%	61%
Eurodollar	1982	57%	52%
Feeder Cattle	1978	67%	65%
GNMA	1978	58%	67%
Gold	1978.5	67%	69%
Heating Oil	1979	78%	58%
Hogs	1977	60%	61%
Japanese Yen	1977	65%	68%
Live Cattle	1980	59%	61%
Lumber	1977	70%	77%
NYMEX Crude Oil	1983	68%	56%
Oats	1978	70%	57%
Orange Juice	1977	69%	64%
Palladium	1980	67%	69%
Platinum	1978.5	74%	71%
Pork Bellies	1978	63%	66%
Silver	1977	63%	66%
Soybeans	1978	62%	68%
Soybean Meal	1978	62%	68%
Soybean Oil	1978	60%	68%
S&P Stock Index	1978.5	66%	53%
Sugar	1977	60%	75%
Swiss Franc	1977	75%	61%
T-bills	1977	71%	60%
T-bonds	1978.5	53%	56%
Value Line Stock Index	1982	73%	67%

WEEKLY

*Markets listed in order of decreasing activity.

Index